STAGE DESIGN
THROUGHOUT THE WORLD
SINCE 1950

INTERNATIONAL THEATRE INSTITUTE PUBLICATIONS

DIRECTOR : RENÉ HAINAUX

stage design

throughout the world

since 1950

texts and illustrations collected by the national centres of the
international theatre institute
chosen and presented by rené hainaux
with the technical advice of yves-bonnat

foreword by
paul-louis mignon
president of the I.T.I. publications committee

theatre arts books
new york

Library of Congress Catalog Card Number : 63-20345
First published 1964
by Theatre Arts Books, 333 Sixth avenue, New York 14
World Copyright 1964 © by Éditions Meddens,
141-143, avenue de Scheut, Bruxelles 7
Printed in Belgium.

FOREWORD

THIS book is a sequel... and it will undoubtedly lead to another. We have not yet journeyed all round the world but here we present fifteen countries not covered by the first volume of *Stage Design Throughout the World*: Austria, Bulgaria, Canada, Cuba, East Germany, Hungary, India, Israel, Peru, Rumania, Spain, Turkey, U.S.S.R., Uruguay, and Venezuela. In addition, eighteen countries from the original panorama are included.

The first group were at liberty to begin their survey in the nineteen thirties and forties, while the second group were asked to take 1950 as their starting point and describe the new developments of the last decade.

The art of the theatre is developing so rapidly today with the spate of experiment and discovery that frequent stocktaking is necessary. In ten years stage-craft has greatly changed through the use of new materials and the exploitation of the possibilities offered by the lighting and stage equipment of newly built theatres. Aesthetically, too, the influence of technical developments can be seen.

The International Theatre Institute has sought to present a comprehensive picture of this experimentation, and it was therefore considered essential to include in this volume a report of the inquiry jointly held by Yves-Bonnat and René Hainaux. The designer may thus find material that will aid him in his own work.

A book of this kind should, in fact, not only assess an historical situation, but at the same time abound in information and suggestions. A book about the theatre must also keep as close as possible to the practical side. At least, this is the aim of the I.T.I. in its publications.

Similarly, another innovation—the Stage Designers' Who's Who—supplies particularly useful information at a time when, through the increase in international exchanges brought about by the Theatre of the Nations and touring companies, an artist can become known and be able to practise his profession outside his own country.

We are aware of the insufficiencies and omissions of this Who's Who; the I.T.I. intends to improve it later on. However, as it is, in addition to designers of world renown, it draws attention for the first time to artists in countries such as Argentina, Canada or Israel whose names until now have been missing from works of this nature.

For those who have no professional concern, the illustrations alone should be of unusual interest. For beyond the stage spectacle and its ephemeral and anecdotal aspect, is it not a glimpse of the artistic sensibility of a nation that is captured by the stage décor in extending into a plastic world the spirit of a play and its characters, common denominators of the public of an epoch?

Paul-Louis MIGNON
Chairman of the Publications Committee of the I.T.I.

ACKNOWLEDGEMENTS

LIKE the first volume of its kind, this one is the result of combined efforts which testify to the vitality and undisputed usefulness of the National Centres of the International Theatre Institute.

The I.T.I. Centres were in most cases responsible for assembling, sometimes with herculean efforts, the mass of material from which Yves-Bonnat and myself have made a selection that, we hope, does justice to the theatrical productivity of each nation. The I.T.I. Centres also tackled the manifold problems to which a book of this kind gives rise. The matter of copyright, in particular, had to be settled before undertaking publication. Thanks to the I.T.I. Centres we were relieved of this burden and now it only remains for us to express our gratitude to the designers, photographers and collectors who have been goodnatured and trusting enough to lend us their often valuable documents. To list all their names would take up too much space, so let this be regarded as a general acknowledgement.

Nevertheless, the following deserve our special thanks : Saulo Benavente of the Argentine Centre, François Mennes and Rudi Van Vlaenderen of the Belgian Centre, Olga Obry and Mauro Francini of Brazil, Mr. Andonov and Mr. Dimitrov of the Bulgarian Centre, David Ongley and Jean-Louis Roux of the Canadian Centre, Eva Soukupova and Karel Kratochvil of the Czechoslovakian Centre, Nora Badia and Salvador Fernandez of the Cuban Centre, Mr. Kohls, Mr. Link and Mr. Rainer of the East German Centre, Marlene Dietrich and Friedrich Schultze of the West German Centre, José Muñoz Fontan, Alfredo Timermans and Manuel Andrès Zabala of the Spanish Centre, Madame Novy of the French Centre, Alexis Minotis, Demeter Murat, Takis Mouzenidis and Stathis Spiliotopoulos of the Greek Centre, Edmond Stadler and Paul Wehrli of the Swiss Centre, Ebrahim Alkazi and Som Benegal of India, Aura Herzog and Manfred Geis of the Israeli Centre, Giacinto Giancola of the Italian Centre, Marijan Matkovic and Mladja Vesélinovic of the Yugoslav Centre, Ferenc Hont of the Hungarian Centre, Françoise Wijckerheld Bisdom-Bruyn and Max Wagener of the Netherlands Centre, Tamotsu Nabeshima of the Japanese Centre, Rigmor Ottho of the Norwegian Centre, Heinrich Schnitzler of the Austrian Centre, Reynaldo d'Amore of the Peruvian Centre, Andrzej Hansbrandt of the Polish Centre, Mircea Acram of the Rumanian Centre, Mr. Denissov and Mr. Goussev of the Soviet Centre, Verneri Veistäja of the Finnish Centre, Margareta Nylander of the Swedish Centre, Irfan Sahinbas of the Turkish Centre, Aubrey Ensor, the British Council, and Kenneth Rae of the British Centre, Charles Elson, Elisabeth Burdick and Ruth Mayleas of the American Centre, Antonia Acevedo Esparza of the Uruguayan Centre, Humberto Orsini of the Venezuelan Centre.

Finally, we were fortunate in securing the services of Ossia Trilling and Jill Pomerance, who were kind enough to supply the English titles of the works listed in the Index and in the Stage Designers' Who's Who.

René HAINAUX

NEW METHODS AND MATERIALS
IN STAGE DESIGN

IN these days, things happen very quickly. Hardly has one decided to adopt a new method, to make use of some recent invention, or to think along new lines, when already other ways, other tools or appliances, and other philosophical systems beckon.

Modern man finds it difficult to get used to handling the products of his crative imagination and particularly to the revolutionary mentality that their use creates.

Which is to say how presumptuous it would be, in the midst of the turmoil of our advancing civilization, to pass even a minor judgment on the meaning of the present trend of stage design throughout the world.

Experience has shown that no true evaluation of artistic movements is possible until they are of long standing. In fact, we are still cavilling about the aptness of the ultra-realistic settings of the Théâtre Libre d'Antoine (or the more moderate ones of Stanislavsky), the modern pictorial contribution of the Diaghilev ballets, and the constructivism of Soviet, German and Czech expressionism. Even today we must be satisfied with recognizing that, each in their time and sometimes in the right place, these movements were necessary because of the stagnation of former practices. However, not one has reached such a point of saturation that we can no longer turn to it for new ideas. This is where this present investigation has to be careful and modest in its conclusions.

These virtues are reflected in the majority of replies received to the inquiry we held, together with Monsieur René Hainaux, among designers of some twenty countries through the medium of the National Centres of the International Theatre Institute.

First of all, why hold this inquiry? To acquaint the public with the problems and specific lines of research of contemporary stage designers? Certainly, but also to spread among these designers information that will help them in their work; to draw the attention of playwrights, producers, directors and even actors to the possibilities, both artistic and practical, offered by modern methods and materials originally made or discovered for uses other than those of the theatre.

Was its purpose propaganda then? Hardly, for nothing is enforced in art. But rather revelation and familiarization.

There again, the replies of designers agree : no prejudice being shown in the decision of each one to use this or that material until then unknown or seldom employed, or some technique differing from that of traditional equipment.

There was rather, on the one hand—as befits the creative spirit of the artist-designer—curiosity, then a desire to convert the alien technique to the needs of the theatre. On the other hand—as befits the professional concerned with success—discovery of an original and improved solution to the difficulties presented by a particular theatrical work or production.

Finally, there was a more or less conscious wish to incorporate design for the stage into the general movement of the plastic arts, which are distinguished in our atomic age by purity of form, hectic rhythm (1) and uniqueness—if not always nobility—of material.

It is therefore certainly a modern concept that is in question, justified both materially and psychologically : a quasi-universal concept which, however, entails no standardization—at least at the moment—since it empowers all personalities, national or individual, to express themselves. Will it give birth to the style of our epoch? Obviously that does not depend upon individual designers. If this trend led to an aesthetic breach with that of production, if one added to the other submerged the written play in an excess of perfection, or if the three together were engulfed in extravagances the audience could not understand, then it would not be a question of style but of decadence.

The natural curb to such dangers lies in the full knowledge that the men of the theatre of our age possess of former styles and methods, which are far from being entirely abandoned. One may prefer to travel by jet aircraft without, by that, refusing at some time to step into a gondola in Venice or go for a horse-ride in the woods.

---

(1) The audience, having become accustomed through the methods of the cinema and television to rapid changes of scene, sometimes instantaneous, sometimes faded, does not tolerate as well as it used to the theatre intervals necessitated by changes of décor. In addition to revolving and sliding stages which offer greater speed, producers and designers are constantly searching for more or less untried procedures that would arrive at the same results.

While admiring a constructivist setting by Teo Otto or Caspar Neher, one can also take pleasure in the painted canvas of Carzou or Bernard Buffet.

As the article on Stage Design in the U.S.S.R. in Vol. X, No. 3 of " World Theatre „ shows, it often happens that two apparently conflicting methods and aesthetic standpoints can be combined with brilliant success.

The essential character of aesthetic modernism arising from the adoption of a modern technique is stylization. Who says " stylization „ says " simplification „ and " selection „. It is not unusual in the stage design of the past twenty years for a single element of décor (a construction, piece of furniture or a property) to represent a complete scene.

If this element is of good proportion, in a suitable material, and if it is set on the stage in the most visible spot and the most obvious one from the point of view of the action, if its shape offers the largest number of surfaces for the reception of pre-arranged lighting, and according to requirements of changing light, then it has all the qualities of a complete set added to which is a greater power of suggestion and often a special fascination.

★

Replies received on first launching our inquiry showed that although considerations concerning this problem are the same the world over, they cannot, at least for the moment, yield any hard and fast theory.

This is just as well, for theory is the enemy of art, and the theatre owes more to artistic inspiration than to technical achievement.

It is still true, however, that a whole field, which had become standardized through the impossibility of improving it imaginatively or practically, has today been opened up to theatre producers and designers. If so far this field has been insufficiently explored, it is because few of the older works for the stage, whose authors could not suspect its extent, lend themselves to it without danger of distortion, and because new writers make no provision for its exploration, no doubt failing sufficient information.

Nevertheless, some modern works not only lend themselves to these mediums, but even seem to invite them.

Such as, for example, Schönberg's *Moses and Aaron* (old in its modernity but so young in spirit), Marcel Landowsky's *The Idiot* and *The Opera of Dust*, to quote only three examples in opera. In drama, most of the plays of Ionesco, Audiberti and Adamov, or any ballet either fantastic or abstract in the modern sense of the word.

One would just as easily find in certain excursions into total theatre by Paul Claudel *(The Satin Slipper, Joan at the Stake* and *Christopher Columbus)* an unconscious and premonitory desire for strange materials and unusual methods.

This amounts to saying that we are now far removed from the equipment, lighting and plastic effects, so ludicrous today, of the comedy-ballets of the Grand Siècle, or the ghostly romanticism of the ballet *Giselle*.

★

Now let us take another look at some of the questions in the inquiry, those that would seem conclusive.

What about new materials? They are innumerable in form, appearance, colour, suggestive or phenomenal properties. They enlarge the field of " effects „ by the exclusion of *trompe-l'œil* painting which has lost its charm for the public and in its effect contradicts the direction of the real light (the shadows, lights and colours changing during the performance). They have an individuality that was not possessed by painted canvas, where the lighting was determined in advance by the brush, either in a semblance of relief or in a purely flat treatment.

The appeal of new materials, or of existing but hitherto unused ones, is attended by enormous possibilities in fashioning, construction and handling.

In this way, the designer comes to the rescue of the producer, the scene shifter and the lighting expert, while at the same time obtaining personal artistic satisfaction.

There are similar advantages regarding costumes. Theatre costume has, as a result, no longer anything to do with historical reconstitution, the finer details of which are lost on the audience, nor with modern dress. It is like a symbol, it is a sign or evidence of personalization through the co-ordination it allows the designer.

In the case of both décor and costume, it becomes possible for the artist to conceive his work in terms of the material used. The material inspires him, as in any other work of plastic art.

His palette no longer consists only of coloured pigments, but also of the whole range of intensities and changing colours offered by electric lighting and the switchboard that controls it.

The " Russian ballet „ style, which consisted of presenting an enlarged easel picture as background to the evolutions of the dancers, and in lighting this picture brightly and effectively (to the detriment of the lighting of the action), appeared on our modern stages as outmoded as the lighting by naked gas flames of the *trompe-l'œil* scenery of the 19th century.

The lavish gift bestowed by electricity entails complete revision of scenic equipment.

In fact, if it enhances what it lights, if it brings out its intrinsic beauties (material, colour, volume), electricity also reveals its defects. It produces unexpected effects with traditional scenery which are usually more embarrassing than desirable. These are, for example, the backings, reveals, cuts and " perspective „ details, tonal changes, unwanted shadows, etc.

For these reasons, a number of designers paint their models and draw their plans with constant thought to the position of the lighting appliances, their power, automation and flexibility. They take full advantage of the qualities of this theatrical electricity while apprehending its freak effects.

One can no longer be a designer without having a sound knowledge of stage lighting.

But once acquired, practised and experimented with, one can achieve a setting with a minimum of strictly decorative elements, the switchboard becoming the paints and brushes of the creative artist.

The designer, initiated into the art of lighting, must now also be initiated into that of sound effects. The introduction into the presentation of opera, drama or ballet of equipment that can provide what is called a " décor sonore „ (or setting in sound)—stereophonic or otherwise, but always conceived in terms of the action—means either the camouflage or visual justification of the presence of such appliances as loudspeakers and sometimes microphones for transmitting and amplifying direct sound.

It is dangerous to think of disguising this apparatus once the scenery is set on the stage and hung in the flies, for the two can only be mutually harmful, in one case for aesthetic reasons, in the other for scientific ones (quality and localization of sound, Larsen effects, etc). In fact, in addition to the permanent sound equipment placed in the auditorium, flies or wings, the production may call for special installations in parts of the stage visible to the audience.

I have personally frequently been faced with this problem, in particular during the creation, with Marcel Lamy producing, of *Chevalier de Neige* (Snow Horseman), an opera by Boris Vian and Georges Delerue. Being forewarned, I worked in conjunction not only with the producer but also the sound engineer in designing the models of my sets. In these circumstances, the piece of sound equipment can become, by the shape of its housing, a plausible item of the décor.

In these circumstances, too, the use of traditional decorative materials may prove ineffective—and there we have one more reason for consulting the catalogue of new materials, or even of inventing new ways of using customary ones.

There is, one might say, a corollary to this problem when it is a question of making constructions or claddings noiseless which, under the tread of actors or dancers, produce sounds that spoil the action or the purity of the music.

One is therefore caught between the desire to modernize the technical aspects of stage settings and to abolish their unwanted resonance.

In France only very few designers concern themselves with these questions (2), preferring in order to solve them to refer to the permanent designers of the theatres where they have been invited to work. It is thus rare that the final result is satisfactory, this kind of co-operation entailing more sterile mutual concessions than creative understanding.

However, these considerations must not lead one to think that tradition has lost all its value. Quite on the contrary, neither the designer nor his immediate chief, the producer, can afford to ignore any of the advantages of the varied and well-tried elements of traditional equipment, even though he uses them for purposes other than those for which they were originally intended.

It is foolish, for example, to do away with the below-stage area because one wants to install revolving or sliding stages. It is equally foolish to do away with or reduce the area for flying equipment, to facilitate the erection of a rigid and over-circular cyclorama.

Many designers, or so-called ones, have so mutilated some stages under the pretext of modernization that the presentation of certain works has become impossible.

In actual fact, anything may be used provided that one does not use just anything without due need.

During some thirty years' theatrical experience, I have often seen young producers, who had previously proved

---

(2) These are : Malclès, Ganeau, Douking, Daydé, Allio, Acquart, Noël, Pace, Rapp, Camurati, Farrah, to quote a few.

their mettle in spite of the poverty of the technical means at their disposal, suffer enormous set-backs as soon as they were able to work in a better equipped theatre.

It is the old story of the indigestion of the starving man suddenly given food.

The work to be performed is in every case the essential guide to the mediums to be used. It dictates the need, it enjoins simplicity.

Till now, I have only discussed this inquiry in the optimistic assumption that there do exist perfectly built and equipped theatres. And I would certainly be dishonest if I seemed to disregard all these countless theatre buildings all over the world that are often only halls, cinemas or even barns, and where the Chariot of Thespis, following a policy of cultural expansionism, decentralization and promotion, is obliged for want of something better to dump its bags.

If this chariot were not the vehicle of shock troops, preaching a gospel, determined to win battles rather than suffer martyrdom, or rather accepting the dangers of martyrdom so that their cause may triumph, it is obvious that bad material conditions would lead to artistic mediocrity.

It is not so, as we know. We even know that their search for solutions to sometimes anticipated difficulties have often enough led to interesting aesthetic discoveries that can be exported to better fitted stages.

This has been seen in France, in the work of the " Jeunes Compagnies „ and in that of the regional Dramatic Centres. In other countries, within the framework of certain American universities and in the work of avant-garde Canadian companies, to quote just a few examples. It will also be seen no doubt, and in even stranger forms, in the experiments in a new theatre to be made by young producers of former colonies.

I could not end my report without bringing up the final question of the inquiry, relating to methods of work, nor without replying to it personally.

I have made several references to it already, whenever a particular question raised its principle, but further mention would not be superfluous.

I am opposed, by experience rather than choice, to any individualism on the part of no matter whom, in the working out and then in the achievement of a production. Each expert in his own special line must try to make himself understood by his partners, to help them and seek their aid. This is the very meaning of team work, and must obtain all the time from the moment the producer is chosen to the first public performances (during which some further improvements may still be made).

This is a general rule for me. But even if I were not completely convinced of its necessity, the development of new methods and the use of new materials, a use which is, for the moment at any rate, experimental, would persuade me.

If the equipment of a theatre had been aptly compared to the rigging of a sailing vessel, the artisans of a production, the producer, designer, stage director, scene shifters, electricians, sound engineer (and in opera and ballet, the choreographer, orchestral conductor and choir master) can also be compared to the members of a ship's crew. No doubt this team spirit is a practical necessity, but it is also a moral insurance against " all risks „.

The more methods improve, the more may accidents be expected. Whether in atomic science or the art of the theatre, man remains the decisive factor, in so far as he knows he can depend upon his fellows.

YVES-BONNAT

NEW MATERIALS
AND NEW METHODS

RESULTS OF AN INQUIRY

Our questionnaire sent to stage designers in some thirty countries, through the medium of the I.T.I. Centres, produced enough material to fill a large file.

We had to make a selection and, most of all, try to disclose the main lines. I hope our correspondents will forgive us if they have at times only been briefly quoted.

I would like to thank Madame Martine Gogneaux-Huens who has assisted me in arranging the comments received in some coherent order.

My gratitude also goes to Mrs. Joan Ashley who had the arduous task of translation.

Finally, this is purely a report. It has no literary pretensions.

René Hainaux

LIST OF STAGE DESIGNERS
FROM WHOM REPLIES WERE RECEIVED

André ACQUART (France)

Arnon ADAR (Israel)

René ALLIO (France)

Seza ALTINDAG (Turkey)

Howard BAY (U.S.A.)

Saulo BENAVENTE (Argentina)

Herta BOEHM (West Germany)

Liviu CIULEI (Rumania)

Veniero COLASANTI (Italy)

Victor Maria CORTEZO (Spain)

Jozsef CSELENYI (Hungary)

Marcelo DAMONTE (Peru)

Georges DOUKING (France)

Charles ELSON (U.S.A.)

Erich ENGEL (East Germany)

Refik EREN (Turkey)

Max FRITZSCHE (West Germany)

Toni GHEORGHIU (Rumania)

Kurt HALLEGGER (West Germany)

Pekka HEISKANEN (Finland)

Sean KENNY (United Kingdom)

Jan KOSINSKI (Poland)

Miroslav KOURIL (Czechoslovakia)

Franco LAURENTI (Italy)

H.W. LENNEWEIT (West Germany)

Ita MAXIMOWNA (West Germany)

Jo MIELZINER (U.S.A.)

Ryotaro MITSUBAYASHI (Japan)

Stellan MORNER (Sweden)

Dan NEMTEANN (Rumania)

Stefan NORRIS (Rumania)

Teo OTTO (Switzerland)

PACE (France)

Erwin PISCATOR (West Germany)

Andrzej SADOWSKI (Poland)

Loudon SAINTHILL (United Kingdom)

Willi SCHMIDT (West Germany)

Wladimir SRAMEK (Czechoslovakia)

Rolf STEGARS (Finland)

Carl Johan STRÖM (Sweden)

Josef SVOBODA (Czechoslovakia)

Harry WICH (Netherlands)

Nicolaas WIJNBERG (Nederlands)

I. MATERIALS

A. — QUESTION :

DO YOU ONLY USE THE TRADITIONAL MATERIALS OF STAGE DÉCOR : PAINTED CANVAS, WOOD, ETC.?

STASTISTICAL ANALYSIS

— The 43 stage designers who replied to the inquiry can be divided into four groups.

First group :	Three admit to using traditional materials solely or mainly.
Second group :	Five believe in traditional materials used judiciously and employ new materials where problems arise that cannot be solved by the use of conventional ones.
Third group :	Thirty, or the majority, are of the opinion that there should be no limitation in this field and they use, as necessary, conventional materials, materials in everyday use, and recently discovered ones.
Fourth group :	Five stand out as dynamic avant-gardists with the declared intention of experimenting above all with new materials.

REASONS GIVEN BY THE FIRST GROUP :

— Their country offers no suitable selection of new materials (no plastics industry, for instance).
— The special case of Hungary.

> " We have a central organization which makes the sets for all theatres in Budapest. Ninety per cent of the productions are old-fashioned in style, so scenic workshops have to be of a conventional nature supplied with suitable but traditional materials. The rare unconventional design only makes trouble for these workshops; it cannot be given to them to execute. This organization is a great drawback in our slow development. " (Jozsef Cselenyi)

REASONS GIVEN BY THE SECOND GROUP :

— Traditional materials are the basic ones : they have been tried and proved and are most generally used.
— Conventional materials can be used in a new spirit. (Victor Maria Cortezo)
— Traditional materials are practical " *in productions that have to be quickly executed*". (Liviu Ciulei)
— Traditional materials = economy. (Netherlands)

REASONS GIVEN BY THE THIRD GROUP :

— " *Anything is good that serves the play's purpose and excites the imagination of the audience.* " (Andrzej Sadowski) This is a plea for a repertoire of materials as extensive as possible.

> " Now, today, the stage designer has at his disposal a wide range of new materials on which he may draw as needs be to meet the demands of his art, whether they be aesthetic or technical. " (Saulo Benavente)

> " The designer today must be able to discriminate *ad infinitum*... He must give his attention, with the same ardour, to every possibility offered, and neglect none... How fortunate if he can forget what he did yesterday and give expression, with all the freshness of originality, to the creation of today. " (Teo Otto)

— Up-to-dateness of means of expression in the theatre is a condition of its very existence.

> " It would be an anachronism to insist on traditional materials and not take advantage of the rapid development of new technology. The theatre would become sterile and in the end would lose its urgent effect on the spectators. " (Wladimir Sramek)

> " A living, creative, up-to-date stage setting designed by a man who moves with the stream of contemporary cultural life... must willy-nilly employ means of expression in line with the other plastic arts. " (Andrzej Sadowski)

— Stage design and dramaturgy mutually influence each other.

> " I believe that contemporary dramatic art and its typical dramatists such as Brecht and Dürrenmatt are partly rooted in the world of plastics, anodized aluminium, steel tube scaffolding, gas filled lamps, nylon, electronic controls and polyethylenes, not to mention still and motion picture projections and mobiles *à la Calder*. As, furthermore, I am convinced that the primordial condition of the existence of the theatre is the contemporaneousness of its forms of expression, I do not think that the designer today can refuse to make use of new materials, new techniques and new methods to lend the work of imagination a true reality, conforming to the times in which we live. " (Saulo Benavente)

> " When I began to work in the D 34 Theatre about thirty years ago, I took a deliberate stand against the traditional materials, wood and canvas. We wished to be militant in everything—plays, production, acting... At the same time we had to discover a new conception of stage design. " (Miroslav Kouril)

> " The drama of our time allows for settings of great audacity—audacity of medium as well as formal design. A great variety of new possibilities results for the designer. Hence the need for him to experiment, but these experiments must not be an end in themselves; he must look on them only as laboratory work for the theatre. " (Teo Otto)

— A new conception of the role of stage design is developing.

> " Contemporary stage design leans more and more towards formal elements, operates by distortion and abstraction, and finally aims at a décor with the purpose, not of defining the time and place of the action, but of suggesting the atmosphere and completing the expression of the play. This stimulates even more the desire to use untraditional materials. " (Andrzej Sadowski)

— New materials are not so cumbersome as conventional ones : they leave more to the spectator's imagination.

> " I think wood and painted canvas are too dull and limited as means of attracting and stimulating the attention of the audience. " (Serza Altindag)

— The audience, being closer to a better lit stage, no longer accepts " tricks ".

> " There is a proliferation of Little Theatres in our country : the proximity of the audience has led to the abandonment of " tricks "; in some cases this abandonment has led to the use of materials in everyday use such as wallpaper, doors and windows in wood and glass, flooring of linoleum imitating parquet or tiles, and so on; in other cases the wildest fancy has blossomed. " (Marcelo Damonte)

REASONS GIVEN BY THE FOURTH GROUP :

— The need for an avant-garde to ensure progress in the theatre.

> " ...Analysis of detail, suggestion of the real by an expressive transposition : one can see we are far from *verism*. This is where the stage crafts take on their true importance and they should be practised energetically. To seek new solutions, use unusual materials, keep up with what industry is producing in this direction, and have the ability to try everything... In this way, the work of the stage carpenter and scene shifter would become a more vital and creative work : a modern work—as one says, modern art. " (René Allio)

B. — QUESTION :

WHAT NEW MATERIALS OR OTHERS NOT USUALLY ASSOCIATED WITH THE THEATRE HAVE YOU EMPLOYED?

a) *For the sets :*

Metals :
: bronze, copper, tin, gold or silversheets, etc.;
perforated sheets;
wire netting;
tubing and sections (iron, aluminium);
brass wire, wrought iron.

> " A material from which I have obtained good results is wrought iron with which one can ' suggest ' walls, roofs and so on in silhouette against a black background. " (Marcelo Damonte)

Glass :
: glass panels;

> " In the very first play presented at the D34 Theatre—it was Molière's *Avare*—the designers Kouril, Novotny and Raban used glass; movable glass panels divided up the stage and Harpagon wasted away over his money in an imaginary lair behind a wall of glass. " (Miroslav Kouril)

mirrors;
ceramics;
powdered glass and glue.

Plastics :

> " Plastic sheeting and extruded plastic forms for three-dimensional forms as designed, i.e. : for capitals, finials, door trim, etc. " (Charles Elson)

Composition boards :
: building materials such as : Multiplex, Linex, porous panelling, etc.;
crumpled papers, etc.

> " Crumpled paper and rough materials attached with glue (esparto, sacking, etc.), or even sand or light cement, offer interesting tactile qualities.
>   Sacking treated with lime or combined with sawdust, paint and plaster can give interesting surfaces. " (Victor Maria Cortezo)

Synthetic materials :
: artificial resins and foams;
polyester foam (latex, etc.);

> " The only complete production cast in latex I designed for an O'Casey drama. Rough brick and flagstone were modelled and then cast in four-by-eight-foot sheets. Even the cyclorama was a gigantic wall of brick—artificial rubber brick. Here the solution was both practical and aesthetic. Strong three-dimensional crumbling and erosion that could be lighted many ways but never escaped a unified flavour of Dublin. " (Howard Bay)

formica, etc.;
Modurit (a Czechoslovak invention);
astralon, celon, Plexiglas;

" Quite recently (at the Opéra-Comique, Paris, 1960) in *Vol de Nuit* (Night Flight), the opera based on Saint-Exupéry's book with music by Dallapiccola and production by Jean Mercure, I devised a set entirely in aluminium and Plexiglas. This gave a sort of stripped-down design for the airline company's offices in Buenos Aires. The numerous Plexiglas windows stopped the actor's voices from becoming los in the stage space and produced, while still allowing the sky to be seen all the time, hundreds of reflections of the characters, but because of the orientation of the surfaces, without reflecting the spotlights. " (Georges Douking)

Jablite.

" Jablite : a new synthetic material I have used with immense effect, especially where the resemblance of age and weathering is required on stone or wood. It is of very light weight (of excellent use in property making) and gives a great impression of weight and solidity and is extremely durable. Those that work the substance are not so enthusiastic as they find it difficult and hard on the hands, but the finished effects I have used in rocky landscapes, early type Roman shields and weathered gravestones in a churchyard could not have been better. " (Loudon Sainthill)

Natural materials : cork;
untanned leather;
plaited straw, osier, rush, reed.

New fabrics and
fibres :
plastics;
Terylene, nylon;
imitation leather;
woven glass materials;
artificial jute, net, fur, down, etc.

Paper :
embossed wall-paper;
newspapers, posters, wrapping paper;
cellophane;
silver paper, etc.;
photographic paper.

Miscellaneous :
rope, netting, coloured ribbon and wire, hose pipe;
stove piping, gas piping, lead pipes;
cardboard boxes, various containers, egg cartons, etc.

" We have had very good results, for instance with ' novodur ' egg trays, which give a surface with a very interesting structure when placed side by side, and offer interesting possibilities for the stage, especially for light treatment. " (Josef Svoboda)

b) *For costumes :*

Traditional fabrics (woollens, etc.) are still in general use but to these should be added :
new fabrics and fibres and the papers described in a);

" Since plastic materials hinder the actor's ease of action and his breathing, I prefer to use them only for ornaments. " (Refik Eren)

various metal sheets;
burlaps, kitchen cloths, etc.

" I very often use sacking (painted or given a bronze patina with a spray or brush) for making costumes. I use string to make coats of mail, or even raffia. I imitate mohair by inserting silk threads in fabrics, snake skin by sequins, and leopard skin by painting shorn sheepskin. I make beads out of whitewood tinted in different shades. " (Liviu Ciulei)

"fabrics with metal threads (woven partly in cotton and partly in metal fibres)... wire frameworks and, generally, any unconventional material that can add to the expressiveness of the costume and so emphasize the corresponding character." (Toni Gheorghiu)

C. — QUESTION :

FOR WHAT REASONS DID YOU USE THESE MATERIALS?

FOR THEIR AESTHETIC QUALITIES (This is the reason most frequently given).

" I choose materials for both their structural qualities and their emotional impact.
...Many materials are interchangeable because of similar structural qualities; each material, however, has unique emotional values for the audience. Since in contemporary art much attention is paid to material *per se*, and stage design is always greatly influenced by the art of the period, modern audiences are becoming more aware of the emotional qualities of materials. " (Arnon Adar)

New materials " *make new kinds of aesthetic effects possible.* " (Max Fritzsche)

— New possibilities of suggestion and expression :

through surface appearance;

" We have been inspired by experiments in modern painting and sculpture to obtain aesthetic effects : roughness, gloss, transparency through compression of the material, improvement and ennoblement of the raw material " (Kurt Hallegger)

through the shapes they allow (stylization);
through the colours they offer;

" Mirrors, with a light fixture that suggests the tinsel atmosphere of old palaces, or crushed coal stuck on to canvas and lit from the side by amber spotlights, give a sombre but rich effect. " (Pace)

through their textures;
some materials have a suggestive power connected with their everyday use.

" I can say from my own experience that it helps to create an atmosphere of poverty to use various packing materials, partly because of their surface and treatment and partly because in themselves these materials are used in such an environment in real life. " (Josef Svoboda)

They allow the designer " *to emphasize the social impressions implicit in the text*". *Documentary Theatre* (Erwin Piscator), or to evoke imaginary worlds (the enchantment of gold lacquer), etc.

*

— Unusual physical properties producing aesthetic effects :

Acoustical qualities : these are very little exploited (unless for the floor to echo or muffle the actors' footsteps), but, according to Max Fritzsche, they will gradually play a more prominent part.

" For the floor : wood, stone, pebbles and velvet. " (Willi Schmidt)

" Personally, I am very interested in sound effects combined with stage-architectural elements and such questions as : how to solve different acoustical problems using the forms and materials of the set; how to enlarge sound dimensions, echoes, etc. for realistic or psychological purposes on the stage.
I also like to use music, through new methods, combined with acting (to parallel, underline, contradict, etc.) and lighting. Form and painting are not unrelated to acoustics (especially in the case of opera). " (Rolf Stegars)

Optical qualities : these are widely exploited : transparency, reflection and absorption of light.

" With such new materials it is easier to achieve an absolutely smooth surface which has widely varied reflecting properties. With movable mirror panels of black plastic we were able to throw reflected light into parts of the stage where direct lighting could not reach or be fixed, but where the actor had to stand under just this light. I used this technique for the ghost scene in *Hamlet*. When using new materials in this way, it is of course important for the panels to be a part of the scenery, a spatial architectural element in the setting. " (Josef Svobada)

" The new materials have allowed us to improve the use of lighting in the theatre and especially to provide projection surfaces. On the other hand, they also helped us to deal with the problem of a shadow zone with almost complete light absorption. The main advantage of the new materials here was that they permitted the reflection of light in the precise direction required. We try to make the floor of the stage as dark as possible from the point of view of the audience, using the incidence of light from low-voltage contra-positioned sources; this was achieved by ridged screening of the material, casting shadow towards the audience and reflecting the light upstage. In this way, the reflected light does not detract from the basic effect of the architectural setting. We obtained the best effects with ridged rubber.
In my setting for Prokofiev's *The Story of a True Man*, I achieved great variability in light-space by using, together with light, a strip of cloth 2 cm wide and 17 metres long (plastic material would have been even better). " (Josef Svoboda)

These optical properties are all the more important in view of the growing prominence of light in the theatre since the introduction of electricity.

FOR THEIR PRACTICAL QUALITIES

— from the technical point of view, the new materials are :

strong and allow greater scope in construction;
lightweight and facilitate rapid scene changes " *without breaking the continuity of the performance.* " (Pekka Heiskanen)
more flexible;
easy to work.

Drawbacks :

> " There are unfortunately few synthetic materials that are satisfactory for sets from the point of view of their practical use. First there are (...) the temperature variations to which scenery is submitted during a performance : on-stage temperature, 20° C and over; scene store, unheated; after the performance, a wait in the road before removal at temperatures in winter of 0° C and below, not to mention rain and fog. In addition, synthetic materials break more easily and are almost impossible to mend. To my mind, synthetic materials are better for scenery that does not have to be moved, like taht for films and television. " (Herta Boehm)

— from the economic nagle : an aspect frequently put forward.
— from the safety angle (in case of fire) : this point is questionable since some new materials are as inflammable as traditional ones, if not more so.
On the whole, the question of being fireproof does not greatly affect the decorator's selection of his material.
— And finally, new materials sometimes solve problems where traditional materials have failed.

Nevertheless, these new materials raise problems in certain aspects and each application calls for special consideration.

> " A certain number of difficulties restrict the freedom of the designer.
> There are objections to the use of Duralumin and aluminium because of their cost and the special knowledge required to weld them.
> There are also objections to the use of rhodoids and Plexiglas (white, opal, variegated or plain colours), for reasons of safety. In this connection, I think manufacturers should turn their attention to the question of fire-proofing. They would, in fact, find important outlets for these materials in exhibition design.
> The use of glass raises difficult problems because of tis weight and, of course, fragility.
> Moreover, the price of coloured plate glass is exorbitant, hence the necessity of using plastics (those admissible on safety frounds). " (André Acquart)

D. — QUESTION :

HAVE YOU FOUND THESE MATERIALS AVAILABLE ON THE MARKET OR HAVE RESEARCHES BEEN CARRIED OUT AT YOUR REQUEST BY ORGANIZATIONS OR LABORATORIES?

The vast majority of designers have sought and found these new materials on the market because :
— the selection offered is big enough to satisfy the most varied requirements, particularly when the designer knows how to make clever use of them;
— from the financial point of view, a setting is costly enough when standard materials already available are used. The funds granted to the designer usually preclude any possibilities of research or special orders.

Exceptionally, people have gone to industrial firms :
— to ask their advice on the use of new materials;

> " Only once did Mr. Wijnberg call upon a materials testing laboratory. This was when he wanted advice about using polyester. The researches were carried out at his request by the Shell Research Laboratory, Rotterdam. " (On behalf of Nicolaas Wijnberg)

— to ask for a new material to be produced that would serve a general purpose and not be used for one particular production.

> " The Czechoslovak ' Modurit ' was specially created for the theatre, and in the theatre, the cinema and exhibition work has proved an excellent modelling material. This is, I think, an exception in that the research work of our scenic laboratories is centred upon materials available on the market and which can be used in the poorest theatres. " (Miroslav Kouril)

This is the place to point out that " research studios " exist in some countries as an adjunct to the theatre for the purpose of studying the use of new materials and techniques for the stage. This is the case in the U.S.S.R. and Czechoslovakia in particular.

> " Thanks to the support given by the present Czech government, I have been working on research in stage materials since 1957 with opportunities for trying out new uses for materials, especially plastics. " (Miroslav Kouril)

E. — QUESTION :

HAVE YOU USED THESE MATERIALS IN THE RAW STATE OR HAVE YOU GIVEN THEM ANY SPECIAL TREATMENT?

Sometimes the one, sometimes the other. It all depends on the play performed and the degree of adequacy of the properties of the material one wants to use.
Usual treatments :
— to fireproof the material;

— to paint, varnish or dye it (for costumes);

— to treat it mechanically or chemically to obtain special aesthetic effects, such as making costumes look old;

> " Through laboratory research, I arrived at quite remarkable effects. For instance, dyeing in shaded tones and the mechanical treatment of some simple materials gave them the rich appearance of velvet or plush. " (Stefan Norris)

— to make a material more supple (e.g., *to soften sacking in a soda bath.* Liviu Ciulei).

A few prefer the material in its raw state.

> " I have a great fancy for materials used in their natural state without having undergone treatments that alter their original appearance. This is for various reasons, but I am chiefly prompted by the desire to obtain ' dramatic realism '; all the forms remaining true and real, not being represented or transposed. I also fear an ' ersatz ' look. For this reason, as part of the stage design course at the University of La Plata, we insist on projects in stage setting being devised only from materials and objects as found in nature or industry. " (Saulo Benavente)

II. STAGE EQUIPMENT

A. — QUESTION :

HAVE YOU FOUND THE TRADITIONAL PICTURE-FRAME STAGE ADEQUATE TO CARRY OUT YOUR IDEAS?

Many designers consider the picture-frame stage inadequate but are satisfied if it is improved (by an adaptable proscenium opening, flexible fore stage or, at least, absence of footlights) and added to by lightweight, mobile mechanisms (not permanently fixed).

> " In an age when dramatic forms have annihilated the theatrical convention of the three unities, the picture-frame stage and equipment cannot be adequate for stage productions. " (Georges Douking)

> " Although I do not consider the former stage equipment as efficient, I make use of everything that could be called classical equipment. Naturally, for the kinetic stage for which I have chosen to work, the existing stage equipment is often not suitable and I try to replace it by other mechanical aids, using small apparatus, which could be described perhaps as small-scale mechanization of the stage. Together with my colleagues, I design certain mechanical apparatus for a play, bearing in mind that it will add to the permanent mechanical devices of the theatre and be available for use in other combinations. In this way, we design conveyor belts, individual hydraulic elevating equipment, mechanized projection surfaces, etc. " (Josef Svoboda)

These requirements are accounted for by the growing importance of " rhythm ", and not merely for ease in scene changing :

> " May I just broach the following problems : that of rapid scene changes. This is not, as one might be tempted to believe, purely a matter of technique or of wanting to transform the stage quickly. The rapid scene change has a quite perceptible aesthetic quality, although not directly conceived for that reason. As much as massive and solidly built scenery paralyses the imaginative potential, so a set that is intentionally little more than sketched in, allows the imagination free rein. The mind must be kept active to preserve its flexibility. This is a creative activity, and to stimulate creative power is an essential, if not the principal, justification of every artistic effort. " (Erich Engel)

> " From the technical point of view, these devices help a performance to proceed rapidly and smoothly, or at least they should... Here, I would nevertheless like to point out one disadvantage : this equipment is clumsy and, more often than not, far too heavy. Stages with variable levels still creak on even in this century of interplanetary travel. " (H.W. Lenneweit)

It sometimes happens that a new piece of equipment participates in the inner workings of the drama and plays a part in the action of a scene (such as revolving or sliding stages accompanying the actors as they walk). In the extreme it becomes the " total theatre " of Piscator.

> " In the modern theatre, stage design together with the other elements used, has the function of communicating to the audience an artistic reality in which everything exactly corresponds to its meaning, so that the stage setting is in perfect harmony with all that takes place on the stage. Thus, fundamentally, it is not a question of accidental composition of elements or even relationships, but the creation of dramatic planes which can be changed in the course of the action, appearing and disappearing as required by the dramatic tension. Modern scenography cannot borrow the means of expression of other branches of art but must create its own language. " (Josef Svoboda)

Novelty in one place, tradition in another.

> " In Japan the case is rather different from that in Europe. Revolving stages and elevator stages are already familiar in the Japanese traditional theatre. " (Ryotaro Mitsubayashi)

At all events, the *style* of the Italian stage is not about to disappear just yet.

> " In Germany, for many years now the traditional ' Italian style ' has been used only in very special cases and then only to give a deliberately historic or ironic effect. " (Max Fritzsche)

HAVE YOU MADE USE OF MORE UP-TO-DATE EQUIPMENT WITH MECHANICAL DEVICES?
IF SO, WHAT WERE THE ADVANTAGES AND DRAWBACKS FROM THE AESTHETIC AND TECHNICAL POINTS OF VIEW?

The majority of designers have had an opportunity, at least once in their lives, of using equipment unknown to the picture-frame stage and have found in it material for personal experiment.

" I personally like to work with a revolving stage, which I often use in my own way. On the turntable I mount a construction which is permanent for the whole length of the play, and I present it from different angles during the performance, like a piece of sculpture, possibly adding, in full view of the audience, elements lowered from the flies or brought in on wagons. This gives a unity as well as a fluidity to the production. " (Jan Kosinski)

But many are of the opinion that this equipment must be used with propriety and that the technical side should not be allowed to predominate :

" ...to free the theatre from everything that only clutters it with the futile appendages of intellectualism. The greatness of the theatre lies in the very fact that it only partially depends on external resources...
...For the first place on the stage goes always to the human being. " (Teo Otto)

Technical hypertrophy threatens to make the visual aspect of the performance pre-eminent.
Another general trend : the preference for light-weight machinery rather than heavy permanent fixtures, which have the disadvantage of inducing the designer to use them even when not perfectly satisfied with them, for reasons of economy or simply slackness. In contrast, light mobile devices do a real service to the designer who can use them when and how he likes.

" It is good for the theatre to possess technical equipment but creative imagination comes first. " (Jozsef Cselenyi)

" I am not a believer in the advantages of permanent revolving stages for the following reasons :
a) they entail a limitation of the stage depth;
b) they entirely, or to a large degree, prohibit the use of below-stage space;
c) they are costly;
d) they can be replaced with advantage, when necessary, by removable turntables, or platforms that both slide and revolve along an axis that is decentred so that they may be moved aside or used in a variety of positions. "
(Saulo Benavente)

Financial reasons are put forward contradictorily. For Piscator, the drawback of modern equipment is that it is expensive; as for Jo Mielziner, he points out that mechanization of the stage in the United States has been hastened through a desire to keep running costs as low as possible.

C. — QUESTION :

HAVE YOU YOURSELF DEVISED ANY SPECIAL TECHNICAL DEVICES?
IF SO, WHAT WERE THEY AND WHAT WAS THEIR PURPOSE?

A large number of designers replied in the affirmative : various small appliances based on the principles of traditional stage machinery and designed with the sole aim of solving special problems. These were makeshifts more than real pieces of machinery.

These inventions aimed at :
1) adding to fixed and inflexible equipment;
2) making up for the insufficiencies of badly designed or ill-equipped stages.

" The miniature theatres used by the ' independent companies ' of Argentina are hot-beds of scenic invention; their precarious installations and small size have obliged designers and technicians to produce devices that are unique and often very ingenious. " (Saulo Benavente)

In this connection, two schools of thought should be mentioned :
some designers complain of being limited in their creations by inadequate mechanization;

" I am all for unlimited technical resources in the theatres (if indeed this is possible); the discipline of choice should not be imposed by the tools, but by the mind of the man who uses them. " (René Allio)

others (without, however, defending unpractical arrangements) admit that limited stages have often stimulated their imagination.

" Certainly, I would like to work in an adaptable theatre, so that every possibility would be within my reach; however, after working for a time on a small stage, I must admit that it was precisely because of its exiguous nature that I was impelled to seek and enabled to find hitherto untried solutions. " (Toni Gheorghiu)

3) obtaining special effects.

> " To mention one detail, I thought of a rail on which a spotlight (its light representing sun or moonlight) could move during the performance. It could be used for other purposes too. " (Rolf Stegars)

> " The cinema prompted me to try the effects of the dolly shot to bring the spectator closer to or farther from the action. In this way, the ship in O'Neill's *Bound East for Cardiff* (Théâtre Pigalle, 1944) appeared and disappeared in the mist and, at the same theatre in 1946, a ' dolly shot ' towards the back of the theatre plunged the characters in *Messalina* into unreality. " (Georges Douking)

> " Just as in the old days the setting consisted of painted drops and wings, props and the classical elements, in which I include the revolving stage and wagons, I have built up my own apparatus of special lighting and mechanical installations. For the play *Their Day* by J. Topol, we built a special kinetic space; for E. Suchon's opera *Svatopluk* we set up new lighting apparatus which created walls of light, and so on.
> From this principle of searching for new means of expression I have built up a collection of scenic equipment, which gives me the opportunity of improvising at the beginning of rehearsals since these individual elements have become permanent features of the theatre. They include special kaleidoscopic projectors, sources of reflected light, mechanized projection surfaces, mechanical equipment combined with various fixed drops, conveyor belts or special film projectors equipped for deflecting the projection axis. The latter enables us to move an image about the stage and mechanically follow an actor or a dancer by means of special louvered surfaces of my own design which can be changed as necessary. This principle, which together with Polyekran was my discovery, was used in the Magic Lantern.
> The principle of the Magic Lantern and Polyekran also gave the stage new means of expression and new possibilities (like the range of new materials). They both came into being in the theatre, as a means of dramatic expression, although Polyekran, which essentially came from the idea of the Magic Lantern, was first seen in pure film form in the film by E. Radok *Prague Spring*. Both the principle of the Magic Lantern and of Polyekran were first seen at the Brussels World Fair, where they were warmly received by the public and won awards. In the Magic Lantern, I and director Alfred Radok tried to create a completely synthetic art combining film and theatre, a projected image and a three-dimensional stage, a live three-dimensional actor and a two-dimensional projected image. An equally important element is the special mechanized stage. This is so equipped as to provide complete freedom to make spatial changes and technically to keep pace with the opportunities afforded by the cinema : so that instantaneous changes on the stage correspond to rapid film cutting, and so that the scenic elements change in harmony with the film as the images succeed one another. For this purpose we use various mechanized projection surfaces (tiltable, movable forward or to the side), fixed drops, conveyor belts and scissor drops of our own design. " (Josef Svoboda)

D. — QUESTION :

WHAT, IN YOUR OPINION, IS THE IDEAL STAGE EQUIPMENT?

Everybody cries out for space and, in the opinion of many, the flexibility of the equipment is more important than its complexity.

> " Lack of storage space on stage I find the greatest difficulty to overcome, in the wings or at the back for stacking scenery. " (Loudon Sainthill)

> " I try to find for each play its proper expression. Since every play demands a special bias, I prefer the stage that offers the greatest number of technical possibilities and therefore the most flexible stage. " (Herta Boehm)

Some give more precise desiderata, such as :

> " First, I want a good floor with a sufficient number of traps; second, a flexible system of suspension (like the synchronized winches of George Izenour); third, a flexible fore stage. " (Arnon Adar)

> " During recent years, I have nearly always found that platform units or ramps have been sufficient for the effects I desired, with at the most a revolving stage for certain plays. " (Max Fritzsche)

> " I believe that the ideal stage equipment should have the maximum variability and should offer the director the greatest number of possibilities : it should have a large revolving stage with a floor densely sectored with lifting and dropping tables, high and fairly strong flies, a back stage with a sliding dance floor and two side stages with sliding floor sections. " (Wladimir Sramek)

Only few aspire to ultra-perfect equipment.

> " Only a sense of proportion, the uses to which the theatre is put and the funds available will set limits to this equipment, which can in any case be improved all the time. " (René Allio)

E. — QUESTION :

HAVE YOU ONLY WORKED IN THE TRADITIONAL PROSCENIUM THEATRES OR HAVE YOU HAD EXPERIENCE OF OTHER ARCHITECTURAL SHAPES? WHAT DO YOU CONSIDER THE ADVANTAGES AND DRAWBACKS?

Many designers have had the opportunity of experiencing various types of architecture. Nevertheless, the majority usually work on a conventional proscenium stage. One almost unanimous regret is the remoteness of the audience. This is why the first step usually taken towards a new architectural style is the theatre with a more or less adaptable fore stage and an adjustable proscenium opening.

" After the war, it was necessary in Germany to adapt oneself to all kinds of stages, and in doing so necessity was the mother of invention. But today nearly all the new theatres that have been built have a spacious stage with an extended fore stage and an adaptable proscenium, which offer many possibilities. " (Max Fritzsche)

Several designers express the wish to bring the actor even further into the auditorium, to establish a continuity between stage and auditorium, and to do away with the proscenium arch. Some raise objections to these steps.

" I prefer the stage with an adaptable proscenium because I am all for separating the world of the stage from that of the spectator. I do not like the mixture of the two worlds. " (Willi Schmidt)

There is undoubtedly a general tendency to attach primary importance to the new auditorium-stage relationship :

" As a designer, I would like to do something about the audience. I would like to arrange them in different ways for different plays because the design and arrangement of the audience and the stage in a particular way is real theatre design. " (Sean Kenny)

" Placing the audience and actors into the correct relationship and using a very minimum of scenery will someday return the theatre to the writers. " (Charles Elson)

" New architectural forms can only bring advantages; drawbacks only occur with reference to a misunderstood tradition. " (Erwin Piscator)

" More than the form of the stage and the theatre, it is the way in which one makes use of this space (from the point of view of decoration as well as production and acting) that will determine whether the nature of the performance given will be one of illusion or not, one of participation or of alienation. The problem of theatre architecture as it is generally raised today is thus seen in its true light : it is a false problem. ' Alienated ' theatre is possible on an Italian-style stage, and make-believe theatre on an apron stage. It depends on what use is made of the stage and has nothing to do with its specifications. " (René Allio)

However, few decorators seem to have used frankly audacious stage structures, or perhaps very occasionally, in the open-air theatre for instance.

III. LIGHTING

A. — QUESTION :

DO YOU PERSONALLY PARTICIPATE IN THE LIGHTING AND THE PREPARATIONS FOR THE LIGHTING?

All designers replied in the affirmative to this question and stressed the increasing importance of light in the conception of the stage spectacle.

" I find the placing of my lights most important. I try to locate all acting area spotlights so that the actors' features are lit at a 45° angle in plan and section from two directions and with two tints of colour. " (Charles Elson)

The primary importance of lighting is due to several factors :
it gives a new kind of relief to the set and greater plasticity;
its effectiveness is unmatched for conveying mood, a sense of unreality or poetry;
it is of first importance in the rhythm of the performance;

" Having learnt from a producer who was also a composer (E.F. Burian), I look at the composition of light as counterpoint, as a rhythmic element in the dramatic action, in harmony with the drama. " (Miroslav Kouril)

it has an influence on the development of stage design by allowing greater economy of means.

" Light should take the place of our cleverness for the sets. Why cannot we have instruments and equipment? We could make fantastic places and spaces which could be brought before your eyes or taken away in a second. A designer uses light anyway when he is designing his sets and probably the reason we over-design and put too much on the stage is because we lack confidence in the lighting engineers' equipment.
There should be no such thing as a lighting designer, this specialized group which has grown up in the theatre. Light is a designer's property and he should use it to simplify his technique. " (Sean Kenny)

The advent of a new specialist, the lighting expert, is not without its problems. Some designers easily accept him, but most are anxious to protect their prerogatives. In the extreme, a few hand over the reins to him completely when the time comes.
" In Japan, there are specialist electricians who work out the lighting plot and control it, quite independently. " (Ryotaro Mitsubayashi)

20

B. — QUESTION :

WHAT LIGHTING SYSTEM DO YOU USUALLY EMPLOY?

In every country, apparently, special consideration has been given in recent years to electrical equipment. Designers are unanimous in wanting it to be as complete as possible.

> " This is the ' star ', the ' angel ' of stage design; everything of the best, and even more, is required. " (Victor Maria Cortezo)

Nearly everywhere it consists of :
— floods (battens and footlights, ground-rows, vertical strips, open floodlights, etc.) to light the environment;
— spotlight of 500, 1000 and 2000 watts, and Fresnels; there is an increasing use of low-voltage spots;

> " I have used all kinds of electrical apparatus—and one needs them all. Recently I have made increasing use of spotlights of low voltage. They give the best possible results. " (Max Fritzsche)

— follow spots;

> " In addition I make use of 3000 and 5000 watt incandescent follow spots in various front-of-house positions to accent principals or significant action, but rarely is the intensity allowed to call attention to itself, rather it must be a useful, obsequious, flexible attendant. " (Charles Elson)

— projection lanterns, etc.;
— dimmers and switchboards which are often electronic.
The following has been selected from a number of examples :

> " Usually, mostly incandescent sources are used, controlled by resistance dimmers, or autotransformers. Soon we shall use thyatron tubes and silicon rectifiers.
> The apparatus includes :
> 1. Ellipsoido-reflector spots;
> 2. Parabolic beam projectors;
> 3. Fresnels;
> 4. Plano-convex spots;
> 5. Strip lights. " (Arnon Adar)

C. — QUESTION :

DO YOU USE ONLY WHITE OR ALSO COLOURED LIGHT, AND WHY?

About one half of the designers who replied to our inquiry use sometimes white and sometimes coloured light according to the style, purpose and aesthetic intentions of the play. " *As required*". (Ita Maximowna)

> " In the classical Kabuki plays, we use white light mostly (and sometimes blue for the night), but in the modern theatre coloured light is used. " (Ryotaro Mitsubayashi)

Of the other half, a majority were in favour of white light, sometimes slightly corrected.

> " ...absolutely white light, made slightly yellow at special times, and on rare occasions white light mixed with a little gold. " (Harry Wich)

The reason given : white light alone gives the colours of the set and costumes their true values without alteration.

> " I use mainly white light because I think it brengs out the colour of the costumes better.
> I use coloured lights sparingly and only if it is necessary to intensify the figure of the actor, or the emotional content of colours and incidents. Sometimes in dream sequences, for example, all the lighting can be coloured. " (Pekka Heiskanen)

A few, however, uphold coloured light :

> " The so-called ' white light ' is of course unfiltered incandescent light; which is not white at all. There is no reason for its use, except only for special effect. Even diffuse daylight has different colour temperatures, so why do worse on stage?
> I am prepared to challenge any ' white light ' apostle to prove his theories in lighting practice. " (Arnon Adar)

> " I prefer coloured light because—in the matter of painting—I prefer colour to monochrome. " (Liviu Ciulei)

D. — QUESTION :

HAVE YOU EVER EMPLOYED ANY SPECIAL EFFECTS : PROJECTED SCENERY (COMPLETE OR PARTIAL), SHADOW PROJECTION, CINEMATOGRAPHIC PROJECTION (FILMS, CARTOONS)...? IF SO, FOR WHAT PURPOSE AND WITH WHAT RESULTS? WHAT ADVANCES WOULD YOU LIKE TO SEE?

With a few rare exceptions—Piscator is one—theatre people enter this field with caution, seeming to fear " spectacle for its own sake ".

WHAT TECHNIQUES DO YOU USE ?

What is now traditional equipment, of course, projecting effects of snow, clouds, sea, fire, fog and so on.
Still or animated pictures (shadow theatre, etc.), *"not as an embellishment in itself, but as part of a complete structure. "* (Teo Otto)

" I consider projections to be valid when they reproduce a designed and created image and are in harmony with the set; if not, they give it a naturalistic flavour. " (Dan Nemteann)

" In *Dead Souls* (Gogol-Adamov), we needed to stress the epic nature of Tchitchikov's travels, and to do so we had to show the journey itself.
This led us to use the technique of the cinema. It was not a question of ' film making ' but of animating one part of the setting only, that part which, above the place represented, depicted the environment. Nor was it a question of vying with the reality of the people and objects on the stage, but of remaining within the sphere of graphic representation. That is why the landscapes and people in the film were drawn, which, moreover, helped to emphasize the style of the setting and its bias. " (René Allio)

Photographic and cinematographic projections.

" My main field of design is the kinetic and light theatre.
One of the new principles of the light theatre is projection onto two projection surfaces at an angle of 45º to each other, with a horizontal contact interstice in the neighbourhood of which perfect diffuse light is obtained. It gives great depth to the stage even when full use is not made of this depth. This technical principle was the basis of the setting for the play *August Sunday* by F. Hrubin and the opera *Rusalka* (Undine) by A. Dvorak.
The greatest interest is naturally aroused by the principles of the Magic Lantern and Polyekran, which were preceded by many years of experiment in the theatre—from 1946 onwards—and in experimental studios, aimed at combining and synchronizing the stage with the cinema. I tried to create a new relationship between the different elements : stage, screen, live acting, dancing and singing. This is no new idea on the stage. In many theatre productions we also tried to bring the separated and differentiated visual phenomena into a new integral composition with a certain theme. We achieve our effect by the placing of images in contrast, by their mutual relationships, and their rhythm in time and space. Thus we can combine them with the platic image, the merging of images and whole scenes, cutting, movement and space rhythm. This means we have dramatic space changing in the course of dramatic action. We achieved the same effect in several recent performances by using other means : pure light reflected from mechanically moved mirror surfaces, or light screens from low-voltage light ramps of our own construction, supplemented by decoration details.
In Czechoslovakia we have an outstanding scenographic laboratory with excellent opportunities for research and development. In addition, the National Theatre has on its staff first-class experts in optics, mechanics and electro-accoustics, which we are planning to make more use of in developing new principles and equipment next season. " (Josef Svoboda)

WHY DO YOU USE THEM ?

As a more tenuous presence than built scenery.

" The projection, on account of its soft and vaguely spherical effect, is one of the most useful mediums in stage design.
The amorphous forms of the projection kindle the audience's imagination. " (Jozsef Cselenyi)

To complete the set in part (according to some, entirely projected scenery would be tedious).
To allow suick scene changes.

" I believe that the main thing (in projected décor) is to enable the scene, and particularly the atmosphere, to be changed in full view of the audience and thus to obtain a plastic setting of great mobility which can closely follow the action and change with it. " (Toni Gheorghiu)

But also as counterpoint to the acting.

" Burian and I ascribed such importance to lighting that in 1936 we invented the Theatergraph, a form of light theatre in which the actor is perceived together with a projected image and a film on a transparent surface downstage. " (Miroslav Kouril)

ONE PROPOSAL THAT WAS FAIRLY GENERALLY PUT FORWARD : " *that light theatre* " be scientifically and experimentally *investigated so that everyone may profit from the experiences of others, and that technical books be published on the subject.* (Miroslav Kouril)

IV. METHOD OF WORK

QUESTION :

CAN YOU BRIEFLY DESCRIBE YOUR METHOD OF WORK, THE EXTENT TO WHICH YOU COLLABORATE WITH THE OTHER TECHNICIANS AND WITH THE PLAYWRIGHT OR COMPOSER? IS THERE CONTINUAL, CLOSE TEAMWORK? DO YOU PERSONALLY SUPERVISE THE EXECUTION OF YOUR SETS AND COSTUMES?

The method of work is much the same for everyone :
1. Reading and discussion of the play, a period of reflection, collaboration with the playwright, if possible, and with the producer, composer, etc. A long period of work.
2. Preliminary ideas in the form of sketches. Discussion.

> " The scheme for the production in its essential features having been decided upon, the work of the stage models starts. I myself always begin with a model made to the scale of 1:50. When this one is ready I make a new model to the scale 1:25. This scale brings out all the defects and flaws. If the model meets the artistic and technical requirements, I pass it on to the workshops of the theatre. I advise all designers to use this method as it saves lots of work and is economical for the theatre. With this method it is seldom necessary to change and remake things, a procedure always expensive and irritating to all concerned. " (Stellan Morner)

3. Preliminary scale models. Discussion.
4. Execution in the workshops.
5. Setting up on the stage, correction, painting. " *I always supervise the setting.* " (Franco Laurenti)
6. Lighting.

Is it a matter of teamwork? Yes, for :
— theatrical art is a composite art, but it must be *homogeneous*;
— better results are obtained when all the participants are involved.

> " The preliminary conferences with the artistic and technical personnel are of great importance. These are usually concerned with a brief outline of the play and how it is to be directed. I find that, as a result, the people do not work mechanically and are more interested in the outcome of their efforts. " (Wladimir Sramek)

This teamwork entails collaboration :
— with the playwright (he must be given an understanding of stage practicalities);
— with the producer (or choreographer) : general conception of the performance, placing, etc.;
— with other designers;

> " For many years, I have worked in collaboration with another stage designer : John Moore. We work in a spirit of complete harmony, and I think that the results of this co-operation are very satisfactory because work in common enables us to employ our reciprocal critical sense more fully and to supervise the work more closely. " (Veniero Colasanti)

— with the technical staff.

> " I talk with the technicians before the scenery is set and work with them in constant co-operation. I try to adapt my ideas to their possibilities. " (Seza Altindag)

Nearly all the designers questioned declare that they themselves direct the execution of their sets and costumes. And all, or nearly all, recognize the need to keep the mind unjaded and the eye fresh.

> " I and my colleagues in this theatre used to say : to start a new task ought to be like starting a new job. Methods, materials and techniques must be strictly adapted to the nature of the work in hand. " (Carl Johan Strom)

Quotations collected by René HAINAUX

KEY TO NUMERALS USED
IN CAPTIONS TO THE ILLUSTRATIONS

First in the caption is the name of the designer. Next, the title of the work in its original language.

The title is preceded by a Roman numeral :

  I : for a play,

 II : for an opera or a musical comedy,

III : for a ballet.

After the title further information is given, as indicated by the following numbers :

1. Name of the author of the play or libretto.

2. Name of the composer.

3. Name of the choreographer.

5. Name of the theatre, followed by the town and the year of production.

6. Name of the photographer.

ARRANGEMENT
OF
ILLUSTRATIONS

THE illustrations are arranged in groups, country by country, the designers' names being, with a few exceptions, arranged in alphabetical order.

The countries are presented in alphabetical order but since this volume is intended for readers of all nations we have preserved their native spelling —for example, Magyarorszag for Hungary or Suomi for Finland.

In the same spirit, captions to the illustrations have been rendered in such a way as to make them universally intelligible. The title of the work is given in its original language. Thus Chekhov's The Seagull, produced in Czechoslovakia, bears its original Russian title Chaïka. On the same principle, Strindberg's A Dream Play, produced in Switzerland, appears as Ett Drömspel.

The English translations of these original titles are given in the Index.

ARGENTINA

SAULO BENAVENTE. I : *Donde la Muerte clava sus Banderas*. **1** : Omar del Carlo. **3** : Orestes Caviglia. **5** : Teatro Nacional Cervantes. Buenos Aires. 1959. **6** : Chaure.

SAULO BENAVENTE. I : *Facundo en la Ciudadela*. **1** : Vicente Barbieri. **3** : Orestes Caviglia. **5** : Teatro Nacional de Comedia. Buenos Aires. 1959. **6** : Serge Nan.

GASTON BREYER. I : *Viaje a la Costa*. **1** : Raul Young. **3** : Raul Young. **5** : Teatro de los Independientes. Buenos Aires. 1956. **6** : Gaston Breyer.

GORI MUÑOZ. I : *El Anzuelo de Fenisa*. **1** : Lope de Vega. **3** : Alejandro Casona. **5** : Teatro Liceo. Buenos Aires. 1958.

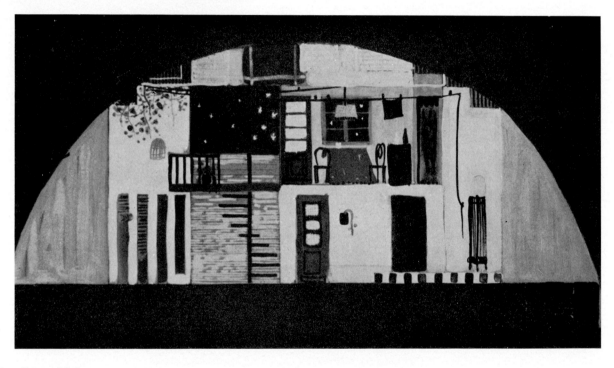

LUIS DIEGO PEDREIRA. I : *Narcisa Garay Mujer para Llorar*. **1** : Juan Carlos Ghiano. **3** : Francisco Silva. **5** : Teatro Carpa Belgrano. Buenos Aires. 1959.

MARIO VANARELLI. I : *Proserpina y el Extranjero*. **1** : Omar del Carlo. **3** : Boyce Diaz Ulloque. **5** : Teatro de Verano. Buenos Aires. 1957.

26

BELGIQUE

THIERRY BOSQUET. II : *Die Zauberflöte*. **2** : Wolfgang Amadeus Mozart. **3** : Jean-Marc Landeir. **5** : Théâtre Royal de la Monnaie. Bruxelles. 1961.

THIERRY BOSQUET. II : *Der Rosenkavalier*.
2 : Richard Strauss. **3** : Herbert Graf.
5 : Théâtre Royal de la Monnaie.
Bruxelles. 1962.

ROGER BROE. II : *Fidelio*. **2** : Ludwig van Beethoven. **3** : Marcel Claudel. **5** : Palais des Beaux-Arts. Charleroi. 1959.
6 : Henry.

SERGE CREUZ. I : *Arlecchino, Servitore di due Padroni*. **1** : Carlo Goldoni. **3** : René Jeauneau. **5** : Comédie de l'Est. Strasbourg. 1962. **6** : Michel Veilhan.

LODE IVO. II : *De Antikwaar*. **1** : Anton van Wilderode. **2** : Jef Maes. **3** : Marc Liebrecht. **4** : Jeanne Brabants. **5** : Koninklijke Vlaamse Opera. Antwerpen. 1963. **6** : J.M. Mertens.

ROBERT GEENENS. I : *Sire Halewijn*. **1** : Herman Closson. **3** : Lode Verstraete. **5** : Nederlands Kamertoneel. Antwerpen. 1957.

ÉMILE LANC. I : *La Malle de Pamela*. **1** : Georges Sion. **3** : Georges Mony. **5** : Rideau de Bruxelles. Bruxelles. 1955.

ÉMILE LANC. I : *La Plage aux Anguilles*. **1** : Paul Willems. **3** : Émile Lanc. **5** : Rideau de Bruxelles. 1959. **6** : Hella.

29

DENIS MARTIN. I : *Barabbas*. **1** : Michel de Ghelderode. **3** : Jacques Huisman. **5** : Théâtre National de Belgique. Bruxelles. 1954. **6** : Hensler.

RENÉ MOULAERT. II : *Aniara*. **2** : Karl-Birger Blomdahl. **3** : Göran Gentele. **5** : Théâtre Royal de la Monnaie. Bruxelles. 1960.

MARC - TOM PAYOT. I : *Teedrinken*. **1** : Jan Christiaens. **3** : André Poppe. **5** : Toneelstudio '50. Arca. Gent. 1958.

MIMI PEETERMANS. I : *Don Gil de las Calzas verdes*. **1** : Tirso de Molina. **3** : Ben Royaards. **5** : Nationaal Toneel van België. Antwerpen. 1962.

RAYMOND RENARD. I : *Arlecchino, Servitore di due Padroni*. **1** : Carlo Goldoni. **3** : Vito Pandolfi. **5** : Théâtre de Poche. Bruxelles. 1958. **6** : Sado.

RAYMOND RENARD. I : *Capitaine Bada*. **1** : Jean Vauthier. **3** : André Reybaz. **5** : Théâtre de Poche. Bruxelles. 1956. **6** : Cayet.

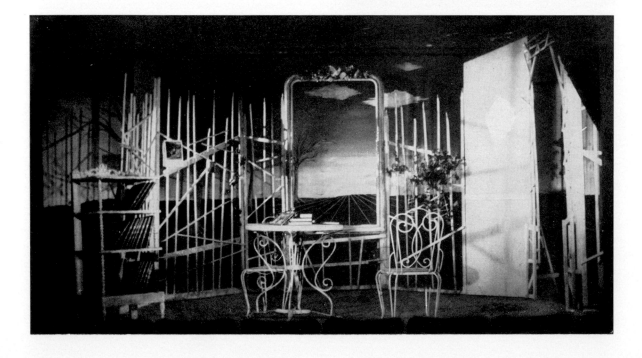

31

LODE SEBREGTS. I : *Spiegel der Minnen.*
1 : Collijn van Rijssele. 3 : Fred
Engelen. 5 : Nationaal Toneel van
België. Antwerpen. 1960.

JACQUES VAN NEROM. I : *De Bruid in de Morgen.*
1 : Hugo Claus. 3 : André Gevrey. 5 : Théâtre
Royal des Galeries. Bruxelles. 1959.
6 : Oscar Vanden Brugge.

JACQUES VAN NEROM. I : *Hamlet.* 1 : William
Shakespeare. 3 : Louis Boxus. 5 : Château de
Beersel. 1953.

ARGENTINA

GORI MUÑOZ. I : *La Hermana Josefina*. **1** : Darthès
y Damel. **3**. : Juan Vehil. **5** : Teatro La Comedia.
Rosario de Santa Fé. 1958.

BELGIQUE

DENIS MARTIN. I : *Peau d'Ours*. **1** : Paul Willems. **3** : Jacques Huisman.
5 : Théâtre National de Belgique. Bruxelles. 1951.

CINO DEL NERI. I : *O Pagador de Promessas.*
1 : Dias Gomes. **3** : Flavio Rangel. **5** : Teatro
Brasileiro de Comédia. São Paulo. 1961.
6 : Carlos.

BRASIL

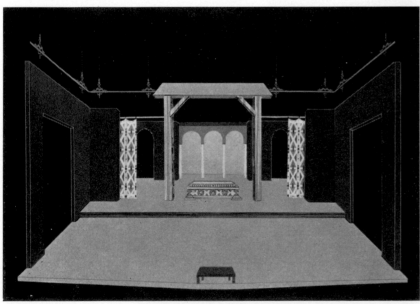

MAURO FRANCINI. I : *Volpone.* **1** : Ben Jonson.
3 : Z. Ziembinski. **5** : Teatro Brasileiro de Comédia.
Rio de Janeiro. 1955. **6** : Dainesi.

MAURO FRANCINI. I : *La Regina e Gli Insorti.* **1** :
Ugo Betti. **3** : Maurice Vaneau. **5** : Teatro Brasileiro
de Comédia. Sao Paulo. 1957.

NAPOLEÃO MONIZ FREIRE. I : *Le Malentendu*. **1** : Albert Camus. **5** : O Tablado. Rio de Janeiro. 1961.

BELLA PAES LEME. I : *Electra no Circo*. **1** : Hermilo Borba Filho. **3** : Geraldo Queiroz. **5** : Movimento Brasileiro de Arte. Rio de Janeiro. 1956.

BEATRICE TANAKA. I : *Le Théâtre de Monsieur Monsieur* (Le Guichet). **1** : Jean Tardieu. **3** : Jorge Lavelli. **5** : Théâtre de l'Alliance Française. Paris. 1962.

BULGARIA

MARIANA POPOVA. II : *Imalo edno vrémé.*
1 : Pavel Spassov. **2** : Parachkev Hadjiev.
3 : Nikolaï Nikolov. **5** : Narodna Opera.
Varna. 1960.

MARIANA POPOVA. I : *Prédlojénié.* **1** : Anton
Chekhov. **3** : Metodi Andonov. **5** : Satiritchen
Téatr. Sofia. 1959.

MARIANA POPOVA. II : *Imalo edno vrémé.*
1 : Pavel Spassov. **2** : Parachkev Hadjiev.
3 : Nikolaï Nikolov. **5** : Narodna Opera.
Varna. 1960.

ASSEN POPOV. I : *King Lear.* **1** : William Shakespeare. **3** : Sacho Soyanov.
5 : Naroden Téatr « Ivan Vazov ». Sofia. 1959.

CANADA

The Festival Shakespeare Theatre. Architectes :
ROUNTHWAITE-FAIRFIELD. Stratford-Ontario.
6 : Herb Nott.

TANYA MOISEIWITSCH. I : *Oidipous Tyrannos.*
1 : Sophocles. **3** : Tyrone Guthrie. **5** : Shakespeare
Festival Theatre. Stratford-Ontario. 1954.
6 : McKague.

TANYA MOISEIWITSCH. I : *Much Ado About
Nothing.* **1** : William Shakespeare. **3** : Michael
Langham. **5** : Shakespeare Festival Theatre.
Stratford-Ontario. 1958.

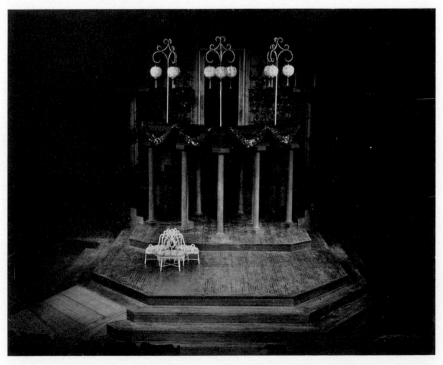

JACQUES PELLETIER. I : *L'Avare*. **1** : Molière.
3 : Jean Gascon. **5** : Théâtre du Nouveau Monde.
Montréal. 1951. **6** : Henri Paul.

ROBERT PREVOST. I : *Le Temps des Lilas*.
1 : Marcel Dubé. **3** : Jean Gascon. **5** : Théâtre du
Nouveau Monde. Montréal. 1958. **6** : Henri Paul.

JEAN-CLAUDE RINFRET. I : *Les
Plaideurs*. **1** : Racine. **3** : Jan
Doat. **5** : Comédie Canadienne.
Théâtre Club. Montréal. 1959.

ČESKOSLOVENSKO

KVETOSLAV BUBENIK. II : *Don Carlos.* **2** : Giuseppe
Verdi. **3** : Karel Jernek. **5** : Smetanovo Divadlo.
Praha. 1960.

JAN HANAK. I : *Bohovia Amsterodamu.* **1** : Jurah Vah.
3 : Jozef Palka. **5** : Statni Divadlo. Kosice. 1959.

VLADIMIR HELLER. II : *Tkalci*. **1** : Gerhart
Hauptmann. **2** : Vit Nejedly. **3** : Bohumir Zoul.
5 : Divadlo J.K. Tyla. Plzen. 1961.

MIKULAS KRAVJANSKY. I : *La Casa de Bernarda Alba*. **1** : Federico Garcia Lorca.
3 : Ivo Lichard. **5** : Slovenské Narodné Divadlo. Bratislava. 1957.

VLADIMIR NYVLT. I : *Kazdy Neco pro Vlast.*
1 : Vaclav Kliment Klicpera. 3 : Emil Frantisek
Burian. 5 : Divadlo D 34. Praha. 1958.

VLADIMIR NYVLT. I : *Sabla Damokla.* 1 : Nazim Hikmet. 3 : Frantisek Stepanek.
5 : Divadlo cs. Armady. Praha. 1959.

JOSEF SVOBODA. II : *Povest o Nastoïachtchem Tchéloveké*. **2** : Sergueï Prokofiev. **3** : Georgij Pavlovic Ansimov. **5** : Narodni Divadlo. Praha. 1961.

JOSEF SVOBODA. I : *Chaïka*. **1** : Anton Chekhov. **3** : Otomar Krejca. **5** : Narodni Divadlo. Praha. 1960.

JOSEF SVOBODA. I : *Hamlet*. **1** : William Shakespeare. **3** : Jaromir Pleskot. **5** : Narodni Divadlo. Praha. 1959.

JOSEF SVOBODA. II : *Die Zauberflöte*. **2** : Wolfgang Amadeus Mozart. **3** : Vaclav Kaslik. **5** : Narodni Divadlo. Praha. 1961.

VLADIMIR SYNEK. I : *Simple Takes a Wife.*
1 : Langston Hughes. 3 : Vaclav Lohnisky.
5 : Divadlo S.K. Neumanna. Praha. 1959.

MILOS TOMEK. I: *Ze Zivota Hmyzu.* 1: Jozef-Karel
Capek. 3 : Ales Podhorsky. 5 : Statni Divadlo.
Brno. 1958.

FRANTISEK TRÖSTER. I : *Dom Juan.* **1** : Molière.
3 : Jaromir Pleskot. **5** : Tylovo Divadlo.
Praha. 1957.

ADOLF WENIG. I : *Le Jeu de l'Amour et du Hasard.* **1** : Marivaux. **3** : Karel Svoboda.
5 : Divadlo komedie. Praha. 1959.

EDUARDO ARROCHA. III : *Entreacto Barroco.*
2 : Jean-Sébastien Bach. **4** : Ramiro Guerra.
5 : Conjunto Nacional de Danza Moderna.
Teatro Garcia Lorca. La Habana. 1963.
6 : Buznego.

CUBA

SALVADOR FERNANDEZ – RAÚL OLIVA. I : *Santa Juana de América.* **1** : Andrés Lizárraga. **3** : Eduardo Manet. **5** : Teatro Nacional de Cuba. Sala Covarrubias. La Habana. 1960. **6** : Mayito.

MARIA ELENA MOLINET. III : *Comparsa Tradicional de Carnaval* (Diablito). **4** : Rodolfo Reyes. **5** : Conjunto Folkorico Nacional. Teatro Mella. La Habana. 1963. **6** : Buznego.

RUBEN VIGÓN. I : *Sempronio, el Peluquero y los Hombrecitos.* **1** : Agustin Cuzzani. **3** : Cuqui Ponce de Léon. **5** : Grupo Rita Montaner. Teatro Nacional de Cuba. Teatro Mella. La Habana. 1962.
6 : Buznego.

OST-DEUTSCHLAND

KARL VON APPEN. I : *Pauken und Trompeten*.
1 : George Farquhar – Bertolt Brecht –
Benno Besson – Elizabeth Hauptmann.
2 : Rudolf Wagner-Régeny. 3 : Benno Besson.
5 : Berliner Ensemble. Berlin. 1955.

KARL VON APPEN. I : *Katzgraben*.
1 : Erwin Strittmatter. 2 : Hanns
Eisler. 3 : Bertolt Brecht – Manfred
Wekwerth. 5 : Berliner Ensemble.
Berlin. 1953. 6 : Percy Paukschta.

FRANZ HAVEMANN. I : *Hamlet.* **1** : William
Shakespeare. **3** : Fritz Bennewitz.
5 : Deutsches Nationaltheater.
Weimar. 1960.

RUDOLF HEINRICH. II : *Lisky Prihody Bystrousky.* **2** : Leos Janacek.
3 : Walter Felsenstein. **5** : Komische Oper. Berlin. 1957.

CANADA

ROBERT PREVOST. I : *Les Femmes Savantes*. **1** : Molière.
3 : Jean Gascon. **5** : Théâtre du Nouveau Monde. Montréal.
1960. **6** : Henri Paul.

OST-DEUTSCHLAND

EBERHARD SCHWENK. III : *Drosselbart*.
1 : Wolfgang Hohensee. **2** : Albert
Burkat. **4** : Veit Büchel. **5** : Städtische
Bühnen. Magdeburg. 1959.

RUDOLF HEINRICH. II : *Die Meistersinger von Nürnberg*. **2** : Richard Wagner. **3** : Joachim Herz. **5** : Opernhaus Leipzig. 1960. **6** : Helga Wallmüller.

RUDOLF HEINRICH. II : *Der brave Soldat Schwejk*. **1** : Lewis Allan. **2** : Robert Kurka. **3** : Joachim Herz. **5** : Komische Oper. Berlın. 1960.

HAINER HILL. II : *Wozzeck*. **2** : Alban Berg. **3** : Werner Kelch.
5 : Deutsche Staatsoper. Berlin. 1955. **6** : Franz Hoffmeister.

HAINER HILL. II : *Elektra*. **2** : Richard Strauss. **3** : Werner
Kelch. **5** : Deutsche Staatsoper. Berlin, 1957.

HEINRICH KILGER. I : *Minna von Barnhelm*. **1** : Gotthold Ephraim Lessing.
3 : Wolfgang Langhoff. **5** : Deutsches Theater. Berlin. 1960.

HEINRICH KILGER. I : *King Lear*. **1** : William Shakespeare. **3** : Wolfgang Langhoff.
5 : Deutsches Theater. Berlin. 1957.

GERHARD SCHADE. I : *Die Heilige Johanna der Schlachthöfe*. **1** : Bertolt Brecht. **3** : Hannes Fischer – Otto-Fritz Gaillard. **5** : Staatstheater. Dresden. 1961. **6** : Jutta Landgraf.

ROMAN WEYL. I : *Pesti Emberek*. **1** : Lajos Mesterhazi. **3** : Fritz Wisten. **5** : Volksbühne. Berlin. 1960.

WEST-DEUTSCHLAND

LENI BAUER-ECSY. I : *Under Milk Wood.* **1** : Dylan Thomas.
3 : Boleslaw Barlog. **5** : Schiller-Theater. Berlin. 1957.
6 : Köster.

HANS AEBERLI. I : *Les Séquestrés d'Altona.* **1** : Jean-Paul
Sartre. **3** : Erwin Piscator. **5** : Städtische Bühnen.
Essen. 1959. **6** : G. Meyer-Hanno.

HERTA BOEHM. I : *El Alcalde de Zalamea.* **1** : Pedro Calderon
de la Barca. **3** : Ulrich Erfurth. **5** : Deutsches Schauspielhaus. Hamburg. 1961. **6** : Rosemarie Clausen.

ROLF CHRISTIANSEN. II : *Antigone*. **1** : Jean Cocteau. **2** : Arthur Honegger.
3 : Reinhard Lehmann. **5** : Städtische Bühnen.
Freiburg. 1955. **6** : G. Meyer-Hanno.

MAX FRITZSCHE. I : *Die Dreigroschenoper*. **1** : Bertolt
Brecht. **2** : Kurt Weill. **3** : Hans Schalla. **5** : Schauspielhaus.
Bochum. Théâtre des Nations. Paris. 1957.

WALTER GONDOLF. II : *Bluthochzeit*. **1** : Federico Garcia
Lorca. **2** : Wolfgang Fortner. **3** : Erich Bormann.
5 : Grosses Haus. Köln. 1957. **6** : Dönitz.

FABIUS VON GUGEL. II : *König Hirsch*. **2** : Hans-Werner
Henze. **3** : Harro Dicks. **5** : Landestheater.
Darmstadt. 1959. **6** : Pini-Optik.

EKKEHARD GRÜBLER. I : *Picnic en Campagne*. **1** : Fernando
Arrabal. **3** : Heinrich Koch – Günter Ballhausen.
5 : Städtische Bühnen. Frankfurt/Main. 1959.
6 : G. Meyer-Hanno.

PAUL HAFERUNG. II : *Moses und Aron*.
2 : Arnold Schönberg. **3** : Karl Heinz Krahl.
5 : Stadttheater. Zürich. 1957. **6** : W.E. Baur.

KURT HALLEGGER. I : *The Wall*. **1** : Millard
Lampell. **3** : Kurt Meisel. **5** : Residenz-
theater. München. 1961.

LENI BAUER-ECSY. II : *Volpone*. **2** : Francis Burt. **3** : Günther
Rennert. **5**: Württembergische Staatstheater. Stuttgart. 1960.

WEST-DEUTSCHLAND

PAUL HAFERUNG. I : *Herr Puntila und sein Knecht Matti*.
1 : Bertolt Brecht. **3** : Anton Krilla. **5** : Theater der Stadt.
Bonn. 1956.

HEIN HECKROTH. III : *Die Sieben Totsünden*. **1** : Bertolt Brecht. **2** : Kurt Weill. **4** : Tatjana Gsovsky. **5** : Städtische Bühnen. Frankfurt/Main. 1960.

HELMUT JÜRGENS. II : *Idomeneo*. **2** : Wolfgang Amadeus Mozart. **3** : Heinz Arnold. **5** : Bayerische Staatsoper. München. 1956. **6** : Rudolf Betz.

HELMUT KONIARSKY. I : *Revizor*. **1** : Nikolaï Gogol. **3** : Günther Rennert. **5** : Schlosspark-Theater. Berlin. 1961. **6** : G. Meyer-Hanno.

H.W. LENNEWEIT. I : *The Women of Trachis.* **1** : Ezra Pound.
3 : Hans Lietzau. **5** : Schiller-Theater. Berlin. 1959.
6 : G. Meyer-Hanno.

H.W. LENNEWEIT. I : *Krieg und Frieden.* **1** : Tolstoï –
Piscator – Prüfer – Neumann. **3** : Erwin Piscator.
5 : Schiller-Theater. Berlin. 1955.

HANNES MEYER. I : *The Women of Trachis*. **1** : Ezra Pound.
3 : Gustav-Rudolf Sellner. **5** : Landestheater.
Darmstadt. 1959.

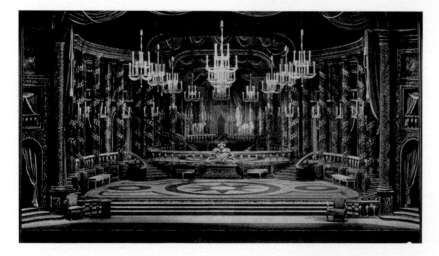

ITA MAXIMOWNA. II : *Un Ballo in Maschera*.
2 : Giuseppe Verdi. **3** : Josef Gielen.
5 : Staatsoper. Wien. 1958. **6** : Paul Macku.

FRANZ MERTZ. I : *Penthesilea*. **1** : Heinrich von Kleist.
3 : Heinrich Koch. **5** : Städtische Bühnen.
Frankfurt/Main. 1961. **6** : Ursula Seitz.

WILFRIED MINKS. I : *Capitaine Bada*. **1** : Jean Vauthier.
3 : Peter Zadek. **5** : Städtische Bühnen. Ulm. 1959.

CASPAR NEHER. II : *Les Contes d'Hoffmann*. **2** : Jacques Offenbach. **3** : Oscar Fritz Schuh – Christian Stange. **5** : Bühnen der Stadt Köln. 1961.

JEAN-PIERRE PONNELLE. 1 : *Il Conte Ory*. **2** : Gioacchino Rossini. **3** : Carl Ebert. **5** : Städtische Oper. Berlin. 1957. **6** : Ilse Buhs.

ROBERT PUDLICH. II : *Don Pasquale*. **2** : Gaetano Donizetti.
3 : Wolf Völker. **5** : Städtische Oper. Berlin. 1954.

WILHELM REINKING. II : *Alkmene*. **2** : Giselher Klebe.
3 : Gustav Rudolf Sellner. **5** : Deutsche Oper. Berlin. 1961.
6 : Ilse Buhs.

WILHELM REINKING. II : *Orpheus und Eurydike*. **2** : Christoph
Willibald Gluck. **3** : Gustav Rudolf Sellner. **5** : Deutsche
Oper. Berlin. 1961. **6** : Harry Croner.

GERD RICHTER. I : *Der Fisch mit dem goldenen Dolch.*
1 : Richard Hey. **3** : Dieter Haugk. **5** : Württembergische
Staatstheater. Stuttgart. 1958. **6** : Winkler – Bezendahl.

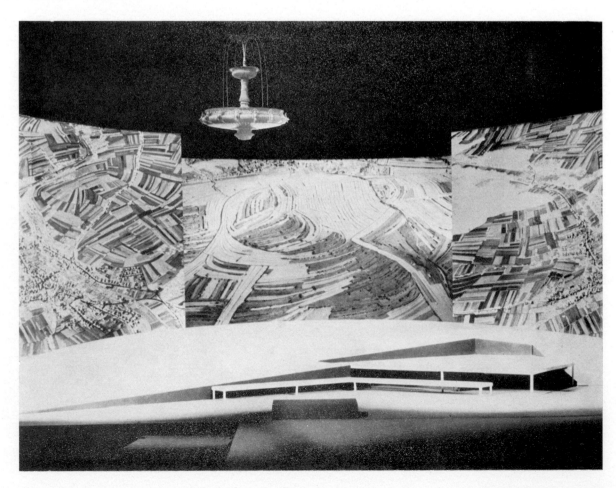

WILLI SCHMIDT. I : *Sei Personnaggi in cerca d'Autore.*
1 : Luigi Pirandello. **3** : Willi Schmidt. **5** : Burgtheater.
Wien. 1959.

G. SCHNEIDER-SIEMSSEN. II : *Die Harmonie der Welt.*
2 : Paul Hindemith. **3** : Albert Lippert. **5** : Theater der
Freien Hansestadt. Bremen. 1957. **6** : Wolle.

JAN SCHLUBACH. I : *Amor de Don Perlimplin con Belisa en su Jardin*. **1** : Federico Garcia Lorca. **3** : Fritz Schmiedel. **5** : Deutsches Theater. Göttingen. 1963. **6** : G. Meyer-Hanno.

RUDOLF SCHULZ. III : *Masques Ostendais*. **1** : Michel de Ghelderode. **2** : Roman Vlad. **3** : Yvonne Georgi. **5** : Opernhaus. Hannover. 1960.

FRIEDHELM STRENGER. I : *Histoire de Vasco*. **1** : Georges Schehadé. **3** : Hans Bauer. **5** : Landestheater. Hannover. 1958. **6** : G. Meyer-Hanno.

ALFRED SIERCKE. II : *Pallas Athene weint.* **2** : Ernst Krenek. **3** : Günther Rennert. **5** : Hamburgische Staatsoper. Hamburg. 1955. **6** : Peyer.

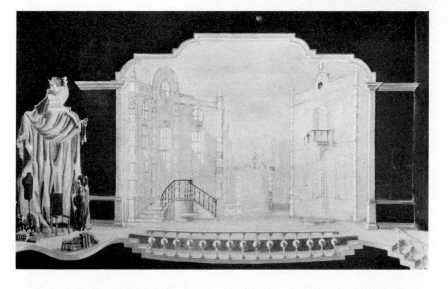

ALFRED SIERCKE. II : *Die Schule der Frauen.* **2** : Rolf Liebermann. **3** : Günther Rennert. **5** : Hamburgische Staatsoper. Hamburg. 1958. **6** : G. Meyer-Hanno.

ALFRED SIERCKE. II : *Cardillac.* **2** : Paul Hindemith. **3** : Hans Schalla. **5** : Hamburgische Staatsoper. Hamburg. 1961.

WIELAND WAGNER. II : *Die Meistersinger von Nürnberg*. **2** : Richard Wagner. **3** : Wieland Wagner. **5** : Festspiele. Bayreuth. 1956. **6** : S. Lauterwasser.

WIELAND WAGNER. II : *Lohengrin*. **2** : Richard Wagner. **3** : Wieland Wagner. **5** : Festspiele. Bayreuth. 1960.

HEINRICH WENDEL. II : *Don Giovanni*. **2** : Wolfgang
Amadeus Mozart. **3** : Georg Reinhardt. **5** : Wuppertaler
Bühnen. Wuppertal. 1959. **6** : Kurt Saurin.

HEINRICH WENDEL. III : *Dritte Sinfonie*. **2** : Hans Werner
Henze. **3** : Erich Walter. **5** : Wuppertaler Bühnen.
Wuppertal. 1960. **6** : Saurin – Sorani.

ESPAÑA

EMILIO BURGOS. I : *Un Soñador para un Pueblo*. **1** : Antonio Buero Vallejo. **3** : José Tamayo. **5** : Teatro Oficial Español. Madrid. 1958. **6** : Gyenes.

LEO ANCHORIZ. I : *La Feria de Cuernicabra*. **1** : Alfredo Mañas. **3** : Manuel Benítez – Sánchez Cortés. **4** : Alberto Portillo. **5** : Teatro Goya. Madrid. 1959. **6** : Basabe.

EMILIO BURGOS. I : *La Cornada*.
1: Alfonso Sastre. **3**: Adolfo Marsillach.
5 : Teatro Lara. Madrid. 1960.
6 : Servicio Fotográfico del Ministerio
de Información y Turismo.

JOSÉ CABALLERO. I : *Don Juan Tenorio*.
1 : José Zorrilla. **3** : José Tamayo.
5: Teatro Oficial Español. Madrid. 1956.
6 : Gyenes.

JOSÉ CABALLERO. I : *Yerma*. **1** : Federico
García Lorca. **3** : Luis Escobar.
5 : Teatro Eslava. Madrid. 1960.
6 : Gyenes.

VÍCTOR MARÍA CORTEZO. I : *Fuente
Ovejuna*. **1** : Lope de Vega. **3** : José
Tamayo Rivas. **5** : Teatro Español.
Madrid. 1962.

SALVADOR DALI. I : *Don Juan Tenorio.*
1 : José Zorrilla. **3** : Luis Escobar.
5 : Teatro María Guerrero. Madrid.
6 : Gyenes.
Segunda versión. 1950.

Primera versión. 1949.

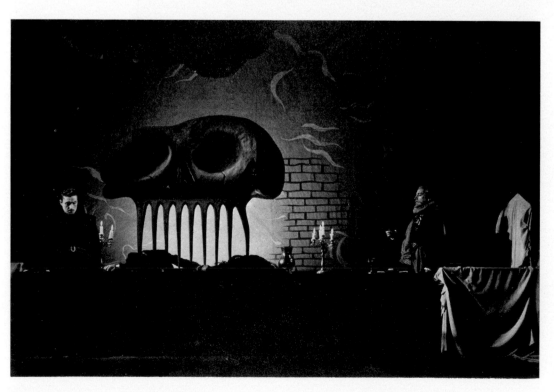

Segunda versión. 1950.

ESPAÑA

SALVADOR DALI. I : *Don Juan Tenorio*. **1** : José Zorrilla. **3** : Luis Escobar. **5** : Teatro María Guerrero. Madrid. 1950 **6** : Servicio Fotográfico del Ministerio de Información y Turismo.

EMILIO BURGOS. I : *Hoy es Fiesta*. **1** : Antonio Buero Vallejo. **3** : Claudio de la Torre. **5** : Teatro María Guerrero. Madrid. 1955. **6** : Servicio Fotográfico del Ministerio de Información y Turismo.

LEO ANCHORIZ. I : *La Feria de Cuernicabra*. **1** : Alfredo Mañas. **3** : Manuel Benítez – Sánchez Cortés. **4** : Alberto Portillo. **5** : Teatro Goya. Madrid. 1959. **6** : Servicio Fotográfico del Ministerio de Información y Turismo.

79

CARLOS PASCUAL DE LARA. I : *Don Juan Tenorio.*
1 : José Zorrilla. **3** : José Tamayo. **5** : Teatro
Oficial Español. Madrid. 1956. **6** : Gyenes.

MANUEL MAMPASO. I : *Don Juan Tenorio.*
1 : José Zorrilla. **3** : José Tamayo.
5: Teatro Oficial Español. Madrid. 1956.
6 : Gyenes.

BENJAMÍN PALECENCIA. I : *Don Juan Tenorio.*
1: José Zorrilla. **3**: José Tamayo. **5**: Teatro Oficial
Español. Madrid. 1956. **6** : Gyenes.

VICENTE VIUDES. I : *La Bella Malmaridada.*
1 : Lope de Vega. 3 : José Luis Alonso. 5 : Teatro
Mar a Guerrero. Madrid. 1961. 6 : Gyenes.

VICENTE VIUDES. I : *La Celestina.* 1 : Fernando de
Rojas. 3 : Luis Escobar. 5 : Teatro Eslava.
Madrid. 1958. 6 : Ortiz.

VICENTE VIUDES. I : *La Celestina.* 1 : Fernando
de Rojas. 3 : Luis Escobar. 5 : Teatro Eslava.
Madrid. 1958.

ANDRÉ ACQUART. I : *Les Nègres.* **1** : Jean Genêt.
3 : Roger Blin. **5** : Théâtre de Lutèce. Paris. 1959.
6 : Acquart.

FRANCE

ANDRÉ ACQUART. I : *L'Histoire de Tobie et Sara.*
1 : Paul Claudel. **2** : Heimo Erbse. **3** : Hans
Lietzau. **5** : Bühnen der Stadt Köln. Kirche
St Maria Himmelfahrt. Köln. 1961. **6** : Preser.

ANDRÉ ACQUART. III : *Pantomime d'un Sou.*
Mimodrame. **3** : Gilles Ségal. **5** : Théâtre de
France. Paris. 1961. **6** : Acquart.

RENÉ ALLIO. I : *Edward II*. **1** : Christopher Marlowe.
3 : Roger Planchon. **5** : Théâtre de la Cité. Villeurbanne-Lyon. 1962. **6** : Pic.

RENÉ ALLIO. I : *Tartuffe*. **1** : Molière. **3** : Roger Planchon.
5 : Théâtre de la Cité. Villeurbanne-Lyon. 1963. **6** : Pic.

RENÉ ALLIO. I : *Les Ames Mortes*.
1 : Gogol-Adamov. **3** : Roger Planchon.
5 : Théâtre de la Cité. Villeurbanne-Lyon. 1960. **6** : Pic.

ROGER BEZOMBES. II : *Sampiero Corso*. **1** : R. Cuttoli.
2 : Henri Tomasi. **3** : Roger Lalande. **4** : Janine Charrat.
5 : Festival de Bordeaux. 1956. **6** : Marc Vaux.

ANDRÉ BOLL. I : *Coriolan*. **1** : William Shakespeare.
3 : Vera Korène. **5** : Théâtre romain de Fourvière.
1953.

JEAN COCTEAU. II : *Pelléas et Mélisande*.
1 : Maurice Maeterlinck. **2** : Claude
Debussy. **3**: Henri Doublier. **5**: Festival
International. Metz. 1962.

CLAUDE BLEYNIE. III : *Suspense*. **1** : Claude Bleynie.
2 : Albert Roussel. **4** : Françoise Adret. **5** : Festival
International de la Danse. Aix-les-Bains. 1957.
6 : Daniel Marc.

YVES BRAYER. II : *Dolorès ou le Miracle de la Femme Laide*. **1** : Henry Ghéon. **2** : André Jolivet. **3**: Louis Erlo. **5**: Opéra de Lyon. 1960. **6**: Marc Vaux.

YVES-BONNAT. II. : *Le Chevalier de Neige*. **1** : Boris Vian. **2** : Georges Delerue. **3** : Marcel Lamy. **5** : Grand Théâtre de l'Opéra. Nancy. 1957.

BERNARD BUFFET. II : *Carmen*. **2** : Georges Bizet. **3** : Louis Ducreux. **5** : Opéra de Marseille. 1962. **6** : Daniel Frasnay.

JACQUES CAMURATI. I : *Prométhée enchaîné*. **1** : Jean de Beer. **3** : Pierre Jolivet. **5** : Théâtre du Tertre. Paris. 1959.

LUCIEN COUTAUD. I : *Protée*. **1** : Paul Claudel. **2** : Darius Milhaud. **3** : Raymond Gérôme. **5** : Comédie de Paris. Paris. 1955. **6** : Marc Vaux.

BERNARD DAYDÉ. II : *Orphée aux Enfers*. **2** : Jacques
Offenbach. **3** : Heinz Rosen. **5** : Städtische Bühnen, Köln
–Volksoper, Wien. 1958. **6** : Liseg.

OLIVIER DECAMP. I : *Prometheus desmotes*. **1** : Aischylos.
3 : Julien Bertheau. **5** : Comédie Française. Festival de
Lyon-Charbonnière. 1954. **6** : Bernand.

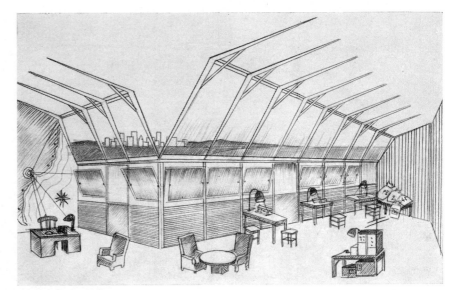

GEORGES DOUKING. II : *Vol de Nuit*. **1** : Saint-Exupéry –
Jacques Bourgeois. **2** : Luigi Dallapiccola. **3** : Jean Mercure.
5 : Opéra-Comique. Paris. 1961.

JACQUES DUPONT. I : *Château en Suède*. **1** : Françoise
Sagan. **3** : André Barsacq. **5** : Théâtre de l'Atelier.
1960. **6** : Marc Vaux.

ABD'EL KADER FARRAH. I : *Mille Francs
de Récompense*. **1** : Victor Hugo.
3: Hubert Gignoux. **5**: Comédie de l'Est.
1961. **6** : Michel Veilhan.

ABD'EL KADER FARRAH. II : *Œdipus Rex*. **1** : Sophocles –
Cocteau – Danielou. **2** : Igor Stravinsky. **3** : Michel Saint-
Denis. **5** : Sadler's Wells. London. 1960. **6** : David Sim.

YVES FAUCHEUR. I : *La Famille Arlequin*.
1 : Claude Santelli. **3** : Jacques Fabbri.
5 : Théâtre du Vieux-Colombier.
Paris. 1956. **6** : Glaeser.

YVES FAUCHEUR. I : *The Merry Wives
of Windsor*. **1** : William Shakespeare.
3 : Guy Lauzin. **5** : Compagnie
Jacques Fabbri. Enghien. 1961.
6 : Glaeser.

LEONOR FINI. I : *Le Garçon d'Honneur*. **1** : Oscar Wilde –
Blondin – Guimard. **3** : Claude Barma. **5** : Théâtre Marigny.
Paris. 1960. **6** : Pic.

ANDRÉ FRANÇOIS. III : *Pas de Dieux*. **1** : Gene Kelly.
2: Georges Gershwin. **4**: Gene Kelly. **5**: Opéra de Paris. 1960.

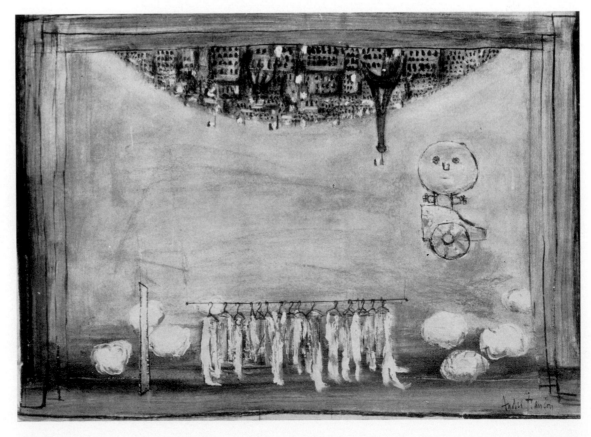

FRANÇOIS GANEAU. I : *La Zapatera Prodigiosa.*
1 : Federico Garcia Lorca. 3 : Maurice Sarrazin.
5 : Grenier de Toulouse. Toulouse. 1960. 6 : Yan.

LÉON GISCHIA. I : *Le Triomphe de l'Amour.* 1 : Marivaux.
3 : Jean Vilar. 5 : Théâtre National Populaire. Paris. 1956.
6 : Bernand.

JEAN JANOIR. II : *Pelléas et Mélisande.* 1 : Maurice
Maeterlinck. 2 : Claude Debussy. 3 : Louis Erlo.
5 : Opéra de Lyon. 1962.

WLADIMIR JEDRINSKI. II : *Carmen*. **2** : Georges Bizet.
3 : Louis Noguera. **5** : Opéra de Nice. 1958.

FÉLIX LABISSE. I : *Oresteia*. **1** : Aischylos.
3 : Jean-Louis Barrault. **5** : Théâtre
Marigny. Paris. 1955. **6** : Bernand.

CHRISTIANE LUCKE. I : Miguel Mañara.
1 : O.V. Milosz. **3** : Guy Suarès.
5 : Comédie de la Loire. Tours. 1963.

JACQUES LAGRANGE. I : *The Shoemaker's Holiday*. **1** : Thomas
Dekker. **3** : Georges Wilson. **5** : Théâtre National
Populaire. Paris. 1959. **6** : Agnès Varda.

RAYMOND DE LARRAIN. III : *La Belle au Bois dormant*.
2 : Tchaïkovsky. **4** : Marius Petipa-Robert Help-
man. **5** : Ballet du Marquis de Cuevas. Théâtre des
Champs-Élysées. Paris. 1961. **6** : Serge Lido.

JEAN-DENIS MALCLÈS. II : *Orphée*. **2** : Christoph Willibald
Gluck. **3**: Jean Meyer. **5**: Festival d'Aix-en-Provence. 1955.
6 : Marcel Arthaud.

JEAN-DENIS MALCLÈS. I : *Becket ou
l'Honneur de Dieu*. **1** : Jean Anouilh.
3 : Jean Anouilh – Roland Pietri.
55 : Théâtre Montparnasse. Paris. 1959.
6 : Lipnitzki.

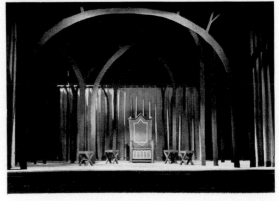

JACQUES MARILLIER. I : *Penthesilea*. **1** : Heinrich von Kleist.
3 : Claude Regy. **5** : Théâtre Hébertot. Paris. 1955.
6 : Bernand.

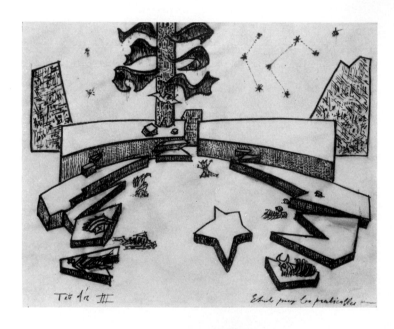

ANDRÉ MASSON. I : *Tête d'Or*. **1** : Paul Claudel.
3 : Jean-Louis Barrault. **5** : Théâtre de France.
Paris. 1959. **6** : Leiris.

MAURICE MÉLAT. I-II-III : *Le Roi
David*. **1** : René Morax. **2** : Arthur
Honegger. **3** : Maurice Sarrazin.
4 : Tony Pardina. **5** : Théâtre du Capitole. Toulouse. 1958. **6** : A. Serres.

95

JACQUES NOËL. I : *Pericles, Prince of Tyre*. **1** : William
Shakespeare. **3** : René Dupuy. **5** : Théâtre de l'Ambigu.
Paris. 1957. **6** : Pic.

JASQUES NOËL. I : *Le Piéton de l'Air*.
1 : Eugène Ionesco. **3** : Jean-Louis Barrault.
5 : Théâtre de France. Paris. 1963. **6** : Pic.

PACE. I : *Rodogune*. **1** : Pierre Corneille. **3** : Antoine
Bourseiller. **5** : Théâtre Sarah Bernhardt.
Paris. 1960. **6** : Weiss.

FRANCE

YVES-BONNAT. II : *Carmen*. 2 : Bizet. 3 : Louis Erlo.
5 : Théâtre Royal de la Monnaie. Bruxelles. 1961.

PACE. I : *Les Parachutistes*. 1 : Jean Cau. 3 : Antoine Bourseiller.
5 : Studio des Champs-Élysées. Paris. 1963.

PACE. I : *La Mort d'Agrippine*. **1** : Cyrano de Bergerac.
3 : Antoine Bourseiller. **5** : Studio des Champs-Élysées.
Paris. 1960. **6** : Bernand.

ÉDOUARD PIGNON. I : *Platonov*. **1** : Anton Chekhov. **3** : Jean Vilar.
Théâtre National Populaire. Paris. 1956. **6** : Agnès Varda.

MICHEL RAFFAELLI. II : *Moses und Aron.*
2 : Arnold Schœnberg. **3** : Gustav Rudolf
Sellner. **4** : Dore Hoyer. **5** : Städtische Oper.
Berlin. 1961.

MICHEL RAFFAELLI. I : *La Fête Noire.*
1 : Jacques Audiberti. **3** : Gustav Rudolf
Sellner. **5** : Landestheater. Darmstadt. 1963.
6 : Pit Ludwig.

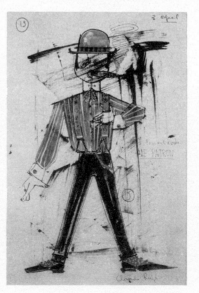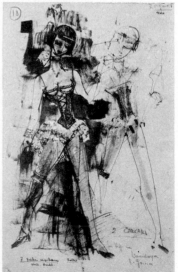

JACQUES RAPP. II : *Simon Boccanegra.* **2** : Giuseppe Verdi.
3 : Jean-Jacques Brothier. **5** : Opéra de Strasbourg. 1963.

JACQUES RAPP. III : *Die Sieben Todsünden.* **1** : Bertolt Brecht.
2 : Kurt Weill. **3-4** : Milko Sparemblek. **5** : Opéra de
Strasbourg. 1963.

100

NINA RIECHETOFF. I : *I Rusteghi*. **1** : Carlo Goldoni.
3 : André Steiger. **5** : Théâtre de Bourgogne. 1960.

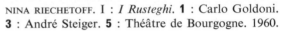
PIERRE SIMONINI. I : *Andromaque*.
1 : Jean Racine. **3** : Marguerite Jamois.
5 : Tournée Georges Herbert. 1961.

PIERRE SIMONINI. I : *Anna d'Eboli*.
1 : Pierre Ordionni **3** : Pierre Valde.
5 : Compagnie Robert Hossein.
Théâtre Charles de Rochefort.
Paris. 1960

MARCEL VERTÈS. III : *La Belle Hélène*.
1 : Marchel Achard – Robert Manuel.
2 : Jacques Offenbach – Manuel Rosenthal. 4: John Cranko. 5: Opéra de Paris.
1955. 6 : N. Mandel.

NINA VIDROVITCH. I : *Les Deux Ogres*. 1 : Guillaume
Kergourlay. 2 : François Serrette. 3 : Jacques Fornier.
5 : Théâtre de Bourgogne. 1958. 6 : Pic.

GEORGES WAKHÉVITCH. II : *Le Dialogue des Carmélites*.
2 : Francis Poulenc. 3 : Margherita Wallmann.
5 : Teatro alla Scala. Milano. 1957. 6 : Piccagliani.

HELLAS

GEORGES ANEMOYANNIS. I : *Odyssia*. **1** : Manolis
Skouloudis. **2** : Jean Macropoulos. **3** : Manos
Catrakis. **4** : Yannis Flery. **5** : Ellinikon Laikon
Théâtron. Théâtron Calouta. Athinai. 1960.

NICOLAS HATZIKYRIAKOS – GHIKAS. I : *Nephelai*. **1** : Aristophanes. **3** : Socratis Carantinos. **5** : Vassilikon Théâtron.
Athinai. 1951.

YANNIS MORALIS. I : *Ploutos*. **1** : Aristophanes.
2 : Manos Hadzidakis. **3** : Karolos Koun. **5** : Théâtron
Technis. Athinai. 1957. **6** : Makis Skiadaressis.

YANNIS MORALIS. I : *La Zapatera prodigiosa*.
1 : Federico Garcia Lorca. **3** : Alexis Solomos.
5 : Vassilikon Théâtron. Athinai. 1958.
6 : Makis Skiadaressis.

ANDRÉAS NOMICOS. I : *Cyclops*. **1** : Euripides.
2 : Manos Hadzidakis. **3** : Alexis Solomos. **4** : Agapi
Evangelidou. **5** : Vassilikon Théâtron. Epidavros.
1959. **6** : Harissiadis.

ANTONIS PHOCAS. I : *Midia*. **1** : Euripides. **2** : Manos
Hadzidakis. **3** : Alexis Minotis. **4** : Agapi Evangelidou. **5** : Vassilikon Théâtron. Epidavros. 1956.
6 : Harissiadis.

JOHN STEPHANELLIS. I : *I Ilikia tis Nychtas.*
1 : Iakovos Kampanellis. **2** : Manos Hadzidakis.
3 : Karolos Koun. **5** : Théâtron Technis.
Athinai. 1959. **6** : Stephanellis.

JOHN TSAROUCHIS. I : *Diadia Vania.* **1** : Anton
Chekhov. **3** : Karolos Koun. **5** : Vassilikon Théâtron.
Athinai. 1953. **6** : Emile.

HELLAS

YANNIS MORALIS. I : *Ploutos*. **1** : Aristophanes.
2 : Manos Hadzidakis. **3** : Karolos Koun.
5 : Théâtron Technis. Athinai. 1957.

MARCEL JANCO. I : *Street Scene*. **1** : Elmer Rice.
3 : Moshe Halevy. **5** : Ohel. Tel Aviv. 1948.

ISRAËL

HELVETIA

MAX BIGNENS. I : *Ett Drömspel*. **1** : August Strindberg.
3 : Rudolf Hofmann. **4** : Stadttheater. Basel. 1957.
6 : H. Stebler.

RUODI BARTH. I : *Bodas de Sangre*. **1** : Federico
Garcia Lorca. **3** : Rolf Müller. **5** : Hessisches
Staatstheater. Wiesbaden. 1958.
6 : G. Meyer-Hanno.

MAX FIRSCH. I : *Herr Biedermann und die Brandstifter.*
1 : Max Frisch. 3 : Oskar Wälterlin. 5 : Schauspielhaus.
Zürich. 1958. 6 : Obrecht.

EDUARD GUNZINGER. I : *Medea.*
1 : Robinson Jeffers. 3 : Rudolf Hofmann.
5 : Stadttheater. Basel. 1959.
6 : H. Stebler.

HANNES MEYER. I : *Ett Drömspel.*
1 : August Strindberg. 2 : Heimo Erbse.
3 : Christoph Groszer. 5 : Stadttheater.
Bern. 1960. 6 : Erismann.

TEO OTTO. I : *Andorra.* **1** : Max Frisch. **3** : Kurt
Hirschfeld. **5** : Schauspielhaus. Zürich. 1961.
6 : René Haury.

TEO OTTO. I : *Requiem for a Nun.*
1 : William Faulkner. **3** : Leopold
Lindtberg. **5** : Schauspielhaus.
Zürich. 1955. **6** : René Haury.

ARY OECHSLIN. I : *Kabale und Liebe*. **1** : Friedrich Schiller. **3** : Hermann Kutscher.
5 : Ateliertheater. Bern. 1959. **6** : Els Saumweber.

MAX RÖTHLISBERGER. II : *Antigone*. **2** : Arthur Honegger. **3** : Hans Hartleb.
5 : Stadttheater. Zürich. 1956. **6** : H. Stebler.

INDIA

Bharatanatyam (Mrinalini Sarabhai –
Serebhendeva Bhopala Kuruvanji).

Mohiniattam (Shanta Rao).

Bharatanatyam (Smt. S.V. Lalitha).

EBRAHIM ALKAZI. I : *Yerma*. **1** : Federico Garcia Lorca.
3 : Ebrahim Alkazi. **5** : Theatre Unit. Bombay. 1960.

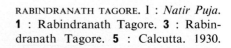

GUL BARDHAN. III : *Panchatantra*.
4 : Shanti Bardhan. **5** : Little Ballet
Troupe. Bombay. 1956.

RABINDRANATH TAGORE. I : *Natir Puja*.
1 : Rabindranath Tagore. **3** : Rabindranath Tagore. **5** : Calcutta. 1930.

INDIA

III : *Kathakali*. **6** : S.H. Vatsyayan.

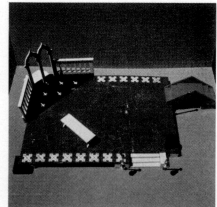

1-2. EBRAHIM ALKAZI. I : *The Merchant of Venice*.
1 : William Shakespeare. **3** : Ebrahim Alkazi.
5 : Theatre Unit, Meghdoot Terrace Theatre.
Bombay. 1958.

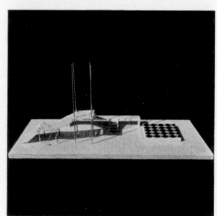

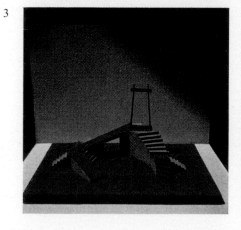

3. EBRAHIM ALKAZI. I : *Macbeth*. **1** : William
Shakespeare. **3** : Ebrahim Alkazi. **5** : Theatre
Unit, Jai Hind College Theatre. Bombay. 1956.

4. EBRAHIM ALKAZI. I : *Volpone*. **1** : Ben Jonson.
3 : Ebrahim Alkazi. **5** : Theatre Unit, Meghdoot
Terrace Theatre. Bombay. 1958.

ISRAËL

ARNON ADAR. I : *A View from the Bridge*. **1** : Arthur Miller. **3** : Hy Kalus. **5** : Habima. Tel Aviv. 1956.

GENIA BERGER. I : *Mihal Bat Shaul*. **1** : A. Ashman. **3** : B. Tchemerinsky. **5** : Habima. Tel Aviv. 1941.

YOSSL BERGNER. I : *Shesh Knafayim L'ehad*.
1 : Hanoch Bartov. 3 : Avraham Ninio.
5 : Habima. Tel Aviv. 1958. 6 : Mirlin-Yaron.

JOSEPH CARL. I : *King Lear*. 1 : William Shakespeare. 3 : Julius Gellner.
5 : Habima. Tel Aviv. 1955. 6 : Mirlin-Yaron.

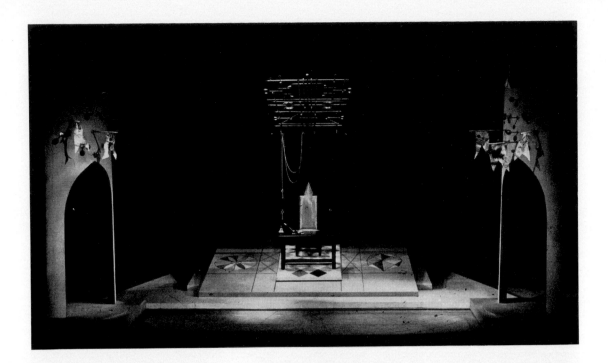

DANI KARAVAN. I : *Maria Stuart.*
1 : Friedrich Schiller. **3** : Gershon
Plotkin. **5** : Cameri. Tel Aviv. 1961.
6 : Keren-Kidron.

E. LUFTGLASS. I : *Sadot Y'rukim.*
1 : Peretz Hirshbein. **3** : Leopold
Lindberg. **5** : Habima. Tel Aviv. 1935.

ARIEH NAVON. I : *Twelfth Night*. **1** : William Shakespeare. **3** : Shmuel Bunim.
5 : Cameri. Tel Aviv. 1959. **6** : Alex Gottlieb.

ARIEH NAVON. I : *Miseria e Nobilta*. **1** : Eduardo Scarpetta. **3** : Shmuel Bunim.
5 : Cameri. Tel Aviv. 1960. **6** : Keren-Kidron.

ITALIA

NICOLA BENOIS. II : *Anna Bolena*. **2** : Gaetano Donizetti.
3 : Luchino Visconti. **5** : Teatro alla Scala.
Milano. 1957. **6** : Piccagliani.

NICOLA BENOIS. II : *Rigoletto*. **2** : Giuseppe Verdi.
3: Ernst Poettgen. **5**: Staatsoper. Wien. 1962. **6**: Macku.

CORRADO CAGLI. II : *Macbeth*. **2** : Ernest Bloch. **3** : Luigi Squarzina.
5 : Teatro alla Scala. Milano. 1959. **6** : Piccagliani.

ERBERTO CARBONI. II : *Agnese di Hohenstaufen*. **2** : Gaspare Spontini. **3** : Maner
Lualdi. **5** : Maggio Musicale Fiorentino. Firenze. 1954. **6** : Maggio Musicale.

MARIO CHIARI. I : *Enrico IV*. **1** : Luigi Pirandello. **3** : Orazio Costa.
5 : Piccolo Teatro della Citta di Milano. Milano. 1961. **6** : Pozzetti.

VENIERO COLASANTI – JOHN MOORE. II : *La Traviata*. **2** : Giuseppe Verdi.
3 : Luigi Piccinato. **5** : Teatro Bellini. Catania. 1959.

ATTILIO COLONNELLO. I : *The Taming of the Shrew*. **1** : William Shakespeare. **3** : Franco Enriquez. **5** : Piccolo Teatro. Trieste. 1959. **6** : de Rota.

GIULIO COLTELLACCI. II : *Amahl and the Night Visitors*. **2** : Gian-Carlo Menotti. **3** : Gian-Carlo Menotti. **5** : Maggio Musicale Fiorentino. Firenze. 1953.

VALERIA COSTA. I : *Venezia Salvata*. **1** : Massimo Bontempelli. **3** : Orazio Costa. **5** : Piccolo Teatro. Roma. 1949. **6** : Bosio.

LUCIANO DAMIANI. I : *El Nost Milan.* **1** : Carlo Bertolazzi. **3** : Giorgio Strehler.
5 : Piccolo Teatro della città di Milano. Milano. 1955. **6** : Pozzetti.

EZIO FRIGERIO. I : *Arlecchino Servitore di due Padroni.* **1** : Carlo Goldoni.
3 : Giorgio Strehler. **5** : Piccolo Teatro della città di Milano. Milano.

SALVATORE FIUME. II : *Nabucco*. **2** : Giuseppe Verdi. **3** : Mario Frigerio. **5** : Teatro alla Scala. Milano. 1958. **6** : Piccagliani.

MARIO GARBUGLIA. I : *A View from the Bridge*. **1** : Arthur Miller. **3** : Luchino Visconti. **5** : Teatro Eliseo. Roma. 1958. **6** : Paul Ronald.

EZIO FRIGERIO. I : *Andromaque*. **1** : Jean Racine. **5** : Radio televisione Italiana. 1960.

PEUGENIO GUGLIELMINETTI. I : *Platonv*. **1** : Anton Chekhov. **3** : Gianfranco De Bosio. **5** : Teatro Stabile. Torino. 1958.

EMANUELE LUZZATI. I : *La Zapatera Prodigiosa*. **1** : Federico Garcia Lorca. **3** : Franco Enriquez. 5 : La Fenice. Venezia. 1959. **6** : Giacomelli.

ITALIA

PIER LUIGI PIZZI. I : *Le Morbinose*. **1** : Carlo Goldoni. **3** : Giorgio De Lulle. **5** : Campagnia dei Giovani. La Fenice. Venezia. 1960. **6** : Bosio.

FRANCO LAURENTI. II : *Il Crescendo*. **2** : Luigi
Cherubini. **3** : Corrado Pavolini. **5** : Teatro Eliseo.
Roma. 1960. **6** : De Antonis.

EMANUELE LUZZATI. II : *Il Cordovano*. **2** : Goffredo
Petrassi. **3** : Franco Enriquez. **5** : Piccola Scala.
Milano. 1959. **6** : Piccagliani.

PIER LUIGI PIZZI. I : *Twelfth Night*. **1** : William
Shakespeare. **3** : Giorgio De Lullo. **5** : Teatro
Eliseo. Roma. 1961.

GIANNI RATTO. II : *The Rake's Progress*. **2** : Igor
Stravinski. **3** : Carl Ebert. **5** : Teatro alla Scala.
Milano. 1951. **6** : Piccagliani.

FRANCO ROGNONI. II : *La Donna è Mobile*. **1** : Guglielmo
Zucconi. **2** : Riccardo Malipiero. **3** : Franco Enriquez.
5 : Teatro alla Scala. Milano. 1957. **6** : Piccagliani.

MISCHA SCANDELLA. I : *Angelica*. **1** : Leo
Ferrero. **3** : Gianfranco de Bosio.
5 : Teatro Stabile. Torino. 1959.
6 : Trevisio.

MISCHA SCANDELLA. I : *La Giustizia*. **1** : Giuseppe Dessi.
3 : Giacomo Colli. **5** : Teatro Stabile. Torino. 1959.

131

GREGORIO SCILTIAN. II : *Il Campanello dello Speziale*. **2** : Gaetano Donizetti. **3** : Margherita Wallmann. **5** : Piccola Scala. Milano. 1957. **6** : Piccagliani.

PIERO TOSI. I : *Diadia Vania*. **1** : Anton Chekhov. **3** : Luchino Visconti. **5** : Teatro Eliseo. Roma. 1955. **6** : Bosio.

FRANCO ZEFFIRELLI – PETER HALL. I : *Romeo and Juliet*. **1** : William Shakespeare. **3** : Franco Zeffirelli. **5** : Old Vic Theatre. London. 1960. **6** : Houston Rogers.

FRANCO ZEFFIRELLI. II : *Rigoletto*. **2** : Giuseppe Verdi. **3** : Franco Zeffirelli. **5** : Théâtre de la Monnaie. Bruxelles. 1960.

133

PIERO ZUFFI. II : *La Vestale*. **2** : Gaspare Spontini.
3 : Luchino Visconti. **5** : Teatro alla Scala.
Milano. 1954. **6** : Piccagliani.

PIERO ZUFFI. II : *Assassinio nella Cattedrale*. **2** : Ildebrando Pizzetti. **3** : Margherita Wallmann. **5** : Teatro alla Scala. Milano. 1957. **6** : Piccagliani.

JUGOSLAVIJA

MILENKO SERBAN. I : *Dundo Maroje*.
1 : Marin Drzic. **3** : Bojan Stupica.
5 : Jugoslovensko Dramsko Pozoriste.
Beograd. 1949.

VLADIMIR MARENIC. I : *Nebeski odred*. **1** : Gjorgje Lebovic – Alek-
sandar Obrenović. **3** : Dimitrije Djurkovic. **5** : Srpsko Narodno
Pozoriste. Novi Sad. 1957.

DORIAN SOKOLIC. III : *Ohridska Legenda.*
2 : Stevan Hristic. **4** : Maks Kirbos.
5: Narodno Kazaliste « Ivan Zajc ». Rijeka. 1957.

MILENKO SERBAN. I : *Macbeth.* **1** : William Shakespeare. **3** : Mata Milosevic.
5 : Jugoslovensko Dramsko Pozoriste. Beograd. 1956.

JUGO-SLAVIJA

DUSAN RISTIC. I : *Héraklès*.
1 : Marijan Matkovic. 3 : Braslav
Borozan. 5 : Narodno Pozoriste.
Beograd. 1959.

NEDERLAND

FRANZ DECKWITZ. II : *Pluk een Ster*.
1 : Mies Bouhuys. 2 : Walter Kous.
3 : Johan Greter. 5 : Amsterdamsche
Vrouwelijke Studenten Vereeniging.
Stadsschouwburg. Amsterdam. 1957.

MAGYARORSZÁG

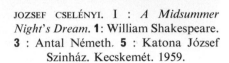

JOZSEF CSELÉNYI. I : *A Midsummer Night's Dream*. **1**: William Shakespeare. **3** : Antal Németh. **5** : Katona József Szinház. Kecskemét. 1959.

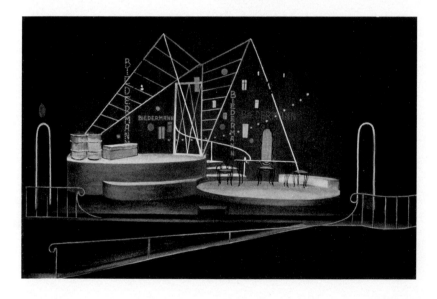

JOZSEF CSELÉNYI. I : *Biedermann und die Brandstifter*. **1** : Max Frisch. **3** : Endre Marton. **5** : Katona József Szinház. Nemzeti Szinhaz. Budapest. 1960.

ISTVAN KÖPECZI-BOCZ. I : *Les Fourberies de Scapin*. **1** : Molière. **3** : László Vamos. **5** : Madach Szinház. Budapest. 1959.

ZOLTÁN FÜLÖP. II : *Furfangos Diákok*. **2** : Ference Farkas.
3 : Gyula Harango. **5** : Allami Operaház. Budapest. 1948.
6 : Toth Laszlo.

ZOLTÁN FÜLÖP. II : *Salome*. **2** : Richard Strauss. **3** : Kálmán
Nadasdy. **5** : Allami Operaház. Budapest. 1958.

GYÖRGY RAJKAI. I : *Aristokrati*. **1** : Nikolaï Pogodin.
3 : Károly Kazimir. **5** : Jókai Szinház. Budapest. 1961.

JÓZSEF PÁN. I : *Diadia Vania*. **1** : Anton Chekhov.
3 : Endre Gellért. **5** : Katona József Szinház.
Budapest. 1952.

EMIL SIKI. I : *Hamlet*. **1** : William Shakespeare. **3** : Laszló
Vámos. **5** : Madách Szinház. Budapest. 1962.
6 : Bartal Ferenc.

GYÖRGY RAJKAI. I : *Prometheus.*
1 : Aischylos. **3** : Károly Kasimir.
5 : Körszinház. 1961.

TIBOR UPOR. I : *Lysistrata.* **1** : Aristophanes. **3** : Károly
Kazimir. **5** : Vigszinház. Budapest. 1959.

MÁTYÁS VARGA. I : *Az Ember Tragédiája.*
1 : Imre Madách. **3** : Tamás Major.
5 : Nemzeti Szinház. Szabadtéri Játékok.
Szeged. 1961.

LEONTIEN VAN BEURDEN. I : *The Merchant of Venice*.
1 : William Shakespeare. **3** : Erik Vos. **5** : Toneelgroep
Arena. Centraal Theater. Amsterdam. 1958.

HEP VAN DELFT. I : *Die Herberge*.
1 : Fritz Hochwälder. **3** : Joris Diels.
5 : De Haagsche Comedie. Koninklijke
Schouwburg. Den Haag. 1960.
6 : Lemaire - Wennink.

JOHAN GRETER. I : *Tueur sans Gages*. **1** : Eugène
Ionesco. **3** : Richard Flink. **5** : Toneelgroep
Theater. Nieuwe de la Mar Theater. Amster-
dam. 1960. **6** : Maria Austria - Henk Jonker.

JOHAN GRETER. I : *L'Histoire de Vasco*. **1** : Georges Schehadé. **3** : Elise Hoomans. **5** : Toneelgroep Theater. Stadsschouwburg. Arnhem. 1959.

HANS VAN NORDEN. I : *De Spaansche Brabander*. **1** : Gerbrand Adriaenszoon Bredero. **3** : Ton Lutz. **5** : Rotterdams Toneel. De Rotterdamse Schouwburg. Rotterdam. 1961. **6** : Lemaire – Wennink.

WIM VESSEUR. I : *Gijsbreght van Aemstel*. **1** : Joost van den Vondel. **3** : Johan de Meester. **5** : Nederlandse Comedie. Stadsschouwburg. Amsterdam. 1960.
6 : Maria Austria – Henk Jonker.

WIM VESSEUR. I : *Troilus and Cressida*. **1** : William Shakespeare. **3** : Johan de Meester. **5** : Holland Festival. Koninklijke Schouwburg. Den Haag. 1959.

HARRY WICH. I : *Rhinocéros*. **1** : Eugène Ionesco.
3 : Henk Rigters. **5** : Nederlandse Comedie. Stadsschouwburg. Amsterdam. 1960.
6 : Lemaire – Wennink.

NICOLAAS WIJNBERG. I : *The Comedy of Errors*.
1 : William Shakespeare. **3** : Ton Lutz. **5** : Rotterdams Toneel. De Rotterdamse Schouwburg.
Rotterdam. 1960. **6** : Lemaire – Wennink.

NICOLAAS WIJNBERG. I : *Moortje*. **1** : Gerbrand
Adriaenszoon Bredero. **3** : Ton Lutz. **5** : Holland
Festival. Koninklijke Schouwburg. Den Haag.
1957. **6** : Lemaire – Wennink.

NIPPON

DANJURÔ XI. *Kanjinchô* (Kabuki). **5** : Kabukiza. Tokyo. 1962.

TATSUO ICHIJÔ. I : *Kaeranu Hito*.
1 : Hideo Honda. **3** : Tetsuji Matsuo.
5 : Mingei. Hitotsubashi Hall.
Tokyo. 1957.

JUICHI ITÔ. I : *Rashomon*. **1** : Ryunosuke
Akutagawa – Takashi Izumo. **3** : Seiichiro
Uchikawa. **5** : Shinkokugeki. Shinjuku
Koma. Tokyo. 1961.

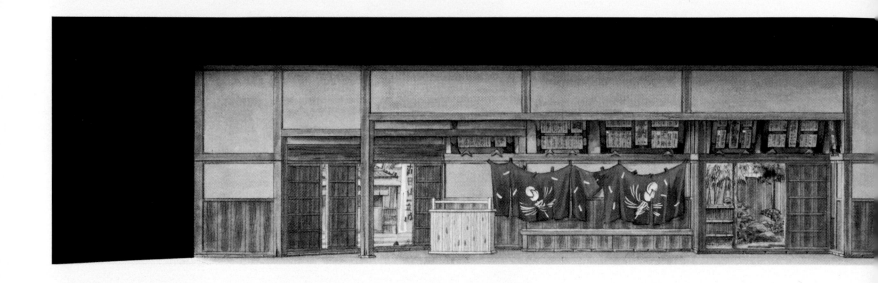

Shimbashi Embujô, Tokyo. 1955.

OTOYA ODA. I : *Tatsumi Kôdan.* **1** : Kyôka Izumi.
3 : Mantarô Kubota. **5** : Shimpa. Shimbashi Embujô.
Tokyo. 1952.

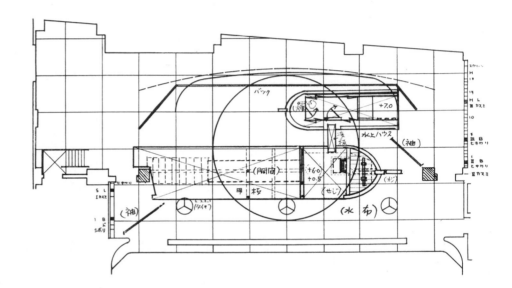

KUNIO KÔNO. I : *Nagare.* **1** : Kazuo Kikuta.
3 : Kazuo Kikuta. **5** : Geijutsuza. Tokyo. 1957.

KISAKU ITÔ. I : *Gashintare*. **1** : Kazuo Kikuta.
3 : Kazuo Kikuta. **5** : Geijutsuza. Tokyo. 1960.

ICHIRÔ TAKATA. I : *Arlecchino, Servitore di due Padroni*. **1** : Carlo Goldoni. **2** : Naozumi Yamamoto - Sumika Hirai. **3** : Eitarô Ozawa. **4** : Noriko Kageyama. **5** : Haiyûza. Tokyo. 1962.

KUNIO KÔNO. I : *Tooi Gaika*. **1** : Naoya Uchimura. **3** : Shirô Okakura. **5** : Mingei. Haiyûza. Tokyo. 1955.

NORGE

GUNNAR ALME. I : *Ze Zivota Hmyzu.* **1** : Josef-Karel
  Capek. **3** : Bjarne Andersen. **5** : Rogaland Teater.
          Stavanger. 1956.

KAI FJELL. I : *Fruen fra Havet.* **1** : Henrik Ibsen. **3** : Gerda
Ring. **5** : Nationaltheatret. Oslo. 1951. **6** : Sturlason.

KAARE HEGLE. I : *Château en Suède*.
1 : Françoise Sagan. 3 : Jens Gunderssen.
5 : Det Nye Teater. Oslo. 1960.
6 : Sturlason.

PAUL RENÉ GAUGUIN. I : *Clochemerle*.
1 : Marcel Aymé. 3 : Hans-Jacob
Nilsen. 5 : Folketeatret. Oslo. 1954.
6 : Sturlason.

GUY KROHG. I : *Nederlaget*. 1 : Nordahl Grieg.
3 : Rönnang Alten. 5 : Folketeatret. Oslo.
1959. 6 : Sturlason.

HERALD MARTIN. I : *Gjengangere*. **1** : Henrik Ibsen. **3** : Ellen
Isefiaer. **5** : Det Nye Teater. Oslo. 1952. **6** : Sturlason.

CARL NESJAR – INGER SITTER. I : *Dom Juan*. **1** : Molière.
3 : Arne Thomas Olsen. **5** : Nationaltheatret. Oslo. 1960.

PER SCHWAB. I : *Galileo Galilei*. **1** : Bertolt Brecht.
3 : Ellen Isefiaer. **5** : Den Nationale Scene. Bergen. 1960.
6 : Sturlason.

CHRISTIAN STENERSEN. I : *Maria Pineda*. **1** : Federico
Garcia Lorca. **3** : Knut Hergel. **5** : Nationaltheatret.
Oslo. 1956.

ARNE WALENTIN. I : *The Tempest*. **1** : William
Shakespeare. **3** : Ivo Cramér. **5** : Det Norske
Teatret. Oslo. 1959. **6** : Sturlason.

ARNE WALENTIN. II : *Lost in the Stars*. **1** : Maxwell
Anderson. **2** : Kurt Weill. **3** : Hans-Jacob Nilsen –
Johan Borgen. **5** : Folketeatret. Oslo. 1952.
6 : Sturlason.

ÖSTERREICH

LOIS EGG. I : *Torquato Tasso*. **1** : Johann Wolfgang Goethe. **3** : Josef Gielen.
5 : Akademietheater. Wien. 1960.

LOIS EGG. I : *Parisian Comedy*. **1** : William Saroyan.
3 : Rudolf Steinböck. **5** : Akademietheater.
Wien. 1960.

STEFAN HLAWA. I : *Don Carlos*. **1** : Friedrich
Schiller. **3** : Josef Gielen. **5** : Burgtheater.
Wien. 1955.

STEFAN HLAWA. I : *La Dama Duende*. **1** : Pedro
Calderon de la Barca. **3** : Ulrich Bettac.
5 : Burgtheater. Wien. 1955. **6** : Macku.

ROBERT KAUTSKY. I : *Take the Fool Away.*
1 : J.B. Priestley. **3** : Adolf Rott.
5 : Burgtheater. Wien. 1956.

OSKAR KOKOSCHKA. I : *Moisasurs Zauberfluch.*
1 : Ferdinand Raimund. **3** : Rudolf Steinböck.
5 : Burgtheater. Wien. 1960. **6** : F. Hausmann.

OSKAR KOKOSCHKA. I : *Die Unheilbringende Krone.*
1 : Ferdinand Raimund. **3** : Rudolf Steinböck.
5 : Burgtheater. Wien. 1961.

GOTTFRIED NEUMANN – SPALLART. II : *Die Zauberflöte.* **2** : Wolfgang Amadeus
Mozart. **3** : Hans Swarowsky. **5** : Staatsakademie für Musik. Wien. 1952.

OSKAR KOKOSCHKA. I : *Die Unheilbringende Krone*. **1** : Ferdinand Raimund. **3** : Rudolf Steinböck. **5** : Burgtheater. Wien. 1961. **6** : Helmut Baar.

POLSKA

ANDRZEJ MAJEWSKI. I : *La Vedova Scaltra*. **1** : Carlo Goldoni. **3** : Maria Malicka. **5** : Teatr J. Slowacki. Krakow. 1959.

GOTTFRIED NEUMANN – SPALLART. I : *Das Spanische Dreieck*. **1** : Kurt Becsi.
3 : Harald Benesch. **5** : Akademietheater. Wien. 1955.

GEORG SCHMID. I : *Die Chinesische Mauer*.
1 : Max Frisch. **3** : Gustav Manker. **5** : Volks-
theater. Wien. 1956. **6** : H. Baar.

WOLFRAM SKALICKI. II : *Die Zauberflöte*.
2 : Wolfgang Amadeus Mozart. **3** : André
Diehl. **5** : Opernhaus. Graz. 1956.

FRITZ WOTRUBA. I : *Oidipous Tyrannos*. **1** : Sophocles. **3** : Gustav Rudolf Sellner.
5 : Burgtheater. Wien. 1960. **6** : Elisabeth Speidel.

PERU

CARLOS AÍTOR CASTILLO. I : *La Endemoniada*.
1 : Carl Schœnherr. **3** : Carlos Aïtor Castillo –
Ofelia Woloshin. **5** : Nuevo Teatro.
Lima. 1959. **6** : Pestana.

CARLOS AÏTOR CASTILLO. I : *Les Bonnes*.
1 : Jean Genet. **3** : Reynaldo D'Amore.
5 : Club de Teatro de Lima. 1959.

MARCELO DAMONTE. I : *An Inspector Calls*. **1** : J.B. Priestley. **3** : José
Velasquez. **5** : Histrion-Teatro de
Arte. Lima. 1961. **6** : Vanotti.

163

MARCELO DAMONTE. I : *Volpone*. **1** : Ben Jonson. **3** : José
Velásquez. **5** : Histrión-Teatro de Arte. Lima. 1961.
6 : Vanotti.

RICARDO GRECO. I : *L'Eternel Mari*. **1** : Dostoievsky – Mauclair.
3 : Reynaldo D'Amore. **5** : Club de Teatro de Lima. 1957.
6 : Pestana.

ITALO NOYA. I : *Persï*. **1** : Aeschylos.
3 : Ricardo Roca Rey. **5** : Asociación
de Artistas Aficionados. Lima. 1953.

OTTO AXER. I : *Iphigenie auf Tauris.*
1 : Johann Wolfgang Gœthe. **3** : Erwin
Axer. **5** : Teatr Wspolczesny.
Warszawa. 1961. **6** : E. Hartwig.

OTTO AXER. I : *Klucz od Przepasci.* **1** :
Krzysztof Gruszczynski. **3** : Adam
Hanuszkiewicz. **5** : Scena Kameralna,
Teatr Polski. Warszawa. 1956.

WLADYSLAW DASZEWSKI. I : *Parady*. **1** : Jan
Potocki. **3** : Ewa Bonacka. **5** : Teatr
Dramatyczny. Warszawa. 1958.

TADEUSZ KANTOR. I : *Saint Joan*. **1** : George
Bernard Shaw. **3** : Wladyslaw Krzeminski.
5 : Teatr Stary. Krakow. 1956.
6 : F. Myszkowski.

JAN KOSINSKI. I : *Policjanci*. **1** : Slawomir Mrozek. **3** : Jan Swiderski. **5** : Teatr Dramatyczny. Warszawa. 1958. **6** : F. Myszkowski.

JAN KOSINSKI. I : *Le Diable et le Bon Dieu*. **1** : Jean-Paul Sartre. **3** : Ludwik René **5** : Teatr Dramatyczny. Warszawa. 1960.

ANDRZEJ MAJEWSKI. I : *La Vedova Scaltra*. **1** : Carlo
Goldoni. **3** : Maria Malicka. **5** : Teatr J. Slowacki.
Krakow. 1959.

JOZEF RACHWALSKI — IRENA ZABOROWSKA.
I : *Akropolis*. **1** : Stanislaw Wyspianski. **3** :
Kazimierz Dejmek. **5** : Teatr Nowy. Lodz. 1959.

TERESA ROSZKOWSKA. I : *Dom Juan*. **1** : Molière.
3 : Bohdan Korzeniewski. **5** : Teatr Polski.
Warszawa. 1951.

ZENOBIUSZ STRZELECKI. I : *Chaika*. **1** : Anton Chekhov.
3 : Roman Zawistowski. **5** : Teatr Polski.
Warszawa. 1959. **6** : F. Myszkowski.

ANDRZEJ SADOWSKI. I : *Ornithes*. **1** : Aristophanes. **3** :
Konrad Swinarski. **5** : Teatr Dramatyczny. Warszawa. 1960.

JOZEF SZAJNA. I : *Imiona Wladzy*. **1** : Jerzy Broszkiewicz. **3** : Krystyna Skuszanka. **5** : Teatr Ludowy.
Nowa Huta. 1957.

JOZEF SZAJNA. I : *W Malym Domku.*
1 : Stanislaw Ignacy Witkiewicz. **3** : Wanda
Laskowska. **5** : Teatr Dramatyczny.
Warszawa. 1959.

JOZEF SZAJNA. I : *Sortie de l'Acteur*. **1** : Michel de Ghelderode. **3** : Andrzej Skupien. **5** : Teatr « 38 ». Krakow. 1960.

JERZY TORONCZYK. I : *Une Fille pour du Vent*. **1** : André
Obey. **3** : Jerzy Golinski. Teatr Osterwy. Lublin. 1957.
              6 : Hartwig-Myszkowski.

ANTONI TOSTA – LILIANA KANKOWSKA. I : *Caligula*.
1 : Albert Camus. **3** : Tadeusz Byrski.
5 : Teatr S. Zeromski. Kielce. 1958.

KRYSTYNA ZACHWATOWICZ. I : *Dziejowa Rola Pigwy*.
1 : Jerzy Broszkiewicz. **3** : Jerzy Krasowski. **5** : Teatr
Ludowy. Nowa Huta. 1960. **6** : W. Plewinski.

LECH ZAHORSKI. I *Porfirion Osielek*. **1** : Konstanty
Ildefons Galczynski. **3** : Jan Ciecierski. **5** : Teatr
Kameralny. Warszawa. 1958. **6** : F. Myszkowski.

ROMANIA

MIRCEA MAROSIN. I : *Ovidiu*. **1** : Grigore Salceanu.
3 : Val Mugur. **5** : Teatrul de Stat. Constanta.
1957. **6** : Agerpres.

MIRCEA MAROSIN. I : *Twelfth Night*. **1** : William
Shakespeare. **3** : Ion Sahighian. **5** : Teatrul
Municipal. Bucuresti. 1956.

MIRCEA MATCABOJI. I : *Hamlet*. **1** : William Shakespeare.
3 : Miron Niculesco. **5** : Teatrul National. Cluj. 1960.
      6 : Meridiane.

JULES PERAHIM. I : *Irkoutskaia Istoria*. **1** : Alexeï Arbuzov.
3 : Radu Beligan. **5** : Teatrul National « I.L. Caragiale ».
        Bucuresti. 1960.

MIHAI TOFAN. I : *Napasta*. **1** : Ion Luca Caragiale.
3 : Miron Niculesco. **5** : Teatrul National « I.L. Caragiale »
Bucuresti. 1958.

VALER VASILESCO. II : *Neamul Soimarestilor*. **1** : Mihail
Sadoveanu. **2** : Tudor Jarda. **3** : Ilie Balea. **4** : Taub
Gabriela. **5** : Opera de Stat. Cluj. 1959. **6** : Meridiane.

S.S.S.R.

NICOLAÏ AKIMOV. I : *Tén.* **1** : Evgheni Chvartz. **3** : Nicolaï Akimov. **5** : Teatr Komedii. Leningrad. 1940.

NICOLAÏ AKIMOV. I : *Délo.* **1** : Soukhovo-Kobyline. **3** : Nicolaï Akimov. **5** : Teatr Lensoveta. Leningrad. 1954.

NICOLAÏ AKIMOV. I : *Revizor.* **1** : Nicolaï Gogol. **3** : Nicolaï Akimov. **5** : Teatr Komedii. Leningrad. 1958.

NATHAN ALTMANN. I : *King Lear*.
1 : William Shakespeare. **3** : Grigori
Kozintzev. **5** : Bolchoï Dramatitcheski
Teatr imeni Gorkovo. Leningrad. 1941.

NATHAN ALTMANN. I : *Hamlet*.
1 : William Shakespeare. **5** : Rousski
Dramatitcheski Teatr. Kiev. 1954.

ANATOLI BOSSOULAEV. I : *Optimistit-cheskaïa Traghédia.* **1** : Vsevolod Vichnevski. **3** : Gheorghi Tovsto-nogov. **5** : Dramatitcheski Teatr imeni Pouchkina. Leningrad. 1955.

NISSON CHIFRINE. I : *Jenitba.* **1** : Nicolaï Gogol. **3** : Alexandre Razinkine. **5** : Tsentralnyi Teatr Sovietskoï Armii. Moskva. 1959.

NISSON CHIFRINE. I : *Stalingradzi*. **1** : Youri Tchépourine. **3** : Alexei Popov. **5** : Tsentralnyi Teatr Sovietskoï Armii. Moskva. 1944.

NISSON CHIFRINE. I : *The Merry Wives of Windsor*. **1** : William Shakespeare. **3** : Youri Zavadski. **5** : Teatr Mossovieta. Moskva. 1957.

NISSON CHIFRINE. I : *Podniataïa Tsélina*. **1** : Mikhaïl Cholokhov. **3** : Alexei Popov – Alexandre Chatrine. **5** : Tsentralnyi Teatr Sovietskoï Armii. Moskva. 1957.

VLADIMIR DMITRIEV. I : *Tri Sestri*. **1** : Anton Chekhov. **3** : Vladimir Némirovitch –
Dantchenko. **5** : МКНАТ. Moskva. 1940.

VLADIMIR DMITRIEV. II : *Pikovaïa Dama*.
1 : Alexandre Poushkine. **2** : Piotr
Tchaïkovski. **3** : Léonide Baratov. **5** :
Bolchoï Teatr. Moskva. 1944.

VLADIMIR DMITRIEV. I : *Diadia Vania.*
1 : Anton Chekhov. **3** : Mikhaïl Kedrov.
5 : MKHAT. Moskva. 1947.

VLADIMIR DMITRIEV. I : *Ounijennié i Oskor-
blionnié.* **1** : Féodor Dostoïevski – Ilia
Olchvanger. **3** : Gheorghi Tovstonogov –
Ilia Olchvanger. **5** : Teatr Léninskovo
Komsomola. Leningrad. 1956.

VLADIMIR DMITRIEV. I : *Bespridannitza.*
1 : Alexandre Ostrovski. **3** : Vassili Sakhnosvki.
5 : MKHAT. Moskva. 1929.

VALERI DORRER. III : *Tropoïou Groma.* **1** : Peter Abrahams. **2** : Kara Karaiev.
4 : Konstantin Sergheev. **5** : Teatr Opery i Baleta imeni Kirova.
Leningrad. 1958.

VLADIMIR FAVORSKI. I : *Twelfth Night.* **1** : William Shakespeare. **3** : Vladimir Gotovtzev – Sophia Ghiatzintova. **5** : MKHAT II. Moskva. 1934.

FEDOR FEDOROVSKI. II : *Kniaz Igor*.
2 : Alexandre Borodine. **3** : Léonide Baratov. **5** : Bolchoï Teatr. Moskva. 1934.

IRAKLI GAMREKELI. I : *Die Räuber*. **1** : Friedrich
Schiller. **3** : Akaki Vassadzé. **5** : Teatr
Roustaveli. Tbilissi. 1934.

DIMITRI POPOV. II : *Lévcha.* **1** : Nicolaï Leskov.
2 : Anatoli Novikov. **3** : Andrei Toutychkine.
5 : Teatr Mouzkomedii. Leningrad. 1959.

VADIM RYNDINE. II : *Voïna i Mir.* **1** : Léon Tolstoï.
2 : Sergueï Prokofiev. **3** : Boris Pokrovski.
5 : Bolshoï Teatr. Moskva. 1959.

S. S. S. R.

185

JOZSAS JANKUS. II : *Franks Kruks.*
1 : Vitauts Grivicks. **2** : Benjamins
Gorbulcks **3** : Vitauts Grivicks.
5 : Kaunas Valsts. Muzikalaja Teatri.
1959.

BORIS KNOBLOCK. I : *Ramayana.*
3 : Valentin Kolessaev. **5** : Tsentralnyi Detski Teatr. Movskva.
1960.

BORIS KNOBLOCK. I : *Droug moï,
Kolka!* **1** : Alexandre Khmélik.
3 : Anatoli Efross. **5** : Tsentralnyi
Detski Teatr. Moskva. 1959.

MIKHAÏL KOURILKO. III: *Krasnyi Mak*. **2**: Reingold
Glière. **4** : Léonide Lavrovski. **5** : Bolchoï Teatr.
Moskva. 1949.

EVGHENI KOVALENKO – VALENTINA KRIVO-
CHEINA. I : *Vessennié Skripki*. **1** : Alexandre
Stein. **3** : Elena Zotova. **5** : Teatr Maïakovs-
kovo. Moskva. 1959.

188

EVGHENI LANSERE. I : *Gore ot Uma*.
1 : Alexandre Griboiedov. **3** : Prov
Sadovski – Ilia Soudakov – Serghei
Alexeev. **5** : Malyi Teatr. Moskva. 1938.

FELIKSS NAVICKS. I : *Generalmeginajums*.
1 : Kaziss Binks. **3** : Genricks Vencevicus.
5 : Kaunas Dramas teatri. 1958.

ALEXANDRE OUSTINOV. I : *Vishnevyi Sad*.
1 : Anton Chekhov. **3** : Valentina Martia-
nova – Serghei Lavrov. **5** : Dramatitcheski
Teatr imeni Chekhova. Taganrog. 1960.

ANATOLI PETRITZKI. I : *Kalinovaïa Rochtcha*.
1 : Alexandre Korneitchouk. 3 : Alexei Diki.
5 : Malyi Teatr. Moskva. 1950.

YOURI PIMENOV. I : *Novogodniaïa Notch*.
1 : Alexandre Gladkov. 3 : Boris Babotchkine.
5 : Teatr Vakhtangova. Moskva. 1945.

YOURI PIMENOV. I : *Vessenni Potok*. 1 : Youri
Tchépourine. 3 : Alexei Popov. 5 : Tsentralnyi
Teatr Sovietskoï Armii. Moskva. 1953.

ISAAC RABINOVITCH. I : *Bolchoï Kirill*. **1** : Ilia
Selvinski. **3** : Rouben Simonov. **5** : Teatr Vakhtangova. Moskva. 1957.

VADIM RYNDINE. I : *Optimistitcheskaïa Traghédia*.
1 : Vsevolod Vichnévski. **3** : Alexandre Taïrov.
5 : Kamernyi Teatr. Moskva. 1933.

VADIM RYNDINE. I : *Much Ado About Nothing*.
1 : William Shakespeare. **3** : Iosif Rappoport.
5 : Teatr Vakhtangova. Moskva. 1936.

191

VADIM RYNDINE. I : *Hamlet*. **1** : William
Shakespeare. **3** : Nicolaï Okhlopkov.
5 : Teatr Maïakovskovo. Moskva. 1954.

VADIM RYNDINE. I : *Mat*. **1** : Maxim Gorki –
Nicolaï Okhlopkov. **3** : Nicolaï Okhlopkov.
5 : Teatr Maïakovskovo. Moskva. 1948.

NICOLAÏ OULIANOV. II : *Carmen*. **2** : Georges
Bizet. **3** : Konstantin Stanislavski.
5 : Operny Teatr Stanislavskovo.
Moskva. 1935.

MARTIROS SARYAN. II : *Khrabryi Nazar*. **2** : Aro
Stépanian. **3** : Archako Bourdjalian. **5** : Teatr
Opery i Baleta imeni Spendiarova. Erevan. 1935.

LIOUBOV SILITCH. I : *Vishnevyi Sad*.
1 : Anton Chekhov. **3** : Victor Stanitsyn.
5 : MKHAT. Paris. 1958. **6** : Official Soviet
Photo.

OTTO SKULME. I: *Uguns un Nakts*.
1 : Janis Rainis. **3** : Eduards
Smilgis. **5** : Dailes Teatri. Riga.
1946.

EVGHENI TCHEMODOUROV. II : *Takhir i Zoukhra.*
1 : Mirzo Tourssoune-Zadé. **2** : Alexandre
Lenski. **3** : Roman Korokh – Saïd Mouradov.
5 : Teatr Opery i Baleta. Stalinabad. 1945.

ALEXANDRE TIMINE. II : *Enhé-Boulat-
bator.* **2** : Markian Frolov. **3** : Iosif
Toumanov. **5** : Teatr Opery i Baleta.
Oulan-Oudé. 1940.

VADIM RYNDINE. I : *Hamlet*. **1** : William Shakespeare. **3** : Nicolaï
Okhlopkov. **5** : Teatr Maïakovskova. Moskva. 1954.

PIOTR VILIAMS. I : *Poslédnié Dni*. **1** : Mikhaïl Boulgakov.
3 : Victor Stanitzine – Vassili Toporkov. **5** : Mkhat.
Moskva. 1943.

ALEXANDRE TYCHLER. I : *Richard III.*
1 : William Shakespeare. **3** : Konstantin
Tverskoï. **5** : Bolchoï Dramatitcheski Teatr
imeni Gorkovo. Leningrad. 1935.

ALEXANDRE TYCHLER. I : *King Lear.*
1 : William Shakespeare.
3 : Serghei Radlov. **5** : Evreiski
Teatr. Moskva. 1935.

ALEXANDRE TYCHLER. I : *Misteria Bouff.*
1 : Vladimir Maïakovski. **3** : Valentin
Ploutchek. **5** : Teatr Satiry. Moskva. 1957.

ALEXANDRE TYCHLER. I : *Ioujnéié 38 parelleli.* **1** : Tkaï Dim Tchoune.
3 : Raphaïl Souslovitch. **5** : Novyi Teatr. Leningrad. 1951.

EDGARS VARDAUNIS. III : *Rigonda*.
1 : Arturs Birnsons – Helena Tangijeva-Birzniec. **2** : Romuald Grinblat.
4 : Helena Tangijeva-Birzniec.
5 : Teatr Opery i Baleta Latviiskoï S.S.R. Riga. 1959.

ALEXANDRE VASSILIEV. I : *Léchii*. **1** : Anton Chekhov. **3** : Youri Zavadski. **5** : Teatr Mossovieta. Moskva. 1960.

PIOTR VILIAMS. I : *Pikwikski Klub*.
1 : Charles Dickens. **3** : Victor Stanitzine. **5** : MKHAT. Moskva. 1934.

GIRTS VILKS. I : *Poéma par Vètru*. **1** : Vilis Lacis. **3** : Eduards
Smilgis. **5** : Dailes Teatri. Riga. 1960.

MILY VINOGRADOV. I : *Striapoukha*.
1 : Anatoli Sofronov. **3** : Rouben
Somonov. **5** : Teatr Vakhtangova.
Moskva. 1959.

SOLIKO VIRSALADZE. III : *Kamennyi Tsvétok*. **1** : Mirra Mendelson-Prokofiéva – Léonide Lavrovski-Bajov. **2** : Serguéï Prokofiev. **4** : Youri Grigorovitch. **5** : Teatr Opery i Baleta imeni Kirova. Leningrad. 1957.

BORIS VOLKOV. II : *Tikhii Don*. **1** : Léonide Dzerjinski. **2** : Ivan Dzerjinski. **3** : Boris Mordvinov. **5** : Mouzikalnyi Teatr imeni Stanislavskovo i Nemirovitcha – Dantchenko. Moskva. 1936.

SOPHIA YOUNOVITCH. I : *V Gloukhom Péréoulké*. **1** : Evgheni Ryss. **3** : Alexandre Rakhlenko. **5** : Teatr Leninskovo Komsomola. Leningrad. 1959.

SOPHIA YOUNOVITCH. II : *Sadko*.
2 : Nicolaï Rimsky-Korsakov.
3 : Evgheni Sokovnine. **5** : Teatr Opery
i Baleta imeni Kirova. Leningrad. 1953.

NICOLAÍ ZOLORATIEV. II : *Povest o nastoïachtchem tcheloveké*. **2** : Sergueï Prokofiev. **3** : Gheorghi Ansimov. **5** : Bolchoï Teatr. Moskva. 1960.

SUOMI

BIRGER CARLSTEDT. I : *L'Œuf*. **1** : Félicien Marceau.
3 : Kerstin Nylander. **5** : Svenska Teatern. Helsinki.
1958. **6** : Rembrandt.

PEKKA HEISKANEN. I : *Fin de Partie*. **1** : Samuel
Becket. **3** : Jack Witikka. **5** : Suomen Kansallisteatteri. Helsinki. 1957. **6** : Kolmio.

LEO LEHTO. I : *Kennen Sie die Milchstrasse*ñ **1** : Karl
Wittlinger. **3** : Edvin Laine. **5** : Suomen Kansallisteatteri.
Helsinki. 1958. **6** : Lehtikuva.

LEO LETHO. I : *Nilkkarengas*. **1** : Artturi Leinonen. **3** : Edvin Laine.
5 : Suomen Kansallisteatteri. Helsinki. 1959. **6** : Lehtikuva.

VEIKKO MÄKINEN. I : *Electre*. **1** : Jean Giraudoux. **3** : Kari Salosaari. **5** : Tampereen Teatteri. Tampere. 1962. **6** : Juhani Riekkola.

SEPPO NURMIMAA. III : *El Sombrero de Tres Picos*. **2** : Manuel de Falla. **4** : Into Lätti. **5** : Suomen Kansallisooppera. Helsinki. 1959. **6** : Taisto Tuomi.

PAUL SUOMINEN. II : *Kniaz Igor*. **2** : Alexander Borodin. **3** : Yrjö Kostermaa. **5** : Suomen Kansallisooppera. Helsinki. 1959. **6** : Taisto Tuomi.

ROLF STEGARS. I : *Ett Drömspel.*
1 : August Strindberg. 3 : Arvi Kivimaa.
5 : Suomen Kansallisteatteri. Helsinki.
1959. 6 : Lehtikuva.

ROLF STEGARS. I : *L'École des Femmes.* 1 : Molière. 3 : Jack
Witikka. 5 : Suomen Kansallisteatteri. Helsinki. 1959.
6 : Lehtikuva.

REINO TAIVASSALO. I : *Viimeiset Kiusauk-set*. **1** : Lauri Kokkonen. **3** : Risto Veste. **5** : Oulun Teatteri. Oulu. 1961.

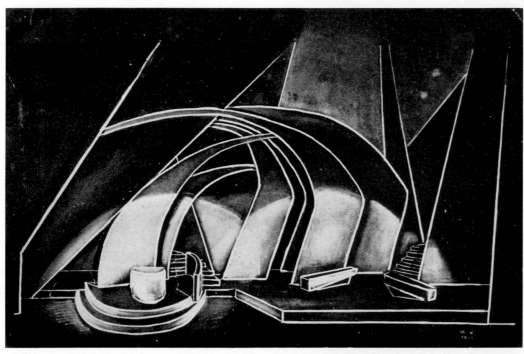

WOLLE WEINER. I : *Dibbuk*. **1** : An-Ski. **3** : Eino Salmelainen. **5** : Työväen Teatteri. Tampere. 1955. **6** : Ahti.

Pyynikin Kesäteatteri. Tampere. **6** : Kuvatoimisto.

SVERIGE

ASMUND ARLE — YNGVE LARSON. I :
Modell Beatrice. **1** : Tore Zetterholm.
3 : Alf Sjöberg. **5** : Dramatiska Teatern.
Stockholm. 1954. **6** : Sven Järlas.

MARTIN AHLBOM. II : *Värmlänningarna*.
1 : Fredrik August Dahlgren. **2** : Andreas
Randel. **3** : Ingmar Bergman. **5** : Stadsteatern.
Malmö. 1958. **6** : Lars Falck.

SVEN ERIXON. II : *Aniara*. **1** : Erik
Lindegren - Harry Martinson. **2** : Karl-
Birger Blomdahl. **3** : Göran Gentele.
4 : Birgit Akesson. **5** : Kungliga Teatern.
Stockholm. 1959. **6** : Rydberg.

YNGVE GAMLIN. I : *Vävaren i Bagdad.*
1 : Hjalmar Bergman. 3 : Arne Forsberg.
5 : Marsyas Teatern. Stockholm. 1955.
6 : Beata Bergström.

KERSTIN HEDEBY-PAWLO. II : *Alcina.* 2 : Marchi-
Haendel. 3 : Bengt Peterson. 4 : Mary
Skeaping. 5 : Kungliga Teatern. Stockholm.
1959. 6 : Rydberg.

ARNE JONES – PIERRE OLOFSSON. I : *Kröningen.*
1 : Lars Forssell. 3 : Bengt Ekerot.
5 : Dramatiska Teatern. Stockholm.
1956. 6 : Beata Bergström.

209

TYR MARTIN. I : *Advokaten Pathelin* (Maître Pathelin). **2** : Ingvar Wieslander. **3** : Mats Johansson. **5** : Stadsteatern. Malmö. 1951. **6** : Skanereportage.

LENNART MÖRK – RANDI FISHER. I : *Drott-ningens Juvelsmycke*. **1** : C.J.L. Almqvist. **3** : Alf Sjöberg. **5** : Dramatiska Teatern. Stockholm. 1957. **6** : Beata Bergström.

STELLAN MÖRNER. I : *A Midsummer Night's Dream*. **1** : William Shakespeare. **2** : Dag Wirén. **3** : Alf Sjöberg. **5** : Kungliga Teatern. Stockholm. 1956.

BARBARA W. ÖBERG. I : *Kristina*. **1** : August Strindberg.
3 : John Zacharias. **5** : Stadsteatern. Norrköping. 1961.
6 : Lennart Jansson.

BARBARA W. ÖBERG. I : *Lysistrata*. **1** : Aristophanes.
2 : Gunnar Hahn. **3** : Olof Thunberg. **5** : Stadsteatern.
Norrköping. 1957. **6** : Einar Jagerwall.

BARBARA W. ÖBERG. I : *Richard II*. **1** : William Shakespeare.
3 : John Zacharias – Olof Widgren. **5** : Stadsteatern.
Norrköping. 1958. **6** : Lennart Jansson.

LENNART RODHE. II : *Der Fliegende Hol-
länder*. **2** : Richard Wagner. **3** : Bengt
Peterson. **5** : Kungliga Teatern.
Stockholm. 1960. **6** : Rydberg.

MARIK VOS. I : *La Zapatera Prodigiosa*. **1** : Federico Garcia Lorca. **3** : Mimi
Pollak. **5** : Dramatiska Teatern. Stockholm. 1956. **6** : Beata Bergström.

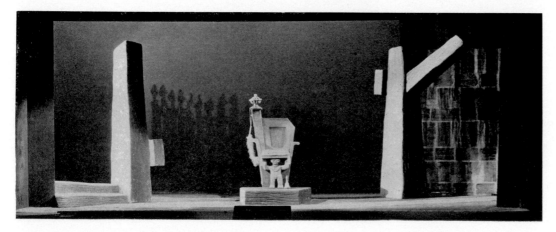

MARIK VOS. I : *Emperor Jones*.
1 : Eugene O'Neill. **3** : Bengt Ekerot.
5 : Dramatiska Teatern. Stockholm.
1958. **6** : Beata Bergström.

TURKIYE

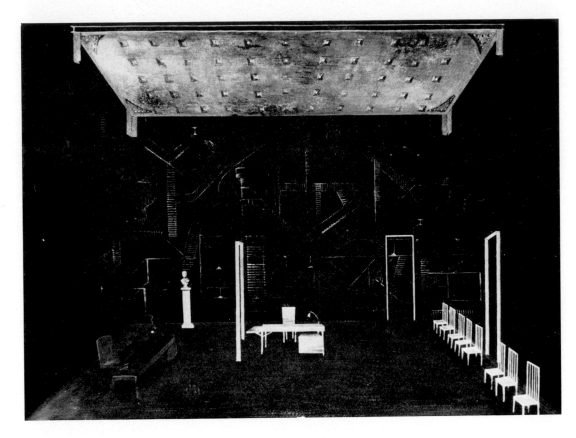

SEZA ALTINDAǦ. I : *Un Caso Clinico*. **1** : Dino Buzzati.
3 : Ziya Demirel. **5** : Devlet Tiyatrosu (Üçüncü Tiyatro).
Ankara. 1960. **6** : Osman Darcan.

REFIK EREN. I : *Hurrem Sultan*. **1** : Orhan Asena. **3** : Sahap
Akalin. **5** : Devlet Tiyatrosu. Ankara. 1959.
6 : Osman Darcan.

REFIK EREN. I : *Oidipous Tyrannos*. **1** : Sophocles. **3** : Takis Mouzenidis. **5** : Devlet Tiyatros. Ankara. 1959. **6** : Osman Darcan.

HÜSEYIN MUMCU. I : *Ask ve Baris*. **1** : Suat Taser. **3** : Suat Taser. **5** : Devlet Tiyatrosu (Küçük Tiyatro). Ankara. 1960. **6** : Osman Darcan.

UNITED KINGDOM

HUGH CASSON. II : *The World of Paul Slickey*. **1** : John Osborne. **2** : Christopher Whelan. **3** : John Osborne. **5** : Palace Theatre. London. 1959. **6** : Corry Bevington.

AUDREY CRUDDAS. I : *Macbeth*. **1** : William Shakespeare. **3** : Michael Benthall. **5** : Old Vic Theatre. London. 1955. **6** : John Vickers.

JAMES BAILEY. III : *Casse Noisette*. **2** : Piotr Tchaikowsky. **4** : Alfred Rodrigues. **5** : Teatro alla Scala. Milano. 1957. **6** : W. Churcher.

PETER BROOK – DESMOND HEELEY. I : *Titus Andronicus*.
1 : William Shakespeare. **3** : Peter Brook. **5** : Royal Shakespeare Theatre. Stratford-upon-Avon. 1955. **6** : Loaned
by the Royal Shakespeare Theatre.

DESMOND HEELEY. III : *Solitaire*. **2** : Malcolm Arnold.
3 : Kenneth Macmilian. **5** : Sadler's Wells Theatre Ballet.
London. 1956. **6** : Denis de Marney.

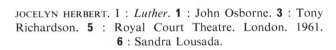

JOCELYN HERBERT. I : *Luther*. **1** : John Osborne. **3** : Tony Richardson. **5** : Royal Court Theatre. London. 1961. **6** : Sandra Lousada.

LESLIE HURRY. I : *Becket*. **1** : Jean Anouilh. **3** : Peter Hall. **5** : Royal Shakespeare Company. Aldwych Theatre. London. 1961. **6** : John Vickers.

SEAN KENNY. I : *The Devils*. **1** : John
Whiting. **3** : Peter Wood. **5** : Royal
Shakespeare Company. Aldwych Thea-
tre. London. 1961. **6** : Engraving
Service Ltd.

SEAN KENNY. II : *Stop the World – I Want to Get Off*. **1-2** : Anthony Newley – Leslie
Bricusse. **3** : Anthony Newley. **5** : Queen's Theatre. London. 1961. **6** : John Vickers.

ISABEL LAMBERT. III : *Jabez and the Devils*. **2** : Arnold
Cooke. **4** : Alfred Rodrigues. **5** : Royal Opera House.
Covent Garden. London. 1961. **6** : Anthony Crickmay.

OSBERT LANCASTER. III : *Tiresias*. **1** : Guillaume Apollinaire.
2 : Francis Poulenc. **4** : John Cranko.
5 : Aldburgh Festival. 1958.

OSBERT LANCASTER. II : *The Rake's Progress*. **1** : Wystan
Auden. **2** : Igor Stravinsky. **3** : Carl Ebert. **5** : Festival
Opera House. Glyndebourne. 1953.

TANYA MOISEIWITSCH. I : *Much Ado About Nothing*. **1** : William Shakespeare. **3** : Douglas Seale. **5** : Royal Shakespeare Theatre. Stratford-upon-Avon. 1958. **6** : T.F. Holt.

SVERIGE

STELLAN MÖRNER. I : *Erik XIV.* **1** : August Strindberg.
3 : Alf Sjöberg. **5** : Dramatiska Teatern. Stockholm. 1950.

UNITED KINGDOM

MOTLEY. I : *A Man for All Seasons.*
1 : Robert Bolt. **3** : Noel Willman.
5 : Globe Theatre. London. 1960.

221

RICHARD NEGRI. I : *The Dream of Peter Mann*. **1** : Bernard Kops. **3** : Frank Dunlop. **5** : Lyceum Theatre. Edinburgh. 1960. **6** : John Vickers.

TIMOTHY O'BRIEN. II : *Der Fliegende Holländer*. **2** : Richard Wagner. **3** : Dennis Arundell. **5** : Sadler's Wells Opera House. London. 1957.

JOHN PIPER. II : *A Midsummer Nights Dream*.
1 : William Shakespeare – Benjamin Britten –
Peter Pears. 2 : Benjamin Britten. 3 : Sir John
Gielgud. 5 : The Royal Opera House. Covent
Garden. London. 1961.

MALCOLM PRIDE. II : *La Vie Parisienne*. 1 : Henri Meilhac –
Ludovic Halevy. 2 : Jacques Offenbach. 3 : Wendy Toye.
5 : Sadler's Wells Opera House. London. 1961.
6 : John Vickers.

PETER RICE. II : *Ariadne in Naxos*. **1** : Hugo van
Hofmannsthal. **2** : Richard Strauss. **3** : Antony Besch.
5 : Sadler's Wells Opera House. London. 1961.
6 : John Vickers.

LOUDON SAINTHILL. I : *Pericles*.
1 : William Shakespeare.
3 : Tony Richardson. 5 : Royal
Shakespeare Theatre. Stratford-
upon-Avon. 1958.

J. HUTCHINSON SCOTT. I : *The Iceman Cometh*. 1 : Eugene
O'Neill. 3 : Peter Wood. 5 : The Arts Theatre Club.
London. 1958. 6 : Corry Bevington.

J. HUTCHINSON SCOTT. I : *The Elder Statesman*.
1 : T.S. Eliot. 3 : Martin Browne. 5 : The
Cambridge Theatre. London. 1958.
6 : Houston Rogers.

ALIX STONE. I : *The Taming of the Shrew*. 1 : William
Shakespeare. 3 : John Barton. 5 : Royal Shakespeare
Theatre. Stratford-upon-Avon. 1960. 6 : Gordon Goode.

ALAN TAGG. I : *The Entertainer*. 1 : John Osborne.
3 : Tony Richardson. 5 : Royal Court Theatre. London.
1957. 6 : Loaned by the British Council.

227

CARL TOMS. III : *La Reja*.
2 : Scarlatti. 3-4 : John Cranko.
5 : Ballet Rambert. Sadler's Wells
Opera House. London. 1959.
6 : John Vickers.

CARL TOMS. II : *New Cranks*. 1 : John Cranko. 2 : David
Lee. 3 : John Cranko. 5 : The Lyric Opera House. Hammersmith. 1960. 6 : John Vickers.

228

HORACE ARMISTEAD. II : *Carmen*. **2** : Georges Bizet. **3** : Sarah Caldwell.
5 : Boston University Theatre. Boston. 1956.

WILL STEVEN ARMSTRONG. I : *Misalliance*. **1** : George Bernard Shaw. **3** : Nikos Psacharopoulos.
5 : Yale University Theatre. New Haven. 1957.

BORIS ARONSON. I : *A View from the Bridge*. **1** : Arthur Miller. **3** : Martin Ritt.
5 : Coronet Theatre. New York. 1955.

BORIS ARONSON. I : *J.B.* **1** : Archibald MacLeish. **3** : Elia Kazan. **5** : Anta Theatre.
New York. 1958. **6** : Robert Galbraith.

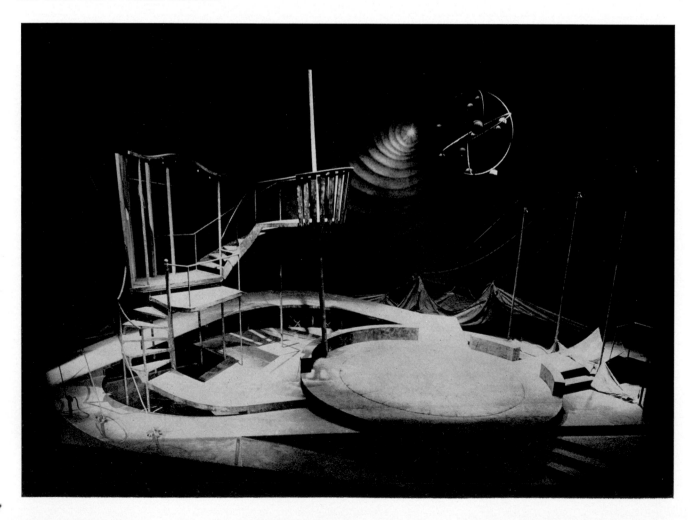

ROUBEN TER ARUTUNIAN. II : *Maria Golovin*. **2** : Gian-
Carlo Menotti. **3** : Kirk Browning. **5** : New York City
Opera. New York City Center. New York. 1959.

U. S. A.

HOWARD BAY. II : *Carmen*. **2** : Georges
Bizet. **3** : Dino Yannopoulos. **5** : Opera
House. San Francisco. 1959.

HOWARD BAY. I : *The Wall*. **1** : Millard
Lampell – John Hersey. **3** : Morton Da Costa.
5 : Billy Rose Theatre. New York. 1960.
6 : Werner J. Kuhn.

WILLIAM – JEAN ECKART. II : *Damn Yankees*.
1 : George Abbott – Douglass Wallop.
2 : Richard Adler – Jerry Ross. **3** : George
Abbott. **4** : Bob Fosse. **5** : Forty-Sixth Street
Theatre. New York. 1955.

WILLIAM – JEAN ECKART. I : *Mister Johnson*.
1 : Norman Rosten – Joyce Cary. **3** : Robert
Lewis. **5** : Martin Beck Theatre.
New York. 1956.

233

ELDON ELDER. I : *Henry V.* **1** : William Shakespeare. **3** : Joseph Papp. **5** : Central Park. New York. 1960. **6** : George E. Joseph.

CHARLES ELSON. II : *Don Giovanni.* **2** : Wolfgang Amadeus Mozart. **3** : Dino Yannopoulos. **5** : Metropolitan Opera. New York. 1955. **6** : Sedge Leblang.

DAVID HAYS. III : *Electronics*. **2** : Remi Gassmann – Oskar Sala. **3** : George Balanchine. **5** : New York City Ballet. New York City Center. New York. 1961. **6** : Fred Fehl.

DAVID HAYS. I : *All the Way Home*. **1** : Tad Mosel – James Agee. **3** : Arthur Penn. **5** : Belasco Theatre. New York. 1960.

PETER LARKIN. I : *No Time for Sergeants*.
1 : Ira Levin – Marc Hyman. 3 : Morton Da
Costa. 5 : Alvin Theatre. New York. 1955.
6 : Fred Fehl.

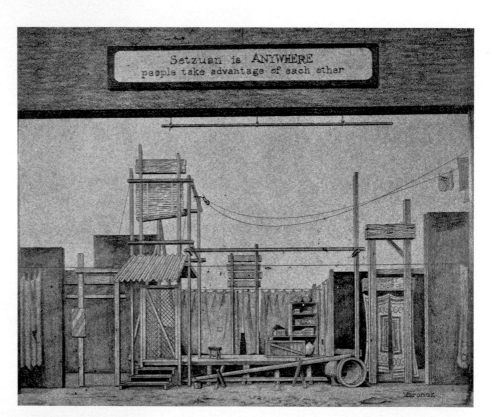

JAMES MARONEK. I : *Der gute Mensch von Sezuan*.
1 : Bertolt Brecht. 3 : Charles McGaw. 5 : The
Goodman Memorial Theatre. Chicago. 1960.

JO MIELZINER. II : *Can-Can*. 1 : Abe Burrows.
2 : Cole Porter. 3 : Abe Burrows. 4 : Michael
Kidd. 5 : Shubert Theatre. New York. 1953.

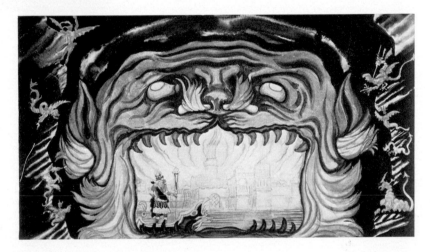

PAUL TRAUTVETTER. I : *Le Chapeau de Paille d'Italie*. **1** : Eugène Labiche. **3**: Lawrence Carra. **5**: Carnegie Institute of Technology. Pittsburgh. 1958.

GARY SMITH. II : *Six Characters in Search of an Author*. **2** : Hugo Weisgall. **3** : William Ball. **5** : New York City Opera. New York City Center. New York. 1959.

238

OLIVER SMITH. I : *Winesburg, Ohio*. **1** : Christopher Sergel – Sherwood Anderson.
3 : Joseph Anthony. **5** : National Theatre. New York. 1958. **6** : Vandamm.

OLIVER SMITH. II : *My Fair Lady*. **2** : Alan Jay Lerner – Frederick Loewe. **3** : Moss
Hart. **4** : Hanya Holm. **5** : Mark Hellinger Theatre. New York. 1956. **6** : Vandamm.

ROUBEN TER-ARUTUNIAN. Basic Set for Drama
Season. **5** : American Shakespeare Festival.
Stratford, Connecticut. 1960.

ROUBEN TER-ARUTUNIAN. I : *Twelfth Night*.
1 : William Shakespeare. **3** : Jack Landau.
5 : American Shakespeare Festival. Stratford,
Connecticut. 1960. **6** : Martha Holmes.

RICHARD WILCOX. I : *The Flowering Peach*.
1 : Clifford Odets. **3** : Nikos Psacharopoulos.
5 : Yale University Theatre. New Haven. 1960.

URUGUAY

JOSÉ ECHAVE. III : *La Danse de Mort.*
2 : Arthur Honegger. **3** : Lamberto
Baldi. **4** : Vaslav Veltcheck. **5** : Teatro
S.O.D.R.E. Montevideo. 1954.

JOSÉ ECHAVE. I : *La Cuisine des Anges.* **1** : Albert
Husson. **3** : Alberto Candeau. **5** : Comedia
Nacional. Teatro Solis. Montevideo. 1956.

MARIO GALUP. I : *Na Dnye.* **1** : Maxim
Gorki. **3** : Atahualpa del Cioppo.
5 : Teatro Universitario. Montevideo.
1957.

MARIO GALUP. I : *Moon on a Rainbow Shawl*. **1** : Errol
John. **3** : Ugo Ulive. **5** : Teatro Universitario.
Montevideo. 1959.

BEATRIZ TOSAR — AIDA RODRIGUEZ. I : *Morir, tal
vez Soñar*. **1** : Carlos Denis Molina. **3** : Orestes
Caviglia. **5** : Comedia Nacional. Teatro Solis.
Montevideo. 1953.

ADOLFO HALTY. I : *Los Intereses Crea-
dos*. **1** : Jacinto Benavente. **3** : Emilio
Acevedo Solano. **5**: Comedia Nacional.
Teatro Solis. Montevideo. 1958.

VENEZUELA

JACOBO BORGES. I : *Bodas de Sangre*. **1** : Federico Garcia Lorca. **3** : Humberto Orsini. **5** : Teatro Ministerio Educacion. Teatro Nacional. Caracas. 1961. **6** : Orsini.

JACOBO BORGES. I : *The Glass Menagerie*. **1** : Tennessee Williams. **3** : Humberto Orsini. **5** : Compañia Mascaras. Teatro La Comedia. Caracas. 1961. **6** : Rosson.

NICOLAS CURIEL. I : *Twelfth Night*. **1** : William Shakespeare. **3** : Nicolas Curiel. **5** : Teatro Universitario de la Universidad Central de Venezuela. Caracas. 1962.

ALBERTO DE PAZ Y MATEO. I : *La Casa de Bernarda Alba.* **1** : Federico Garcia
Lorca. **3** : Alberto de Paz y Mateo. **5** : Teatro Municipal. Caracas. 1954.

JOSÉ SALAS. I : *Lo que dejo la Tempestad.* **1** : Cesar Rengifo. **3** : Humberto Orsini.
5 : Compañia Mascaras. Teatro Nacional. Caracas. 1961. **6** : Rosson.

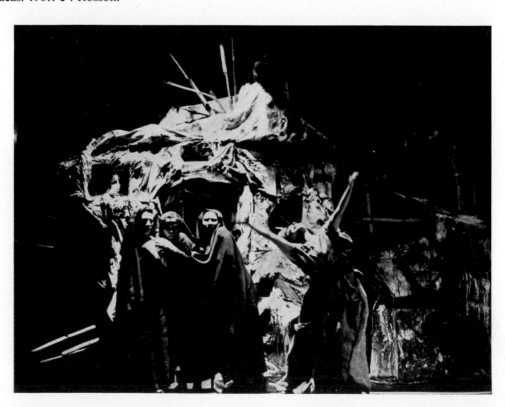

STAGE DESIGNERS' WHO'S WHO

B

BAILEY, James. (Great Britain)
Born : London. 7 March 1922.
Educated : Byam Shaw School of Art and Slade School. Disciple of Randolphe SCHWABE and Vladimir POLUNIN.
Stage Designs : 17.
AS YOU LIKE IT, Shakespeare. M : Michael Benthall. Theatre Guild, New York. 1950. – THE WAY OF THE WORLD, William Congreve. M : John Gielgud. Lyric Theatre, Hammersmith, London. 1953. – A MIDSUMMER NIGHT'S DREAM, Shakespeare. M : Michael Benthall. Old Vic., London. 1958.

BARTH, Ruodi. (Switzerland)
Born : Basle. 16 June 1921.
Educated : Gewerbeschule, Basle.
Stage Designs : Over 100.
THE BARBER OF SEVILLE, Rossini. M : Friedrich Schramm. City Theatre, Basle. 1950. – LYSISTRATA, Aristophanes. M : Erich-Fritz Brücklmeier. City Theatre, Basle. 1953. – THE FIREBIRD, Igor Stravinsky. M : Robert Peyer. City Opera, Zurich. 1958.

BAUER-ECSY, Leni.
(West Germany)
Born : Hamburg.
Educated : Kunxthochschule, Hamburg. Disciple of Professor CZECHKA.
Stage Designs : Over 250.
UNDER MILK WOOD, Dylan Thomas. M : Boleslaw Barlog. Schiller Theatre, West Berlin. 1956. – COSI FAN TUTTE. Mozart. M : Günther Rennert. Salzburg Festival, 1960. – BLOOD WEDDING, Wolfgang Fortner, after Federico Garcia Lorca. M : Günther Rennert. State Opera, Stuttgart. 1961.

BAY, Howard. (U.S.A.)
Born : Centralia. 3 May 1912.
Stage Designs : About 150.
FINIAN'S RAINBOW, E.Y. Harburg - Fred Saidy. Mu : Burton Lane. M : William Hammerstein. Ch : Herbert Ross. City Centre, New York. 1957. – SHOW BOAT, Oscar Hammerstein. Mu : Jerome Kern. M : E. Goldberg. Ch : Ernest Flatt. Philharmonic Auditorium, Los Angeles. 1959. – TOYS IN THE ATTIC, Lillian Hellman. M : Arthur Penn. Hudson Theatre, New York. 1959.

BENAVENTE, Saulo. (Argentina)
Born : Buenos Aires. 11 Feb. 1916.
Educated : High School of Fine Arts, Buenos Aires.
Stage Designs : Over 400.
THE GARDENER'S DOG, Lope de Vega. M : Osvaldo Bonet. Odeon Theatre, Buenos Aires. 1958. – DONDE LA MUERTE CLAVA SUS BANDERAS (Where Death fastens his Flags). Omar del Carlo. M : Orestes Caviglia. Cervantes National Theatre Buenos Aires. 1959. – FACUNDO EN LA CIUDADELA (Facundo in the Citadel), Vicente Barbieri. M : Orestes Caviglia. Cervantes National Theatre, Buenos Aires. 1959.

BENOIS, Nicholas. (Italy)
Born : St. Petersburg (Russia). 2 May 1901.
Educated : Fine Arts Academy, Leningrad. Disciple of Alexandre BENOIS and Oreste ALLEGRI.
Stage Designs : About 200.
BORIS GODUNOV, Mussorgsky. M : Alexander Sanin – Issai Dobroven. Scala, Milan. 1927 and 1953. – ANNA BOLENA, Donizetti. M : Luchino Visconti. Scala, Milan. 1957. – POLIUTO, Donizetti. M : Herbert Gref. Scala, Milan. 1961.

BERGNER, Yossl. (Israel)
Born : Vienna (Austria). 13 Oct. 1920.
Educated : Royal Academy of Art, Melbourne (Australia).
Stage Designs :
THE VISIONS OF SIMONE MACHARD, Bertolt Brecht. M : Israel Becker. Habima Theatre, Tel Aviv. 1957. – BIGDEY HAMELEH (The Emperor's New Clothes), Nisim Alony. M : Nisim Alony. Habima Theatre, Tel Aviv. 1961. – HANSIHA HA 'AMERIKAIT (The American Princess), Nisim Alony. M : Nisim Alony. Theatre of the Seasons, Tel Aviv. 1963.

BEURDEN, Leontien van.
(Netherlands)
Born : Amsterdam. 17 June 1930.
Educated : Kunstnijverheidschool, Amsterdam, and the Central School of Arts and Crafts, London. Disciple of Jeannetta COCHRANE.
Stage Designs : 15.
TROILUS AND CRESSIDA, Shakespeare. M : Johan de Meester. Royal Theatre, The Hague. 1959. – THE LITTLE FOXES, Lillian Hellman. M : Robert de Vries. City Theatre, Amsterdam. 1960.

BEZOMBES, Roger. (France)
Born : Paris. 17 Jan. 1913.
Stage Designs :
SAMPIERO CORSO. Mu : Tomasi. M : Roger Lalande. Ch : Janine Charrat. Grand Theatre, Bordeaux, and Holland Festival. 1956. – THE AMAZONS. Mu : Semenoff. M-Ch : Janine Charrat. Grand Colon Theatre, Buenos Aires. 1957. – CONCERTO. Mu : Tchaikovsky. M-Ch : Herbert Ross. Metropolitan Opera (American Ballet), New York. 1958.

BIGNENS, Max. (Switzerland)
Born : Zurich. 9 June 1912.
Educated : Kunstgewerbeschule, Zurich, Kunstakademie, Munich, and Academy of Fine Arts, Florence.
Stage Designs : Over 300.
FAUST I, Gœthe. M : Paul Kalbeck. City Theatre, Berne. 1944. – ŒDIPUS REX, Igor Stravinsky. M : Friedrich Schramm. City Theatre, Basle. 1952. – LES MAMELLES DE TIRÉSIAS (The Breasts of Tiresias), Francis Poulenc. M : Rudolf Lansky. City Theatre, Basle. 1957.

BLEYNIE, Claude. (France)
Born : Paris. 1923.
Educated : École des Beaux-Arts, Paris.
Disciple of SOUVERBIE.
Stage Designs : 15.
GISELLE. Mu : Adam. M : F. Adret. Ch : Marius Petipa. Amsterdam Opera. 1956. – BLUE-BEARD. Book : F. Guillot de Rode. Ch : Marise Desèvres. Casino, Aix les Bains. 1958. – THE WOLF AND THE LAB. Book : Edmond Audran. Ch : Ludmila Tchérina Sarah Bernhardt Theatre Paris. 1960.

BOLL, André. (France)
Born : Paris. 25 Apr. 1896.
Pupil of NAUDIN (design), LAFOLLYE (architecture) and AMABLE (stage design).
Stage Designs : About 250.
ŒDIPUS, Enesco. M : Rouché-Boll. Paris Opera. 1936. – CORIOLANUS, Shakespeare. M : Véra Korène. Fourvières. 1953. – THE MYSTERY OF THE PASSION. M : Pierre Aldebert. Performed in front of the Cathedral of Notre-Dame, Paris, since 1936.

BONNAT, Yves. (France)
Born : Voiron. 20 Feb. 1912.
Educated : École des Beaux-Arts, Paris. Disciple of Suzanne VALADON and E.O. FRIESZ (painting) and DULLIN and PITOËFF (theatre).
Stage Designs : Over 120.

JOAN AT THE STAKE, Claudel-Honegger. M : Jan Doat. Ch : Serge Lifar. Paris Opera. 1951. – CARMEN, Bizet. M : Louis Erlo. Théâtre Royal de la Monnaie, Brussels. 1961. – SAINT JOAN, Bernard Shaw. M : Pierre Valde. Comédie de Genève. 1963.

BORGES, Jacobo. (Venezuela)
Born : Caracas. 28 Nov. 1931.
Educated : School of Plastic Arts in Caracas and Paris.
Stage Designs : 10.
HERNANI, Victor Hugo. M : Román Chalbaud. City Theatre, Caracas. 1958. – THE GLASS MENAGERIE, Tennessee Williams. M : Humberto Orsini. La Comedia Theatre. 1960. – BLOOD WEDDING, Federico Garcia Lorca. M : Humberto Orsini. National Theatre, Caracas. 1961.

BOSQUET, Thierry. (Belgium)
Born : Brussels. 2 May 1937.
Educated: École Nationale Supérieure d'Architecture et des Arts Décoratifs, Brussels.
Stage Designs : 5.
THE MAGIC FLUTE, Mozart. M : Jean-Marc Landier. Théâtre Royal de la Monnaie, Brussels. 1960. – DON GIOVANNI, Mozart. M : Jean-Marc Landier. Théâtre Royal de la Monnaie, Brussels. 1961. – DER ROSENKAVALIER, Richard Strauss. M : Herbert Graf. Théâtre Royal de la Monnaie, Brussels, 1962.

BOSSULAYEV, Anatoli. (U.S.S.R.)
Born : Kerch. 15 June 1904.
Educated: Fine Arts School, Kharlov, and Proletkult Studio. Disciple of Isaac RABINOVITCH.
Stage Designs : About 200.
THE SAILORS OF CATTARO, Friedrich Wolf. M : Alexei Diki. V.T.S.P.S. Theatre, Moscow. 1932. – THE SUMMER VISITORS, Maxim Gorki. M : Boris Babochkin. Gorki Grand Dramatic Theatre, Leningrad. 1937. – THE OPTIMISTIC TRAGEDY, Vsevolod Vishnevski. M : Georgi Tovstonogov. Pushkin Academic Theatre, Leningrad. 1955.

BRAYER, Yves. (France)
Born : Versailles. 18 Nov. 1907.
Educated : École des Beaux-Arts, Paris.
Stage Designs : 13.
JOAN OF ZARISSA. Mu : Werner Egk. Ch : Serge Lifar. Paris Opera. 1942. – MITHRIDATE, Jean Racine. Comédie Française, Paris. 1952. – DOLORÈS OU LE MIRACLE DE LA FEMME LAIDE (Dolores, or the Miracle of the Plain Woman). Mu : André Jolivet. Lyons Opera. 1960.

BROË, Roger. (Belgium)
Born : Brussels. 6 Sep. 1925.
Educated : Académie des Beaux-Arts and École Nationale Supérieure d'Architecture et des Arts Décoratifs, Brussels. Disciple of Joris MINNE.
Stage Designs : 55.
THE MASK OF THE RED DEATH. Mu : Jongen. Ch : Etcheverry. Théâtre Royal de la Monnaie, Brussels. 1957. – THE UNICORN. Mu : Menotti. Ch : Etcheverry. Théâtre Royal de la Monnaie, Brussels. 1958. – GISELLE. Mu : Adam. Ch. : Skibine. Palais des Beaux-Arts, Charleroi. 1962.

BROOK, Peter. (Great Britain)
Born : London. 21 March 1925.
Stage Designs :
TITUS ANDRONICUS, Shakespeare. M : Peter Brook. Royal Shakespeare Theatre, Stratford-upon-Avon. 1955. – CAT ON A HOT TIN ROOF, Tennessee Williams. M : Peter Brook. Antoine Theatre, Paris. 1956. – KING LEAR, Shakespeare. M : Peter Brook. Royal

Shakespeare Theatre, Stratford-upon-Avon. 1962.

BUBENIK, Květoslav.
(Czechoslovakia)
Born: Kostelec na Hané. 29 May 1922.
Educated : Vysoká Skola Umelecko-Prumyslová. Disciple of Josef KAPLICKY and Antonin STRNADEL.
Stage Designs : Over 100.
POOP (The Button). Mu : Otakar Zich. M : Ladislav Stros. National Theatre, Prague. 1959. – MUSA DZALIL. Mu : Nazib Ziganov. M : Ladislav Stros. National Theatre, Prague. 1960.

BUFFET, Bernard. (France)
Born : Paris. 10 July 1928.
Educated : École des Beaux-Arts, Paris.
Stage Designs : 5.
LA CHAMBRE (The Room), Georges Simenon. Mu : Georges Auric. M-Ch : Roland Petit. Champs-Élysées Theatre, Paris. 1955. – LE RENDEZ-VOUS MANQUÉ (The Missed Appointment), Françoise Sagan. Mu : Michel Magne. M : Vadim. Ch : John Taras-Don Lurio. Monte Carlo Opera. 1958. – CARMEN, Bizet. M : Louis Ducreux. Marseilles Opera. 1962.

BURGOS, Emilio. (Spain)
Born : Madrid. 18 Feb. 1912.
Stage Designs : About 30.
THE CARMELITES, Georges Bernanos. M : José Tamayo. Teatro Español, Madrid. 1954. – DOÑA FRANCISQUITA, Romero-Fernandez-Shaw. Mu : Amadeo Vives. M : José Tamayo. Teatro Zarzuela, Madrid. 1956. – THE DEAD QUEEN. Henry de Montherlant. M : Claudio de la Torre. Teatro Maria Guerrero, Madrid. 1957.

C

CABALLERO, José. (Spain)
Born : Huelva. 11 June 1916.
Stage Designs : 21.
BLOOD WEDDING, Federico Garcia Lorca. M : Federico Garcia Lorca. Teatro Poliorama. 1935. – LOVE, THE MAGICIAN, Manuel de Falla. M-Ch : Antonio, Saville, London - Champs Élysées, Paris - Scala, Milan. 1955 - 1956. – YERMA, Federico Garcia Lorca. M : Luis Escobar. Teatro Eslava, Madrid. 1960.

CAGLI, Corrado. (Italy)
Born : Ancona. 23 Feb. 1910.
Stage Designs : 6.
THE MEDIUM, Gian-Carlo Menotti. M : Gian-Carlo Menotti. 1947. – THE TRIUMPH OF BACCHUS AND ARIADNE, Balanchine. 1948.

CAMURATI, Jacques. (France)
Born : Paris. 11 Feb. 1925.
Educated: École Nationale Supérieure des Arts Décoratifs et Atelier d'Essai. Disciple of Yves-BONNAT and Félix LABISSE.
Stage Designs :
DRUMS IN THE NIGHT, Bertolt Brecht. M : André Steiger. Lutèce Theatre, Paris, 1958. – TRISTAN AND ISOLDA, Jean de Beer. M : Pierre Jolivet. Tertre Theatre, Paris 1959.

CARLSTEDT, Birger-Jarl. (Finland)
Born : Helsinki. 12 July 1907.
Educated : Fine Arts Academy, Finland.
Stage Dessigns : 30.
DE BESATTA (The Possessed), Martin Söderhjelm. Mu : Einar Englund. M : Gerde Wrede. Swedish Theatre, Helsinki. – PIECES OF A MODEL, Soya. M : Vivica Bandler. Little Theatre, Helsinki. – GRÄSBUREN (The Grass Cape), Mary Mandelin. M : Vivica Bandler. Litle Theatre, Helsinki.

CASSON, Sir Hugh Maxwell.
(Great Britain)
Born : London. 23 May 1910.
Educated : Eastbourne College, St.
John's College, Cambridge, and British
School, Athens.
Stage Designs : 5.
ALCESTE, Gluck. M : Carl Ebert.
Glyndebourne. 1953. – TROILUS AND
CRESSIDA. Mu : William Walton. M :
George Devine. Royal Opera House,
Covent Garden, London. 1954. – THE
WORLD OF PAUL SLICKEY, John
Osborne. M : John Osborne. Palace
Theatre, London. 1959.

CASTILLO, Carlos Aïtor. (Peru)
Born : Lima. 6 June 1913.
Non-figurative painter, teacher and art
critic.
Stage Dessigns : 20.
THE MAIDS, Jean Genet. M : Reynaldo
d'Amore. Theatre Club, Lima. 1956. –
TARTUFFE, Molière. M : Carlos Tosi.
National Theatre Company, Lima.
1961. – YERMA, Federico Garcia
Lorca. M : Philippe Toledano. Nuevo
Theatre, Lima. 1963.

CHIARI, Mario. (Italy)
Born : Florence. 14 July 1909.
Educated : Faculty of Architecture,
University of Florence.
Stage Designs : 35.
A TRIP TO THE COUNTRY, Carlo
Goldoni. M : Giorgio Strehler. Piccolo
Teatro, Milan. 1954. – IL DIAVOLO
PETER (Peter the Devil), Salvato
Cappelli. M : Alessandro Fersen.
Teatro Stabile, Genoa. 1957.

CHIFRINE, Nisson. (U.S.S.R.)
See Shifrin, Nisson.

CIULEI, Liviu. (Rumania)
Born : Bucharest. 7 July 1923.
Educated : Faculty of Architecture,
Bucharest, and Institute of Dramatic
Art and Cinematography, Bucharest.
Disciple of Marioana VOICULESCU
(actress) and Ion SAVA (director).
Stage Designs : Over 60.
THE DARK YEARS, Aurel Baranga -
Nicolae Moraru. M : Sica Alexan-
drescu. National Teatre I.L. Caragiale,
Bucharest. 1958. – SAINT JOAN,
Bernard Shaw. M : Liviu Ciulei. City
Theatre, Bucharest, 1959. – THE
LOWER DEPTHS, Maxim Gorki. M :
Liviu Ciulei. City Theatre, Bucharest.
1960.

COLASANTI, Veniero. (Italy)
Born : Rome. 21 July 1910.
Educated : Rome.
Stage Designs : 60 to 70.
TURANDOT, Puccini. M : Vassallo.
Torre del Lago. 1958. – THE TALES OF
HOFFMANN, Jacques Offenbach. M :
Herbert Graf. Rome Opera. Scala,
Milan. 1959. – OTELLO, Verdi. M :
Herbert Graf. Doges' Palace, Venice.
1960.

COLONNELLO, Attilio. (Italy)
Born : Milan. 9 Nov. 1931.
Educated : Faculty of Architecture,
University of Milan. Disciple of
Ernesto N. ROGERS and Gio PONTI.
Stage Designs : 30 to 35.
ORFEO, Monteverdi. M : Aurel M.
Millos. Maggio Musicale Fiorentino,
Florence. 1958. – BEATRICE. Mu :
Vincenzo Bellini. M : Franco Enriquez.
Scala, Milan. 1960. – OTELLO, Verdi.
M : John Houseman. Civic Opera
Company, Dallas. U.S.A.

COLTELLACCI, Giulio. (Italy)
Born : Rome. 12 April 1916.
Educated : Fine Arts Academy, Rome.
Pupil of Aldo CALVI.
Stage Designs : About 100.

RINALDO IN CAMPO (Rinaldo in the
Field), Garinei-Giovannini. Mu : Do-
menico Modugno. M : Garinei -
Giovannini. Ch. Herbert Ross. Sistina
Theatre, Rome. 1961. – RUGANTINO,
Garinei - Giovannini. Mu : Armando
Trovaioli. M : Garinei - Giovannini.
Ch : Dania Krupska. Sistina Theatre,
Rome. 1962.

COSTA, Tullio. (Italy)
Born : Rome. 16 Nov. 1916.
Stage Designs : About 500.
THE LOWER DEPTHS, Gorki. M :
Flaminio Bollini. Teatro Brasilero de
Comédia, São Paulo. 1951. – THE
HOUSE OF BERNARDA ALBA, Federico
Garcia Lorca. M : Flaminio Bollini.
Popular Art Theatre, São Paulo. 1956.

COSTA, Valeria. (Italy)
Born : Rome. 15 Dec. 1917.
Stage Designs : 40.
HIPPOLYTUS. Euripides. M : Orazio
Costa. Greek Theatre, Syracuse.
1954. – THE CARMELITES, Georges
Bernanos. M : Orazio Costa. Art
Theatre. Rome. 1955. – THE GIANTS
OF THE MOUNTAIN, Luigi Pirandello.
M. Orazio Costa. Brussels National
Theatre. 1963.

COUTAUD, Lucien. (France)
Born : Meynes. 13 Dec. 1904.
Educated : École des Beaux-Arts,
Nîmes.
Stage Designs : 17.
THE BIRDS, Aristophanes. M : Charles
Dullin. Atelier Theatre, Paris. 1928. –
THE SATIN SLIPPER, Paul Claudel. M :
Jean-Louis Barrault. Comédie Fran-
çaise, Paris. 1943. – MEDEA, Cherubini.
M : André Barsacq. Maggio Fioren-
tino, Florence. 1953.

CREUZ, Serge. (Belgium)
Born : Molenbeek. 4 May 1924.
Educated : Académie des Beaux-Arts
and École Nationale Supérieure d'Ar-
chitecture et des Arts Décoratifs,
Brussels. Worked with Christian
BÉRARD and Félix LABISSE.
Teacher at École Supérieure d'Art
Dramatique, Strasbourg.
Stage Designs : About 50.
LA BOHÈME, Puccini. M : Bronislaw
Horowicz. Théâtre Royal de la
Monnaie, 1960. – THE VISIT OF THE
OLD LADY, Friedrich Dürrenmatt. M :
Hubert Gignoux. Comédie de l'Est,
Strasbourg. 1961. – THE CAUCASIAN
CHALK CIRCLE, Bertolt Brecht. M :
Paul Anrieu. Rideau de Bruxelles,
Brussels. 1962.

CSELÉNYI, József. (Hungary)
Born : Budapest. 1928.
Educated : High School of Decorative
Arts. Budapest. Disciple of Gyula
KACS and László HORNICSEK.
Stage Designs : 150.
OTHELLO, Shakespeare. M : Antal
Németh. Katona József Theatre, Buda-
pest. 1957. – BIEDERMANN AND THE
FIRE RAISERS, Max Frisch. M : Endre
Marton. Katona József Theatre,
Budapest. 1959. – ROMEO AND JULIET,
Shakespeare. M : Zoltán Várkonyi.
Gaiety Theatre, Budapest. 1963.

CURIEL, Nicolas. (Venezuela)
Born : Caracas. 23 Apr. 1928.
Disciple (influence) of APPIA, GRAIG,
BATTY, Caspar NEHER, etc.
Stage Designs : 8.
LES MISÉRABLES, Victor Hugo. M :
Nicolas Curiel. Aula Magna, Caracas.
1957. – JUAN FRANCISCO DE LEON,
José Ignacio Cabrujas. M : Nicolas
Curiel. Aula Magna, Caracas. 1959. –
TWELFTH NIGHT, Shakespeare. M :
Nicolas Curiel. Aula Magna, Caracas.
1961.

D

DAMIANI, Luciano. (Italy)
Born : Bologna. 14 July 1923.
Educated : Fine Arts Academy.
Stage Designs : 78.
CORIOLANUS, Shakespeare. M: Giorgio
Strehler. Piccolo Teatro, Milan. 1957. –
THE GOOD WOMAN OF SETZUAN,
Bertolt Brecht. M : Giorgio Strehler.
Piccolo Teatro, Milan. 1958.

DAMONTE, Marcelo. (Peru)
Born : Buenos Aires (Argentina).
8 Nov. 1930.
Stage Designs : Over 20.
LIFE'S A DREAM, Calderon de la Barca.
M : Sergio Arrau, San Marco Univer-
sity Theatre, Lima. 1961. – PETER THE
DEVIL, Salvato Cappelli. M : Reynaldo
d'Amore. Lima Theatre Club. 1961. –
THE MAKER OF DEBTS, Sebastián
Salazar Bondy. M : José Velasquez.
Histrión Arts Theatre, Lima. 1962.

DAYDÉ, Bernard. (France)
Born : Paris. 3 Feb. 1921.
Stage Designs : 95.
ORPHEUS IN THE UNDERWORLD, Jac-
ques Offenbach. M-Ch : Heinz Rosen.
Bühnen der Stadt Köln, Cologne.
1957. – LES VICTOIRES DE L'AMOUR,
Harald Lander. Mu : Lulli. M-Ch :
Harald Lander. Royal Opera, Copen-
hagen. 1962. – THE MISFORTUNES OF
ORPHEUS, Armand Lunel. Mu : Darius
Milhaud. M : Louis Ducreux. Ch :
Joseph Lazzini. Piccola Scala, Milan.
1963.

DECKWITZ, Franz. (Netherlands)
Born : Schermerhorn. 25 Feb. 1934.
Stage Designs : 8.
THE MOON IN THE TRAPEZE. Mu :
Benjamin Britten. Ch : Hans van
Manen. City Theatre. Utrecht. 1959. –
FEAR AND MISERY IN THE THIRD
REICH, Bertolt Brecht. M : Walter
Kous. Hypokriterion, Amsterdam.
1961.

DEL CASTILLO PÉREZ, Efren.
(Cuba)
Born : Guines. 19 Nov. 1932.
Educated : Escuela Nacional de Bellas
Artes " San Alejandro " and Univer-
sity Theatre. Pupil of J.M. BALMASEDA
and Rubén VIGON.
Stage Designs :
LA FABULA DEL SECRETO bien GUAR-
DADO (The Fable of the Well-Kept
Secret), Alejandro Casona. M :Enrique
Ramos. Sociedad " Brage ", Guines,
Cuba. 1957. – ABDALA, José Marti.
M : Bertilio Pérez Alpizar. Sociedad
Liceo, Guines, Cuba. 1960.

DELFT, Hep van. (Netherlands)
Born : Amsterdam. 12 May 1921.
Educated : Normaalschool voor Te-
kenleraren. Disciple of Gerrit VAN
'T NET.
Stage Designs : About 70.
THE ENTERTAINER, John Osborne. M :
Paul Steenbergen. Theatre Royal,
The Hague. 1958. – BIEDERMANN AND
THE FIRE RAISERS, Max Frisch. M :
Joris Diels. Ch : Albert Mol. Theatre
Royal, The Hague. 1959.

DE PAZ Y MATEO, Alberto.
(Venezuela)
Born : Corunna (Spain).
Disciple (influence) of Gordon CRAIG.
Stage Designs : 30.
THE HOUSE OF BERNARDA ALBA,
Federico Garcia Lorca. M : Alberto
de Paz y Mateo. City Theatre, Caracas.
1955. – CAIN ADOLESCENTE (Young
Cain), Román Chalbaud. Casa Sindi-
cal Theatre, Caracas. 1956. – YERMA,
Federico Garcia Lorca. M : Alberto
de Paz y Mateo. City Theatre, Caracas.
1961.

D

DEVINE, Sophia. (Great Britain)
(Sophia DEVINE together with Marga-
ret HARRIS and Elizabeth MONT-
GOMERY make up the trio of designers
called MOTLEY).
Born : Hayes. Kent. 2 July 1902.
Educated : Chelsea.
Stage Designs : About 600.
ROMEO AND JULIET, Shakespeare. M :
John Gielgud. New Theatre, London.
1936. – THE COUNTRY WIFE, Wycherley.
M : George Devine. Royal Court,
London. 1955. – Ross, Terence
Rattigan. M : Glen Byam Shaw.
Haymarket Theatre, London. 1960.

DMITRIEV, Vladimir. (U.S.S.R.)
Born : Moscow. 13 Aug. 1900.
Educated : Fine Arts Academy, Petro-
grad. Disciple of Kuzma PETROV -
VODKIN.
Stage Designs : Over 150.
THE FLAMES OF PARIS, ballet by
Boris Asafiev, Libretto by Nicolai
Volkov and Vladimir Dmitriev. D :
Vasili Vainonen. M : Serge Radlov.
Kirov Opera and Ballet Theatre,
Leningrad. 1932. – THE THREE
SISTERS, Chekhov. M : Vladimir Nemi-
rovich - Danchenko. Moscow Art
Theatre. 1940. – THE MAID OF ORLEANS,
Tchaikovsky. M : Ilia Shlepianov.
Kirov Opera and Ballet Theatre,
Leningrad. 1945.

DORRER, Valeri. (U.S.S.R.)
Born : Leningrad. 22 Feb. 1928.
Disciple of Mikhail ZANDIN.
Stage Designs : About 150.
THE PATH OF THUNDER, ballet by
Kara Karayev. Ch : Konstantin Ser-
geyev. Kirov Opera and Ballet Theatre,
Leningrad. 1958. – THE BANK OF
HOPE, ballet by Andrei Petrov and
Yuri Slonimski. Ch : Igor Belski.
Kirov Opera and Ballet Theatre,
Leningrad. 1959. – GOLYI KOROL
(The Emperor's New Clothes), Evghe-
ni Shvartz. M : Margarita Mikaelian.
Contemporary Studio Theatre (Sovre-
mennik), Moscow. 1960.

DOUKING, Georges. (France)
Born : Paris. 6 Aug. 1902.
Stage Designs : 101.
JEANNE AVEC NOUS (Jeanne with Us),
Claude Vermorel. M : Georges Dou-
king. Compagnie des Champs-Élysées,
Paris. 1942. – FILUMENA MARTURANO,
Eduardo de Filippo. M : Jean Darcante.
Renaissance Theatre, Paris. 1942. –
RAMEAU'S NEPHEW, Diderot. M : J.-
H. Duval. Michodière Theatre, Paris.
1963.

DUPONT, Jacques-Henri. (France)
Born : Chatou. 16 Jan. 1909.
Stage Designs : 30.
LES CAPRICES DE MARIANNE (Marian-
ne's Whims), Jean-Pierre Grédy, after
Alfred de Musset. Mu : Henri Sauguet.
M : Jean Meyer. Aix-en-Provence
Festival. 1954. – LA FOURMI DANS LE
CORPS (The Ant in the Body), Audi-
berti. M : André Barsacq. Comédie
Française, Paris. 1962. – DIDO AND
AENEAS, Purcell. M-Ch : Margherita
Wallmann. Scala, Milan. 1963.

E

ECHAVE, José. (Uruguay)
Born : Salto. 27 Nov. 1921.
Stage Designs :
DANCE OF DEATH, Paul Claudel. Mu :
Arthur Honegger. M : Lamberto
Baldi. Ch : Vaslav Veltchek. S.O.D.R.E.
1954. – FAUST, Gounod. M : Juan José
Brenta. Ch : Yurek Shabelevski.
S.O.D.R.E. 1960. – BECKET OR THE
HONOUR OF GOD, Jean Anouilh. M :
Ruben Yañez. Comedia Nacional.
Teatro Solis, Montevideo. 1961.

ECKART, Jean. (U.S.A.)
Born : Chicago. 18 Aug. 1921.
Educated : Newcomb College then Yale University (Stage Design).
Stage Designs : About 20.
THE GOLDEN APPLE, John Latouche. Mu : Jerome Moross. M : Norman Lloyd. Ch : Hanya Holm. Phoenix Theatre, New York. 1954. – DAMN YANKEES, George Abbott - Douglas Wallop. Mu : Richard Adler - Jerry Ross. M : George Abbott. Ch : Bob Fosse. 46th Street Theatre, New York. 1955. – FIORELLO. Jerome Weidman - George Abbott. Mu : Sheldon Harnick - Jerry Bock. M : George Abbott. Ch : Peter Gennaro. Broadhurst Theatre, New York. 1959.

ECKART, William. (U.S.A.)
Born : New Iberia. 21 Oct. 1920.
Educated : Tulane University (Architecture) and Yale University (Stage Design).
Stage Designs : 20.
(See ECKART, Jean.)

EGG, Lois. (Austria)
Born : Innsbruck. 11 Oct. 1913.
Educated: Arts Academy, Prague, and Akademie der Bildenden Künste, Vienna. Disciple of Emil PIRCHAN and Clemens HOLZMEISTER.
Stage Designs : About 500.
NEUES VOM TAGE (News of the Day), Paul Hindemith. M : Martin Bormann. People's Opera, Vienna. 1955. – LILY DAFON, William Saroyan. M : Rudolf Steinböck. Akademie Theatre, Vienna. 1960. – DER BAUER ALS MILLIONÄR (The Peasant a Millionaire), Ferdinand Raimund. M : Rudolf Steinböck. Salzburg Festival. 1961.

ELSON, Charles. (U.S.A.)
Born : Chicago. 5 Sep. 1909.
Educated : University of Illinois and Yale.
Stage Designs : 220.
LOHENGRIN, Wagner. M : Dino Yannopoulos. Metropolitan Opera, New York. 1951. – TITUS, Mozart. M : Boris Goldowsky. Tanglewood, Lenox (Mass.) 1952. – THE LOVERS, Leslie Stevens. M : Michael Gordon. Martin Beck Theatre, New York. 1956.

EREN, Refik. (Turkey)
Born : Siran. 1922.
Educated : Academy of Fine Arts, Istanbul, and École des Beaux-Arts, Paris. Disciple of BRIANCHON, BARSACQ and LHOTE.
Stage Designs : Over 60.
HÜRREM SULTAN (Sultana Hürrem), Orhan Asena. M : Sahap Akalin. State Theatre, Ankara. 1959. – THE CRUCIBLE, Arthur Miller. M : Cüneyt Gökcer. State Theatre, Ankara. 1959. – ŒDIPUS REX, Sophocles. M : Takis Muzenidis. State Theatre, Ankara. 1960.

ERIXON, Sven Leonard. (Sweden)
Born : Tumba. 23 Nov. 1899.
Educated : Konstakademien, Stockholm. Disciple of Olle HJORTZBERG.
Stage Designs : 10.
CARMEN, Bizet. M : Göran Gentele. Ch : Birgit Akesson. Royal Opera, Stockholm. 1954. – WOZZECK, Alban Berg. M : Göran Gentele. Ch : Birgit Akesson. Royal Opera, Stockholm. 1957.

ESTERCAM, Vic. (Belgium)
Born : Antwerp. 29 Apr. 1920.
Educated : Antwerp Academy and Académie Julian, Paris. Disciple of the director, Étienne DEBEL.
Stage Designs : 10 and designs for Television.
ELIEZER AND SARAH, Marcel Falmagne. M : Étienne Debel, Palais des Beaux-Arts, Brussels. 1958. – VASCO, Georges Schéhadé. M : Jeanne Geldof. 1959.

F

FARRAH, Abd' El Kader. (France)
Born : Boghari (Algeria). 28 Mar. 1926.
Stage Designs : 33.
THE CAUCASIAN CHALK CIRCLE, Bertolt Brecht. M : John Blatchley - Jean Dasté. Comédie de Saint-Étienne. – ANDROMAQUE, Jean Racine. M : Daniel Leveugle, Comédie de l'Est, Strasbourg. – THE TEMPEST, Shakespeare. M : Clifford Williams - Peter Brook. Royal Shakespeare Theatre, Stratford-upon-Avon. 1963.

FAUCHEUR, Yves. (France)
Born : Pont à Mousson. 21 July 1924.
Stage Designs : About 40.
LA FAMILLE ARLEQUIN (Harlequin and his Family), Claude Santelli. M : Jacques Fabbri. Vieux Colombier Theatre, Paris. 1952. – POVERTY AND NOBILITY, Scarpetta. M : Jacques Fabbri. Alliance Française, Paris. 1954. – THE MERRY WIVES OF WINDSOR, Shakespeare. M : Guy Lauzun. Ambigu Theatre, Paris. 1961.

FAVORSKI, Vladimir. (U.S.S.R.)
Born : Moscow. 15 Mar. 1886.
Educated : Moscow University and Simon HOLOSI Academy (Munich).
Stage Designs : About 20.
TWELFTH NIGHT, Shakespeare. M : Sophia Giatsintova - Vladimir Gotovtsev. Mu : Nicolai Rakhmanov. Moscow Art Theatre. 1934. – VELIKI GOSSUDAR (The Great Sovereign), Vladimir Soloviev. M : Boris Zakhava. Mu : Nicolai Sizov. Vakhtangov Theatre, Moscow. 1945.

FEDOROVSKI, Fedor. (U.S.S.R.)
Born : Chernigov. 27 Dec. 1883.
Educated: Stroganov School, Moscow. Disciple of Konstantin KOROVIN and Mikhail VRUBEL.
Stage Designs : About 70.
TIKHI DON (Quiet Flows the Don). Mu : Ivan Dzerzhinski. M : Nicolai Smolich. Bolshoi Theatre, Moscow. 1936. – BORIS GODUNOV, Mussorgsky. M : Leonid Baratov. Bolshoi Theatre, Moscow. 1948. – KHOVANSCHCHINA, Mussorgsky. M : Leonid Baratov. Bolshoi Theatre, Moscow. 1950.

**FERNANDEZ MARTINEZ,
Salvador.** (Cuba)
Born : Havana. 10 Nov. 1937.
Educated : University of Havana (architecture).
Stage Designs :
SAINT JOAN OF AMERICA, Lizarraga. Cuban National Theatre. 1959. – THE TWO GREAT TALKERS, Cervantes. Teatro Estudio, Sala Covarrubias, Havana. 1960. – THE FAMOUS 702, A. Mirodan. Sala Hubert de Blanck, Havana. 1962.

FINI, Léonor. (France)
Born : Buenos Aires (Argentina).
Stage Designs : About 40.
THE PLEASURE OF HONESTY, Pirandello. M : Jean Mercure. Saint-Georges Theatre, Paris. 1950. – THE TAMING OF THE SHREW, Shakespeare. M : Georges Vitaly. Athénée Theatre, Paris. 1957. – A HONEYMOON CALL, Dumas fils. M : Raymond Gérôme. Comédie Française, Paris. 1961.

FISHER, Randi. (Sweden)
Born : Melbourne (Australia). 1 Apr. 1920.
Educated : Konstfackskolan and Konstakademien, Stockholm.
Stege Design :

DROTTNINGENS JUVELSMYCKE (The Jewels of the Queen), Jonas Love Almqvist. M : Alf Sjöberg. Royal Dramatic Theatre, Stockholm. 1958.

FIUME, Salvatore. (Italy)
Born : Comiso (Sicily). 23 Oct. 1916.
Educated : Urbino.
Stage Designs : 10.
MEDEA, Cherubini. M : M. Wallmann. Scala, Milan. 1952. – NABUCCO, Verdi. M : Mario Frigerio. Scala, Milan. 1958. – AIDA, Verdi. M : M. Wallmann. Covent Garden, London. 1957.

FJELL, Kai. (Norway)
Born : Skoger. 2 March 1907.
Educated : Statens Haandverks-og Kunstindustriskole, Oslo, and Kunstakademiet, Oslo. Disciple of Axel REVOLD.
Stage Designs : 6.
FRU SYLVIA, Ernst Orvil. M : Olafr Havrevold. National Theatre, Oslo. 1950. – PEER GYNT, Henrik Ibsen. M : Alfred Maurstad. National Theatre, Oslo. 1955.

FRANÇOIS, André. (France)
Born : Timisoara (Rumania). 9 Nov. 1915.
Educated : École des Beaux-Arts, Paris. Disciple of A.M. CASSANDRE.
Stage Designs : 6.
LE VÉLO MAGIQUE (The Magic Bike), Raymond Queneau. M-Ch : Roland Petit. Théâtre de Paris. Paris. 1956. – PAS DE DIEUX, Gene Kelly. Mu : Gershwin. M-Ch : Gene Kelly. Paris Opera. 1960.

FRIGERIO, Ezio. (Italy)
Born : 1930.
Educated : Brera Academy.
Stage Designs : 20.
BECKET OR THE HONOUR OF GOD, Jean Anouilh. M : Mario Ferrero. Teatro Eliseo, Rome. 1961. – SAINT JOAN, Bernard Shaw. M : Mario Ferrero. Teatro Quirino, Rome. 1962.

FRITZSCHE, Max. (West Germany)
Born : Karlsruhe. 19 July 1906.
Educated: Kunstgewerbeschule, Hamburg, and Kunstakademie, Düsseldorf. Disciple of Professor Walter V. WECUS.
Stage Designs : About 650.
DER GÜNSTLING (The Favourite), Caspar Neher. Mu : Wagner - Régeny. M : Bruno Heyn. Hessisches Landestheater, Darmstadt. 1936. – DON CARLOS, Friedrich Schiller. M : Hans Schalla. Hessisches Landestheater, Darmstadt. 1937. – ANTONY AND CLEOPATRA, Shakespeare. M : Hans Schalla. Schauspielhaus, Bochum. 1955.

FÜLÖP, Zoltán. (Hungary)
Born : Péczel. 1907.
Educated : High School of Decorative Arts, Budapest.
Stage Designs : 600.
THE FLAMES OF PARIS, Boris Asafiev. Ch-M : Vasili Vainonen. Hungarian National Opera, Budapest. 1961. – PRINCE IGOR, Alexander Borodin. M : Pavel Zlatogorov. Ch : Gyula Harangozó. Hungarian National Opera, Budapest. 1961. – C'EST LA GUERRE, Emil Petrovics. Libretto : Miklós Hubay. M : Miklós Szinetár. Hungarian National Opera, Budapest. 1962.

G

GALUP, Mario. (Uruguay)
Born : Montevideo. 16 Dec. 1924.
Stage Designs : Over 50.
DOÑA ROSITA, Federico Garcia Lorca. M : Antonio Larreta. Club de Teatro, Montevideo. 1956. – THE GIANTS OF THE MOUNTAIN, Luigi Pirandello. M : Antonio Larreta. Comedia Nacional.

Teatro Solis, Montevideo. 1957. – THE WOULD-BE GENTLEMAN, Molière. M : Pedro Orthous. Teatro El Galpón, Montevideo. 1960.

GAMLIN, Yngve. (Sweden)
Born : Strömsund. 17 Mar. 1926.
Stage Designs : Over 150.
THE SLEEPING BEAUTY. Mu : Tchaikovsky. Ch : Mary Skeaping. Royal Opera, Stockholm. 1955. – TARTUFFE, Molière. M : Börje Mellvig. State Travelling Theatre (Sweden). 1956. – AMPHITRYON 38, Jean Giraudoux. M : Erling Schröder. Royal Dramatic Theatre, Copenhagen. 1959.

GAMREKELI, Irakli. (U.S.S.R.)
Born : Gori. 17 May 1894.
Educated : School of Design.
Stage Designs : Over 100.
ANZOR, Sandro Shanshiashvili (after " Armoured Train 14-69 " by Vsevolod Ivanov). M : Sandro Akhmeteli. Shota Rustaveli Theatre, Tbilisi. 1928. – THE ROBBERS, Schiller. M : Sandro Akhmeteli - Shalva Agsabadze. Shota Rustaveli Theatre, Tbilisi. 1933. – ABESSALOM AND ETERI. Mu : Zakharia Paliashvili. M : Shalva Agsabadze. Paliashvili Opera and Ballet Theatre, Tbilisi. 1937.

GANEAU, François. (France)
Born : Paris. 1 May 1912.
Educated : École Boulle.
Stage Designs :
THE DOUBLE INCONSTANCY, Marivaux. M : Jacques Charon. Comédie Française. Paris. 1947. – PELLEAS AND MELISANDE, Maurice Maeterlinck. Mu : Claude Debussy. M : Michel Crochot. Maggio Fiorentino, Florence. 1957. – THE DIARY OF ANNE FRANK, Goodrich - Hackett. M : Marguerite Jamois. Montparnasse Theatre, Paris. 1958.

GARBUGLIA, Mario. (Italy)
Born : Portocivitanova. 27 May 1927.
Stage Designs : 5.
LOOK HOMEWARD ANGEL, Ketty Frings. M : Luchino Visconti. Teatro Quirino, Rome. 1958. – FIGLI D'ARTE (Children of the Theatre), Diego Fabbri. M : Luchino Visconti. Teatro Eliseo, Rome. 1959.

GAUGUIN, Paul René. (Norway)
Born : Copenhagen (Denmark). 27 Jan. 1911.
Stage Designs :
CAESAR AND CLEOPATRA, Bernard Shaw. M : Agnes Mowinckel. National Theatre, Oslo. 1951. – CLOCHEMERLE, Marcel Aymé. M : Hans Jacob Nilsen. Nye Theatre, Oslo. 1960.

GEENENS, Robert. (Belgium)
Born : Ghent. 20 Aug. 1896.
Educated : Académie des Beaux-Arts, Ghent, and Fine Arts Academy, Rotterdam.
Stage Designs : 2.
SIRE HALEWIJN, Herman Closson. M : Lode Verstraeten. Nederlands Kamertoneel, Antwerp. 1956. – NU HET DORP NIET MEER BESTAAT (Now The Village Is No More), Tone Brulin. M : Maurits Balfoort. Koninklijke Nederlandse Schouwburg, Antwerp. 1956.

GILLETTE, Arnold S. (U.S.A.)
Born : Phœnixville. 4 June 1904.
Educated : Universities of Montana and Yale.
Stage Designs : Over 100.
THE BEGGAR'S OPERA, John Gay. M : Harold Crain. University Theatre, Iowa City. 1952. – WAITING FOR GODOT, Samuel Beckett. M : W.M. Reardon. University Theatre, Iowa City. 1957. – THE WHITE DEVIL, John Webster. M : Glynne Wickham. University Theatre, Iowa City. 1960.

GISCHIA, Léon. (France)
Born : Dax. 8 June 1903.
Stage Designs : About 30.
ŒDIPE, André Gide. M : Jean Vilar.
3rd. Avignon Festival. 1949. —
MURDER IN THE CATHEDRAL, T.S.
Eliot. M : Jean Vilar. People's National
Theatre, Paris. 1952. — LORENZACCIO,
Alfred de Musset. M : Gérard Philipe.
6th. Avignon Festival. 1952.

GONDOLF, Walter.
(West Germany)
Born : Düsseldorf. 19 June 1912.
Educated : Kunstakademie, Düssel-
dorf. Disciple of Walter von WELUS.
Stage Designs : 350.
THE SEAGULL, Chekhov. M : Gustav
Gründgens. Stadt. Bühnen, Düssel-
dorf. 1950. — DANTON'S DEATH,
Georg Büchner. M : Hans Scalla.
Schauspielhaus, Bochum. 1953. — IF
FIVE YEARS PASS, Federico Garcia
Lorca. M : Hans Bauer. Kammer-
spiele der Städt. Bühnen, Cologne.
1955.

GRETER, Johan. (Netherlands)
Born : Amsterdam. 23 Apr. 1927.
Stage Designs : 22.
CAT ON A HOT TIN ROOF, Tennessee
Williams. M : Richard Flink. City
Theatre, Arnhem. 1956. — THE DEAD
QUEEN, Henry de Montherlant. M :
Elise Hoomans. City Theatre, Arn-
hem. 1958. — VASCO, Georges Sché-
hadé. M : Elise Hoomans. City
Theatre, Arnhem. 1959.

GRÜBLER, Ekkehard.
(West Germany)
Born : Berlin. 29 Jan. 1928.
Educated : Berlin and Yale University.
Assistant and collaborator of Caspar
NEHER.
Stage Designs : 105.
IL MONDO DELLA LUNA, Joseph
Haydn. M : Bohumil Herlischka.
Bayerisches Staatstheater, Munich.
1959. — DIE FRAU OHNE SCHATTEN
(The Woman without a Shadow), H.
von Hofmannsthal. Mu : Richard
Strauss. M : Hans Neugebauer. Staats-
theater, Kassel. 1962. — KONIG HIRSCH
(King Stag), Heinz von Cramer. Mu :
Hans Werner Henze. M : Hans
Hartleb. Staatstheater, Kassel. 1963.

GUGEL, Fabius von.
(West Germany)
Born : Worms.
Is above all a painter.
Stage Designs :
THE AFFECTED LADIES, Molière. Mu :
Felice Lattuada. M : Felice Lattuada.
Ch : Attila Radice. Rome Opera.
1950. — THE PRINCE OF THE PAGODAS.
Mu : Benjamin Britten. M-Ch : Alan
Carter. Bavarian State Opera, Mu-
nich. 1958. — KÖNIG HIRSCH (King
Stag). Mu : Hans Werner Henze. M :
Harro Dicks. Landestheater, Darm-
stadt. 1959.

GUGLIELMINETTI, Eugenio.
(Italy)
Born : Asti. 17 July 1921.
Stage Designs : 30.
ANTIGONE, Alfieri. M : Gianfranco
De Bosio. National Alfieri Study
Centre, Asti. 1959. — MILES GLORIOSUS,
Plautus. M : Giovanni Poli. Teatro
Stabile, Turin. 1960.

GUNZINGER, Eduard.
(Switzerland)
Born : Basle. 18 Dec. 1897.
Educated : Akademische Hochschule
für die Bildenden Künste, and Verei-
nigte Stadtschulen für freie und
angewandte Kunst, Berlin. Disciple of
César KLEIN.
Stage Designs : Over 300.
MURDER IN THE CATHEDRAL, T.S.
Eliot. M : Wilfried Scheitlin. City

Theatre, Basle. 1939. — ROMULUS THE
GREAT, Friedrich Dürrenmatt. M :
Ernst Ginsberg. City Theatre, Basle.
1949. — AIDA, Verdi. M : Ulrich
Reinhard. City Theatre, Basle. 1957.

H

HALLEGGER, Kurt.
(West Germany)
Born : Mähr (Schönberg). 8 July 1901.
Educated : Academies of Decorative
Arts, Breslau. Vienna and Prague.
Disciple of Otto MÜLLER, Oskar
MOLL and F. THIELE.
Stage Designs : About 120 (theatre,
cinema, television).
THE DREAM PLAY, August Strinberg.
M : Paul Verhoeven. Staatsschauspiel,
Munich. 1947. — LIFE IS A DREAM,
Calderon de la Barca. M : Peter Lühr.
Staatsschauspiel, Munich. 1949. —
THE WALL, Millard Lampell. M : Kurt
Meisel. Staatstheater, Munich. 1962.

HANÁK, Ján. (Czechoslovakia)
Born : Bánovce nad Bebravou. 17
Feb. 1931.
Educated : Vysoká Skola Muzickych
Umeni Bratislava. Disciple of L.
VYCHODIL (architect).
Stage Designs : Over 80.
IT HAPPENED IN IRKUTSK, Alexei
Arbuzov. M : Josef Palka. City
Theatre, Kosice. 1960. — SVATOPLUK,
Eugen Suchon. M : Kornel Hájek.
City Theatre, Kosice. 1960. — BETRO-
THAL IN THE CONVENT. Mu : Serguei
Prokofiev. M : Branislav Kriska. City
Theatre, Kosice. 1961.

HAVEMANN, Franz.
(East Germany)
Born : Neukloster. 4 Aug. 1933.
Educated : Hochschule für Bildende
und Angewandte Kunst, Berlin -
Weissensee. Disciple of Heinrich
KILGER.
Stage Designs : About 30.
HAMLET, Shakespeare. M : Fritz Ben-
newitz. German National Theatre,
Weimar. 1960. — EGMONT, Gœthe -
Beethoven. M : Fritz Bennewitz. Ger-
man National Theatre, Weimar. 1961.
— THE MAN WITH THE GUN, Nikolai
Pogodin. M : Horst Schönemann.
Deutsches Theater, East Berlin. 1962.

HAYS, David. (U.S.A.)
Born : New York. 1930.
Educated : Universities of Harvard,
Yale and Boston. Worked in London
with Roger FURSE and Leslie HURRY.
Stage Designs : About 50.
LONG DAY'S JOURNEY INTO NIGHT,
Eugene O'Neill. M : Jose Quintero.
Helen Hayes Theatre, New York.
1956. — THE TENTH MAN, Paddy
Chayefsky. M : Tyrone Guthrie. Booth
Theatre, New York. 1959. — EPISODES
(Ballet). Mu : Anton Webern. Ch :
George Balanchine - Martha Graham.
New York City Ballet. City Centre.
New York. 1959.

HECKROTH, Hein.
(West Germany)
Born : Giessen. 24 Apr. 1901.
Educated : Germany, Paris and Spain.
Stage Designs : About 500.
THE GREEN TABLE, Jooss. Mu : F.A.
Cohen. M-Ch : Jooss. Champs Élysées
Theatre, Paris. 1932. — FALSTAFF,
Verdi. M : Carl Ebert. Cambridge
Theatre, London. 1947. — ORFEO,
Gluck. Scala, Milan. 1957.

HEDEBY-PAWLO, Kerstin.
(Sweden)
Born : Linköping. 12 Feb. 1926.
Educated : Konstakademien, Stock-
holm. Disciple of Sven ERIXON.
Stage Designs : 12.
LE MISANTHROPE, Molière. M : Ingmar
Bergman. City Theatre, Malmö.

1957. — ALCINA, Handel. M : Bengt
Peterson. Ch : Mary Skeaping. Royal
Opera, Stockholm. 1959. — THE
TALES OF HOFFMANN, Jacques Offen-
bach. M : Beqgt Peterson. Royal
Opera, Stockholm. 1960.

HEGLE, Kaare. (Norway)
Born : Steinkjaer. 15 March 1909.
Educated : Technical School and
Statens Haandverks-og Kunstindus-
triskole, Oslo. Disciple of Alf BJOERN.
Stage Designs : About 250.
GEHENNA, Jarl Hemmer. M : Ellen
Isefiaer. Trondelag Theatre, Trond-
heim. 1938. — HAMLET, Shakespeare.
M : Alfred Solaas. Nye Theatre,
Oslo. 1951. — KISS ME KATE, Sam and
Bella Spewack. Mu : Cole Porter. M :
Sven Aage Larsen. Ch : Ivo Cramer.
Nye Theatre, Oslo. 1952.

HEINRICH, Rudolf. (Germany)
Born : Halle. 10 Feb. 1926.
Educated : Kunstschule, Halle. Disci-
ple of P. PILOWSKI and M. ELTEN.
Stage Designs : About 80.
THE CUNNING LITTLE VIXEN. Mu :
Janacek. M : Walter Felsenstein.
Komische Oper, East Berlin. 1956. —
THE TALES OF HOFFMANN. Mu :
Offenbach. M : Walter Felsenstein.
Komische Oper, East Berlin. 1958. —
A MIDSUMMER NIGHT'S DREAM. Mu :
Benjamin Britten. M : Walter Felsen-
stein. Komische Oper, East Berlin.
1961.

HEISKANEN, Pekka. (Finland)
Born : Lappeenranta. 5 May 1929.
Educated : Arts and Crafts Institute
and Finnish National Theatre.
Disciple of Karl FAGER.
Stage Designes : About 50.
IPHIGENIA IN AULIS, Euripides. M :
Arvi Kivimaa. Finnish National
Theatre, Helsinki. 1957. — KARKURIT
(The Deserters), Aleksis Kivi. M :
Jack Witikka. Finnish National Thea-
tre, Helsinki. 1959. — A VIEW FROM
THE BRIDGE, Arthur Miller. M : Jack
Witikka. Finnish National Theatre.
Helsinki. 1960.

HELLER, Vladimir.
(Czechoslovakia)
Born : Bratislava. 2 June 1922.
Educated : Akademie Muzickych Ume-
ni, Prague.
Stage Designs : About 100.
FIDELIO, Beethoven. M : Bedrich
Kramosil. Ch : Jirí Nemecek. J.K.
Tyl Theatre, Pilsen. 1953. — THE
BATH HOUSE, Vladimir Mayakovski.
M : Václav Lohnicky. J.K. Tyl
Theatre, Pilsen. 1954. — INVASION,
Leonid Leonov. M : Václav Spidla.
J.K. Tyl Theatre, Pilsen. 1960.

HERBERT, Jocelyn.
(Great Britain)
Born : London. 22 Feb. 1917.
Educated : London Theatre Studio.
Disciple of Michel SAINT-DENIS.
Stage Designs : 20.
THE CHAIRS, Ionesco. M : Tony
Richardson. Royal Court, London.
1957. — LUTHER, John Osborne. M :
Tony Richardson. Royal Court, Lon-
don. 1961. — BAAL, Bertolt Brecht.
M : William Gaskill. Phœnix Theatre,
London. 1963.

HILL, Hainer. (Germany)
Born : Darmstadt-Eberstadt. 28 July
1913.
Educated : Staatsschule für Kunst und
Handwerk, Mainz, and Staedelsche
Kunstschule, Frankfurt.
Disciple of Caspar Neher.
Stage Designs :
THE RING OF THE NIBELUNG,
Richard Wagner. M : Frank De

Quell. Rome Opera. 1961. — WOZZECK.
Büchner. Mu : Alban Berg. M :
Werner Kelch. German State Opera,
East Berlin. — FIDELIO, Beethoven. M :
Otto Klemperer. Royal Opera House,
Covent Garden. London. 1961.

HLAWA, Stefan. (Austria)
Born : Vienna. 2 Feb. 1896.
Educated : Akademie der Bildenden
Künste, Vienna. Disciple of Professor
BACHER.
Stage Designs : About 250.
DON CARLOS, Schiller. M : Josef
Gielen. Burg Theatre, Vienna. 1955. —
INTERMEZZO, Jean Giraudoux. M :
Rudolf Steinböck, Akademie Theatre,
Vienna. 1957. — IDOMENEO, Mozart.
M : Paul Hager. Salzburg Festival.
1961.

HURRY, Leslie. (Great Britain)
Born : London. 10 Feb. 1909.
Educated : St. John's Wood Art
School and Royal Academy Schools.
Stage Designs : About 70.
THE RING OF THE NIBELUNG, Wagner.
Royal Opera House, Covent Garden,
London. 1956. — SWAN LAKE, Tchai-
kovsky. Royal Ballet, Covent Garden,
London. (Three revivals.)

I

ICHIJÔ, Tatsuo. (Japan)
Born : Tokyo. 25 Aug. 1924.
Educated : Industrial School, Yasuda.
Disciple of Juichi ITÔ.
Stage Designs : 40.
SANNEN NETARÔ (Taro the Sleeper),
Junji Kinoshita. M : Shirô Okakura.
Budô-no-Kai, Tokyo. 1952. — ICHI-
KAWA UMAGORÔ ICHIZA (Ichikawa
and His Troupe), Miho Mayama.
M : Miho Mayama. Shin-Seisakuza.
1953. — IT HAPPENED IN IRKUTSK,
Alexei Arbuzov. M : Jûkichi Uno.
Mingei, Tokyo. 1960.

ITÔ, Juichi. (Japan)
Born : Tokyo. 10 Jan. 1911.
Educated : University of Waseda.
Disciple of Kisaku ITÔ.
Stage Designs : 700.
THE POWERS OF DARKNESS, Tolstoi.
M : Yoshi Hijikata. Mingei, Tokyo.
1954. — AKAI CARDIGAN (The Red
Cardigan), Eijirô Hisaita. M : Koreya
Senda. Haiyûza, Tokyo. 1955. — TÔ
(The Tower), Tadasu Iizawa. M :
Tadasu IIzawa. Bungakuza, Tokyo.
1960.

ITÔ, Kisaku. (Japan)
Born : Tokyo. 1 Aug. 1899.
Educated : Arts School, Tokyo.
Stage Designs : Over 2,500.
YOAKEMAE (Before Dawn), Tôson
Shimasaki - Tomoyoshi Murayama.
M : Sakae Kubo. Shinkyô Gekidan, To-
kyo. 1935. — YUHZURU (The Twilight
Crane), Junji Kinoshita. M : Shirô
Okakura. Budô-no-Kai, Tokyo. 1950.
— YUME NO ONNA (The Dream
Woman), Kafû Nagai - Mantarô
Kubota. M : Mantarô Kubota. Shim-
pa, Tokyo. 1959.

IVO, Lode. (Belgium)
Born : Berchem-Antwerp. 26 Aug.
1899.
Educated : Antwerp Academy and
Malines Academy.
Stage Designs : Over 1,000.
MATHIS DER MALER (Mathis, the
Painter), Hindemith. M : K. Schmidtz.
Royal Flemish Opera, Antwerp. —
DIE ANTIKWAAR (The Second-hand
Dealer). Mu : Jef Maes. M : Marc
Liebrecht. Ch : J. Brabants. Royal
Flemish Opera, Antwerp. 1963. — THE
MAGIC FLUTE, IL SERAGLIO, etc. Royal
Opera, Antwerp.

J

JANKUS, Jozsas. (U.S.S.R.)
Born : Sereikonis (Lithuania). 4 Apr. 1912.
Educated : High School of Fine Arts, Kaunas.
Stage Designs : Over 20.
AUDRONE, ballet by Jozs Indra. Libretto by V. Grivicks. Ch : V., Grivicks. Lithuanian Republic Opera and Ballet Theatre, Vilnius. 1957. – PILENAI. Mu : Vitauts Klov. M : Jozs Gustaits. Lithuanian Republic Opera and Ballet Theatre, Vilnius. 1957.

JANOIR, Jean. (France)
Born : Mâcon. 26 Oct. 1929.
Stage Designs : 2.
PELLEAS AND MELISANDE, Maurice Maeterlinck. Mu : Claude Debussy. M : Louis Erlo. Lyons Opera. 1962. – SAMSON AND DELILAH, Saint-Saëns. M : Louis Erlo, Teatro Colon, Buenos Aires. 1963.

JEDRINSKY, Wladimir. (France)
Born : Moscow (Russia). 30 Mai 1899.
Educated : Fine Arts Academy, Kiev. Disciple of Leonid BRAILOWSKY.
Stage Designs : Over 400.
CARMEN, Bizet. M : Branko Gavella. Brno National Opera. 1936. – THE QUEEN OF SPADES, Tchaikovsky. M : W. Jedrinsky. Zagreb National Opera. 1946. – RESURRECTION, after Tolstoi. Mu : Alexandre Tansmann. M-Ch : Françoise Adret. Nice Opera. 1962.

JONES, Arne. (Sweden)
Born : Borgsjö. 20 Oct. 1914.
Educated : Kungliga Konsthögskolan, Stockholm. Disciple of Eric GRATE.
Stage Designs : 4.
NARREN (The Fool), Lars Forsell. M : Hans Dahlin. City Theatre, Uppsala. 1953. – KRÖNINGEN (The Coronation), Lars Forsell. Mu : G. Bucht. M : Bengt Ekerot. Ch : Birgit Cullberg. Royal Dramatic Theatre, Stockholm. 1958.

JUDTMANN, Fritz. (Austria)
Born : Vienna. 15 June 1899.
Educated : Architecture at the Technische Hochschule, Vienna.
Stage Designs : 120.
DER HAUPTMANN VON KÖPENICK (The Captain from Köpenick), Carl Zuckmayer. M : Adolf Rott. Burg Theatre, Vienna. 1950. – CYRANO DE BERGERAC, Edmond Rostand. M : Adolf Rott. Burg Theatre, Vienna. 1951. – KÖNIG OTTOKARS GLÜCK UND ENDE (The Fate and Fall of King Ottokar), Franz Grillparzer. M : Adolf Rott. Burg Theatre, Vienna. 1955.

JÜRGENS, Helmut. (West Deutschland)
Born : Höxter. 19 June 1902.
Educated : Kunstakademie, Düsseldorf. Disciple of Prof. VON WECHS.
Stage Designs : About 500.
JULIUS CAESAR, Handel. M : Rudolf Hartmann. State Opera, Munich. 1955. – CARMINA BURANA, Carl Orff. M : Heinz Rosen. State Opera, Munich. 1959. – MATHIS, THE PAINTER, Paul Hindemith. M : Hans Hartleb. State Opera, Munich. 1960.

K

KARAKACHEV, Georgi. (Bulgaria)
Born : Russé. 23 Apr. 1899.
Educated : Institute of Fine Arts, Sofia. Disciple of Tseno TODOROV.
Stage Designs : Over 200.
SNAHA (The Beauty), G. Karaslavov - A. Hadjihristov. M : Krastu Mirski. " Ivan Vazov " National Theatre, Sofia. 1950. – LEIPZIG 33, Kompane-

hets Kronfeld. M : B.A. Babochkin. " Ivan Vazov " National Theatre, Sofia. 1952. – IVANKO, Vasil Drumev. M : Boris Spirov. National Theatre. Kolarovgrad. 1958.

KARAVAN, Dani. (Israel)
Born : Tel Aviv. 7 Dec. 1930.
Educated : Israeli artists, ARDON, STREICHMAN, AVNI, and Fine Arts Academy, Florence. Disciple of E. LUFTGLASS and Paul LEVY.
Stage Designs : About 10.
THE STORY OF RUTH. Ch : Sara Levy - Tanai. Inbal Dance Troupe, Tel Aviv. 1961. – KINNERET (Galilee), Natan Alterman. M : Gershon Plotkin. Cameri Theatre, Tel Aviv. 1961. – THE LEGEND OF JUDITH. Ch : Martha Graham. Martha Graham Dance Troupe. 1962.

KAUTSKY, Robert. (Austria)
Born : Vienna. 26 Oct. 1895.
Educated : Kunstakademie, Berlin. Disciple of Alfred ROLLER and Oskar STRNAD.
Stage Designs : 160.
THE BARTERED BRIDE, Smetana. M : Hans Duhan. Vienna State Opera. 1935. – DER ROSENKAVALIER, Richard Strauss. M : Herbert von Karajan. Scala, Milan. 1948. – CHRISTOPHER COLUMBUS, Paul Claudel. M : Adolf Rott. Burg Theatre, Vienna. 1957.

KENNY, Sean. (Great Britain)
Born : Tipperary (Ireland). 23 Dec. 1932.
Educated : Dublin School of Architecture and in the U.S.A. Disciple of Frank LLOYD-WRIGHT.
Stage Designs : 40.
THE HOSTAGE, Brendan Behan. M : Joan Littlewood. Theatre Workshop, London. 1958. – OLIVER, Bart. M : Coe. New Theatre, London. 1959. – BLITZ, Bart. M : Fazan. Adelphi Theatre, London. 1962.

KILGER, Heinrich. (East Germany)
Born : Heidelberg. 8 Mar. 1907.
Stage Designs : About 70.
THE FLIES, Jean-Paul Sartre. M : Jürgen Fehling. Hebbel Theatre, West Berlin. 1948. – MOTHER COURAGE AND HER CHILDREN, Bertolt Brecht. M : Bertolt Brecht - Erich Engel. Deutsches Theater, East Berlin. 1951. – FAUST 1, Gœthe. M : Wolfgang Langhoff. Deutsches Theater, East Berlin. 1958.

KNOBLOCK, Boris. (U.S.S.R.)
Born : Moscow. 19 Apr. 1903.
Educated : Art Studios (Vkhutemas) and the Studio of Vasili YAKOVLEV and Pavel SHUKHMIN.
Stage Designs : Over 100.
THE ARISTOCRATS, Nicolai Pogodin. M : Nicolai Okhlopkov. Realistic Theatre, Moscow. 1935. – THE BARBARIANS, Gorki. M : Konstantin Zubov - Ilia Sudakov. Maly Theatre, Moscow. 1941. – DRUG MOI, KOLKA (My friend, Kolka), Arkadi Khmelik. M : Anatoli Efros. Central Childrens' Theatre, Moscow. 1959.

KOKOSCHKA, Oskar. (Austria)
Born : Pöchlarn - on - the - Danube. 1 March 1886.
Educated : Kunstgewerbeschule, Vienna. Disciple of W. LÖFFLER.
Stage Designs : 4.
THE MAGIC FLUTE, Mozart. M : Herbert Graf. Salzburg Festival. 1955. – MOISASURS ZAUBERFLUCH (The Magic Circle), Ferdinand Raimund. M : Rudolf Steinböck. Burg Theatre, Vienna. 1960. – DIE UNHEILBRINGENDE KRONE (The Cursed Crown), Ferdinand Raimund. M : Rudolf Steinböck. Burg Theatre,

Vienna. 1961. – DIE GEFESSELTE PHANTASIE (Fancy in Chains), Ferdinand Raimund. M : Hans Thimig. Burg Theatre, Vienna. 1962.

KOLÁŘ, Zbyněk. (Czechoslovakia)
Born : Katerinky u Opavy, 10 July 1925.
Educated : Vysoka Skola Umelecko-Prumyslová, Prague. Disciple of J. FISÁREK.
Stage Designs : Over 150.
PELLEAS AND MELISANDE, Maurice Maeterlinck. Mu : Claude Debussy. M : Miroslav Fiser. Slovakian National Theatre, Bratislava. 1958. – THE FOX AND THE GRAPES, Guilherme Figueiredo. M : Ota Ornest. Comedy Theatre, Prague. 1959. – FIDELIO, Beethoven. M : Miroslav Fiser. Slovakian National Theatre, Bratislava. 1960.

KONIARSKY, Helmut. (West Germany)
Born : Berlin. 14 Oct. 1913.
Educated : Höhere Grafische Fachschule, Berlin. Disciple of Professor FREESE and Traugott MÜLLER.
Stage Designs : About 250.
SIMONE BOCCANEGRA, Verdi. M : Alfred Noller. State Opera, Hamburg. 1941. – THE GREAT GOD BROWN, O'Neill. M : Paul Stoffmann, Staatstheater, Stuttgart. 1952. – THE PHYSICISTS, Friedrich Dürrenmatt. M : Hans Lietzau. Schlosspark Theatre, West Berlin. 1962.

KÔNO, Kunio. (Japan)
Born : Los Angeles (U S A). 22 Feb. 1914.
Educated : Technical High School, Tokyo.
Disciple of Kisaku ITô.
Stage Designs : 200.
CRIME AND PUNISHMENT, Dostoievsky-Baty. M : Yukiyo Yamakawa. Tokyo Seinen Gekijô, Tokyo. 1947. – HAMLET, Shakespeare. M : Tsuneari Fukuda. Bungakuza, Tokyo. 1955. – TOOI GAIKA (Triumphal Songs from Afar), Naoya Uchimura. M : Shirô Okakura. Mingei, Tokyo. 1956.

KÖPECZI-BÓCZ, István. (Hungary)
Born : Budapest. 1919.
Educated : High School of Decorative Arts and Fine Arts, Budapest. Disciple of Vilmos ABA NOVAK and Aurel BERNATH.
Stage Designs : 360.
THE TRICKS OF SCAPIN, Molière. M : László Vámos. Madách Chamber Theatre, Budapest. 1959. – A KÉT BÓLYAI (The Two Bolyais), László Németh. M: Zoltán Várkonyi. Katona József Theatre, Budapest. 1961. – A ELVESZETT PARADICSOM (Paradise Lost), Imre Sarkadi. M : Géza Pártos. Madách Chamber Theatre, Budapest. 1961.

KOURILKO, Mikhaïl. (U.S.S.R.)
See KURILKO, Mikhaïl.

KOVALENKO, Evgheni. (U.S.S.R.)
Born : Kharkov. 11 Nov. 1910.
Educated : Institue of Fine Arts, Kharkov. Disciple of Professor Alexander KHVOSTOV.
Stage Designs : About 140.
THE SEAGULL, Chekhov. M: Alexander Taïrov - Leonid Lukianov. Kamerny Theatre, Moscow. 1944. – THE TRAVELLERS, Ewan MacColl. M : Josif Tumanov. Mu : Vano Muradeli. Pushkin Dramatic Theatre, Moscow. 1954. – THE LITTLE CLAY CART, Shudraka. M : Josif Tumanov. Mu : Vano Muradeli. Pushkin Dramatic Theatre, Moscow. 1956.

KRAVJANSKÝ, Mikulás. (Czechoslovakia)
Born : Rudnany. 3 May 1928.
Educated : Vysoka Skola Muzickych Umeni, Bratislava. Disciple of Ladislav VYCHODIL (architect).
Stage Designs :
ALZBETA BÁTHORICKA, Jonás Záborsky - Julo Zborovjan. M : Mikulás Stefan Godja. Jonás Záborsky Theatre, Presov. 1958. – MANON LESCAUT, Vitezslav Nezval. M : Vladimir Petruska. Jonás Záborsky Theatre, Presov. 1958. – THE BLACK PIT, Albert Maltz. M : Pavol Haspra. Slovakian National Theatre. Bratislava. 1960.

KRIVOSHEÏNA, Valentina. (U.S.S.R.)
Born : Kharkov. 17 Nov. 1909.
Educated : Institute of Fine Arts, Kharkov. Disciple of Professor Alexander KHVOSTOV.
Stage Designs : About 140.
THE FAIRY LADY, Pedro Calderon. M : Victor Ganshin. Mu : Alexander Medtner. Kamerny Theatre, Moscow. 1945. – THE IMPORTANCE OF BEING EARNEST, Oscar Wilde. M : Nicolai Petrov. Pushkin Theatre, Moscow. 1957. – VESENNYE SKRIPKI (Spring Violins), Alexander Shtein. M : Yelena Zotova. Mu : Vasili Soloviev - Sedoi. Mayakovski Theatre, Moscow. 1960.

KROHG, Guy. (Norway)
Born : Oslo. 27 July 1917.
Educated : Oslo and Paris. Disciple of GROMAIRE.
Stage Designs : 25.
THE MAD WOMAN OF CHAILLOT, Jean Giraudoux. M : Hans Jacob Nilsen. Norwegian Theatre, Oslo. 1951. – THE MAID WOMAN OF CHAILLOT, Jean Giraudoux. M : Holger Gabrielsen. Royal Theatre, Copenhagen. 1951. – CARMINA BURANA, Carl Orff. M : Ivo Cramer. Norwegian Opera, Oslo. 1960.

KURILKO, Mikhaïl. (U.S.S.R.)
Born : Kamenets - Podolskiy. 11 June 1880.
Educated : Fine Arts Academy, St. Petersburg and Institute of Architecture.
Stage Designs : About 30.
A NIGHT IN MAY, Rimsky-Korsakov. M : Konstantin Stanislavski - Vladimir Alexeyev. Stanislavski Opera Theatre, Moscow. 1928. – THE RED POPPY, ballet by Reinhold Glière. Libretto by Mikhail Kurilko. M : Vasili Tikhomirov - Alexander Lashchilin. Bolshoi Theatre, Moscow. 1927. Revived in 1949. Bolshoi Theatre, Moscow.

L

LABISSE, Félix. (France)
Born : Douai. 9 Mar. 1905.
Stage Designs : About 50.
THE TRIAL, Kafka - Gide. M : Jean-Louis Barrault. Marigny Theatre, Paris. 1947. – LUCIFER AND THE LORD, Jean-Paul Sartre. M : Louis Jouvet. Antoine Theatre. Paris. 1951. – THE MARTYRDOM OF SAINT SEBASTIAN, Gabriele d'Annunzio. Mu : Claude Debussy. M : Maurice Jacquemont. Ch : Serge Lifar. Paris Opera. 1957.

LAGRANGE, Jacques. (France)
Born : Paris. 28 July 1917.
Educated : École des Arts Décoratifs.
Stage Designs :
UBU, Alfred Jarry. M : Jean Vilar. People's National Theatre, Paris. 1958. – THE SHOEMAKER'S HOLIDAY, Thomas Dekker. M : Georges Wilson. People's National Theatre, Paris. 1959. – JOUR DE FÊTE Á L'OLYMPIA (Holiday in the Olympia). M : Jacques Tati. Ch : Georges Reich. Olympia Theatre, Paris. 1961.

LAMBERT, Isabel. (Great Britain)
Born : London. 10 July 1912.
Educated : Royal Academy Schools.
Stage Designs : 7.
ELEKTRA, Richard Strauss. M : Hartmann. Royal Opera House, London. 1954. – MADAME CHRYSANTHÈME, Rawsthorne. M : Ashton. Royal Opera House, London. 1956.

LANC, Émile. (Belgium)
Born : Uccle. 27 May 1922.
Educated : Académie Royale des Beaux-Arts, Brussels, Pupil of Jean CANNEEL and disciple of Jean-Denis MALCLÈS.
Stage Designs : Over 200.
THE ASTRONOMER'S DREAM. Mu : René Defossez. Ch : André Leclerc. Tnéâtre Royal de la Monnaie, Brussels. 1950. – THE COMPASS-CARD, Claude Spaak. M : Raymond Gérôme. National Theatre, Brussels. 1953. – THE MIDDAY BREAK, Paul Claudel. M : André Berger. Rideau de Bruxelles. 1957.

LANCASTER, Osbert.
(Great Britain)
Born : London. 4 Aug. 1908.
Educated : Slade School, London. Disciple of Vladimir POLUNIN.
Stage Designs : 19.
BONNE BOUCHE, Arthur Oldham. Ch : John Cranko. Royal Opera House, Covent Garden, London. 1952. – THE RAKE'S PROGRESS, Igor Stravinsky. M : Carl Ebert. Glyndebourne Opera Company, Edinburgh. 1953. – HOTEL PARADISO, Georges Feydeau. M : Peter Glenville. Winter Garden. London. 1956.

LANSERE, Evgheni. (U.S.S.R.)
Born : Pavlovsk. 23 Aug. 1875.
Educated : Society for the Encouragement of Fine Arts and Académie Julien, Paris. Pupil of I. TSYONGLINSKI, E. LIPHARDT, Jean-Paul LAURANCE and Benjamin CONSTANT. Disciple of Alexandre BENOIS.
Stage Designs :
JULIUS CAESAR, Shakespeare. M : Ivan Platon. Maly Theatre, Moscow. 1923. – WOE FROM WIT, Griboyedov. M : Prov Sadovski. Maly Theatre, Moscow. 1938. – BARYSHNYA-KRESTYANKA (The Young Peasant Lady). Ballet by Boris Asafiev. Libretto by Nicolai Volkov. M : Rostislav Zakharov. Bolshoi Theatre, Moscow. 1946.

LARKIN, Peter S. (U.S.A.)
Born : Boston. 1925.
Educated : Deerfield School and Yale University.
Stage Designs : 25.
INHERIT THE WIND, Jerome Lawrence - Robert E. Lee. M : Herman Shumlin. National Theatre, New York. 1955. – COMPULSION, Meyer Levin. M : Alex Segal. Ambassador Theatre, New York. 1957.

LARRAIN, Raymundo de. (France)
Born : Santiago (Chile). 9 June 1931.
Stage Designs : About 30.
SNOW BIRD. Mu: Tchaikovsky. M-Ch: Larrain. Waldorf Astoria, New York. 1959. – THE SLEEPING BEAUTY. Mu : Tchaikovsky. M-Ch : Helpmann - Larrain. Champs-Élysées Theatre, Paris. 1960.

LARSON, Yngve. (Sweden)
Born : Gothenburg. 11 Feb. 1913.
Stage Designs : About 120.
ANTIGONE, Sophocles. M : Olof Molander. Royal Dramatic Theatre, Stockholm. 1948. – MISS JULE, August Strindberg. M : Alf Sjöberg. Royal Dramatic Theatre, Stockholm. 1949.

LAURENTI, Franco. (Italy)
Born : Sestino (Arezzo). 27 March 1928.

Educated : Fine Arts Academy, Rome. Disciple of Enrico PRAMPOLINI.
Stage Designs : 30.
ELECTRA, Sophocles. M : Giulio Pacuvio. Greek Theatre, Syracuse. 1956. – THE CREATURES OF PROMETHEUS. Mu : Beethoven. Ch : Aurel M. Millos. Maggio Musicale Fiorentino, Florence. 1957.

LEHTO, Leo. (Finland)
Born : Jämsänkoski. 26 June 1912.
Disciple of Jussi KARL.
Stage Designs : About 300.
THE TEMPEST, Shakespeare. Mu : Sibelius. M : Jorma Nortimo. Ch : Thelma Tuulos. Turku City Theatre, 1947. – THE SEAGULL, Chekhov. M : Eino Kalima. Finnish National Theatre, Helsinki. 1959. – THE SEVEN BROTHERS, Aleksis Kivi. M : Wilho Ilmari. Finnish National Theatre, Helsinki. 1960.

LENNEWEIT, Hans-Walter.
(West Germany)
Born : Elbing (West Prussia).
Educated : Königsberg, Weimar and Berlin. Disciple of Professor KLEIN.
Stage Designs : About 300.
AMPHITRYON, Kleist. M : Walter Henn. Schiller Theatre, Berlin. 1961. – A STROLL IN THE AIR, Eugène Ionesco. M : Walter Henn. Schiller Theatre, Berlin. 1963.

LUCKE, Christiane. (France)
Born : Berlin (Germany). 17 Nov. 1935.
Educated : Fine Arts Academy, Berlin.
Stage Designs : About 15.
THIS MEANS WAR, HARLEQUIN, Goldoni - Arnaud. M : Gabriel Monnet. Bourges. 1962. – THE BARBER OF SEVILLE, Beaumarchais. M : Edmond Tamiz. Carcassonne Theatre. Sarah Bernhardt Theatre, Paris.

LUZZATI, Emanuele. (Italy)
Born : Genoa. 3 June 1921.
Stage Designs : 80.
LEA LEBOVITZ, Alessandro Fersen. M : Alessandro Fersen. Teatro Nuovo, Milan. 1946. – THE MAGIC FLUTE, Mozart. M: Franco Enriquez. Glyndebourne Festival. 1963.

M

MÄKINEN, Veikko. (Finland)
Born : Helsinki. 11 July 1928.
Educated : Free School of Fine Arts, Helsinki. Disciple of Erkki KOPONEN, Sven GRÖNVALL, Tomas VON BOEHM and Tauno MANNINEN.
Stage Designs : About 100.
ARVOTTOMAT (The Worthless), Reino Lahtinen. M : Kalervo Nissilä. Tampere Theatre. 1959. – A MIDSUMMER NIGHT'S DREAM, Shakespeare. M : Kalervo Nissilä. Tampere Theatre. 1960. – ORPHEUS IN THE UNDERWORLD, Jacques Offenbach. M: Kalervo Nissilä. Tampere Theatre. 1961.

MALCLÈS, Jean-Denis. (France)
Born : Paris. 15 May 1912.
Educated : École Boulle.
Stage Designs : 100 to 150.
LA PARADE – LILIOM. M : Jean-Pierre Grenier. Compagnie Grenier - Hussenot. 1948. – LES CAVES DU VATICAN (The Vatican Cellars), André Gide. M: Jean Meyer. Comédie Française, Paris. 1951. – THE LARK, Jean Anouilh. M : Roland Piétri. Montparnasse Theatre, Paris. 1953.

MARENIĆ, Vladimir. (Yugoslavia)
Born : Caglin. 15 Sept. 1921.
Educated : Academy of Applied Arts, Belgrade. Student of Ivan TABAKOVIC and disciple of Milenko SERBAN.
Stage Designs : Over 80.
THE ROSE TATTOO, Tennessee Williams. M : Braslav Borozan. Narodno Pozorište, Belgrade. 1959. – KRISTOFOR

KOLUMBO (Christopher Columbus), Miroslav Krleza. M : Ivan Lešic. Serbian National Theatre, Novi Sad. 1961.

MARILLIER, Jacques. (France)
Born : Marseilles. 2 July 1924.
Educated : École Nationale Supérieure des Arts Décoratifs, Paris. Disciple of Maurice BRIANCHON and Roland OUDOT.
Stage Designes : 80 to 90.
DON GIOVANNI, Mozart. M : José Beckmans. Paris Opera. 1956. – THE CARMELITES, Georges Bernanos. M : Marcelle Tassencourt. Comédie Française, Paris. 1961. – ARMS AND THE MAN, Bernard Shaw. M : René Dupuy. Gramont Theatre, Paris.

MARONEK, James E. (U.S.A.)
Born : Milwaukee. 4 Dec. 1931.
Educated : Chicago Art Institute.
Stage Designs : More than 130.
CAMINO REAL, Tennessee Williams. M : Charles MacGaw. Ch : Frances Allis. Goodman Theatre, Chicago. 1958. – THE TAMING OF THE SHREW, Shakespeare. M : Charles MacGaw. Ch : Frances Allis. Goodman Theatre, Chicago. 1960. – THE GOOD WOMAN OF SETZUAN, Bertolt Brecht. Mu : Stefan Wolpe. M : Charles MacGaw. Goodman Theatre, Chicago. 1960.

MAROSIN, Mircea. (Rumania)
Born : Bucharest. 16 March 1921.
Educated : Faculty of Arts, University of Bucharest.
Stage Designs :
TWELFTH NIGHT, Shakespeare. M : Ion Sahighian. City Theatre, Bucharest 1956. – UNCLE VANYA, Chekhov. M : Ion Olteanu. National Theatre of Iassy. 1960. – RICHARD III, Shakespeare. M : Ion Sahighian. National Theatre of Iassy. 1963.

MARTIN, Denis. (Belgium)
Born : Uccle. 13 Dec. 1909.
Educated : Académie des Beaux-Arts and Institut Supérieur des Arts Décoratifs, Brussels. Disciple of Herman TEIRLINCK.
Stage Designs : Over 300.
THE DUCHESS OF MALFI, John Webster. M : Louis Ducreux. Rideau Gris, Marseilles. 1935. – BOBOSSE, André Roussin. M : François Périer. Michodière Theatre, Paris. 1950. – THE GAMBLER, Ugo Betti. M : Jacques Huisman. Théâtre National de Belgique, Brussels. 1955.

MARTIN, Harald. (Norway)
Born : Fana (Bergen). 16 Oct. 1918.
Educated : Statens Haandverks-og Kunstindustriskole, Oslo.
Stage Designs : 102.
GHOSTS, Henrik Ibsen. M : Ellen Isefiaer. Nye Theatre, Oslo. 1954. – MOURNING BECOMES ELECTRA, Eugene O'Neill. M : Claes Gill. Nye Theatre, Oslo. 1960.

MARTIN, Tyr. (Sweden)
Born : Stockholm. 16 Mar. 1915.
Educated : Konstakademien, Stockholm. Disciple of Otte SKÖLD and Emil JOHANNES-THOR.
Stage Designs : Over 100.
THE DANCE OF DEATH, August Strindberg. M : John Zacharias. City Theatre, Norrköping-Linköping. 1954. THE CHERRY ORCHARD, Chekhov. M : John Zacharias. City Theatre, Norrköping-Linköping. 1955.

MASSON, André. (France)
Born : Balagny. 4 Jan. 1896.
Educated : Académie Royale, Brussels (Teacher, MONTALD) and École des Beaux-Arts, Paris (Teachers, Raphael COLIN and Paul BAUDOIN).
Stage Designs : 14.

LES PRÉSAGES, Ballet by Léonide Massine. Monte Carlo Opera. 1932. – NUMANCIA, Cervantes. M : Jean-Louis Barrault. Antoine Theatre, Paris. 1937. – GOLDEN HEAD, Paul Claudel. M : Jean-Louis Barrault. Théâtre de France, Paris. 1959.

MATCABOJI, Mircea. (Rumania)
Born : Andriseni (Iassy). 30 Sept. 1921.
Educated : Fine Arts Academy, Iassy. Disciple of the painters Corneliu BABA and Ion IRIMESCU.
Stage Designs : Over 90.
HECUBA, Euripides. M : Stefan Braborescu. National Theatre, Cluj. 1957. – HAMLET, Shakespeare. M : Miron Nicolescu. National Theatre, Cluj. 1960. – FEBRE (Fever), Horia Lovinescu. M : Constantin Anatol. National Theatre, Cluj. 1962.

MAXIMOWNA, Ita.
(West Germany)
Educated : Paris and Berlin.
Stage Designs : About 150.
CARMEN, Bizet. M : Herbert von Karajan. Ch : Massine. Scala, Milan. 1955. – LA CENERENTOLA, Rossini. M : Günther Rennert. State Opera, Vienna. 1959. – DER PRINZ VON HOMBURG. M : Hans Werner Henze. M : Hans Hartleb. City Theatres, Frankfurt. 1960.

MÉLAT, Maurice. (France)
Born : Epernay. 24 May 1910.
Educated : École Nationale Supérieure des Arts Décoratifs, Paris. Disciple of Gustave CORLIN and Raymond LEGUEULT.
Stage Designs : About 40.
LES AMANTS DE VÉRONE (The Lovers of Verona). Mu : Edmond Gaujac. M : Serval. Capitole Theatre, Toulouse. 1956. – KING DAVID, René Morax. Mu : Arthur Honegger. M : Maurice Sarrazin. Capitole Theatre, Toulouse. 1958. – HOP! SIGNOR, after Michel de Ghelderode. Mu : Manuel Rosenthal. M : Jan Doat. Capitole Theatre, Toulouse. 1962.

MEYER, Hannes. (Switzerland)
Born : Arbon. 16 Nov. 1923.
Disciple of Teo OTTO.
Stage Designs : Over 100.
WAITING FOR GODOT, Samuel Beckett. M : Roger Blin. Playhouse, Zurich. 1954. – MOURNING BECOMES ELECTRA, Eugene O'Neill. M : Walter Oberer. City Theatre, Lucerne. 1958. – BORIS GODUNOV, Mussorgsky. M : Christof Groszer. City Theatre, Berne. 1961.

MIELZINER, Jo. (U.S.A.)
Born : Paris (France). 19 Mar. 1901.
Educated : National Academy of Design, New York City, Pennsylvania Academy of Fine Arts, Philadelphia, in Paris and in Vienna.
Stage Designs : About 250.
WINTERSET, Maxwell Anderson. M : Guthrie McClintic. Martin Beck Theatre, New York. 1935. – DEATH OF A SALESMAN, Arthur Miller. M : Elia Kazan. Morosco Theatre, New York. 1949. – THE LARK, Jean Anouilh - Lillian Hellman. Mu : Leonard Bernstein. M : Joseph Anthony. Plymouth Theatre, New York. 1955.

MINKS, Wilfried.
(West Germany)
Born : Binai (Czechoslovakia). 21 Feb. 1930.
Educated : Hochschule für Bildende Künste, Berlin. Disciple of Willi SCHMIDT.
Stage Designs : 12.
DON CARLOS, Friedrich Schiller. M : Kurt Hübner. – CAPTAIN BADA, Jean Vauthier. M : Peter Zadek.

MOISEIWITSCH, Tanya.
(Great Britain)
Born : London. 3 Dec. 1914.
Educated : Central School of Arts and Crafts. Disciple of Jeanetta COCHRANE.
Stage Designs : 190.
PETER GRIMES, Benjamin Britten. M : Tyrone Guthrie. Royal Opera House, Covent Garden, London. 1947. – HISTORIES CYCLE, Shakespeare. M : Anthony Quayle. Royal Shakespeare Theatre, Stratford-upon-Avon. 1951. – ŒDIPUS REX, Sophocles. M : Tyrone Guthrie. Festival Theatre, Stratford, Canada. 1954.

MOLINET de la PENA, Maria Elena.
(Cuba)
Born : Oriente. 30 Sep. 1919.
Educated : Academia San Alejandro and Academia Interamericana, Dibujo.
Stage Designs :
THE KNIGHT OF OLMEDO (costumes), Lope de Vega. M : Andres Castro. Grupo La Mascaras. Sala Teatro Farsero, Havana. 1957. – CANTATA A CHIRINOS (costumes), Román Chalbaud. M : Alberto de Paz y Mateos. Popular National Theatre, Caracas. 1960.

MOORE, John.
(Italy)
Born : Tryon (North Carolina, U.S.A.). 22 Jan. 1924.
Educated : Oxford and Rome.
Stage Designs : 10 to 15.
SCHOOL FOR WIVES, Molière. Mu : Virgilio Mortali. M : Margherita Wallmann. Piccola Scala, Milan. 1958. – LA TRAVIATA, Verdi. M : Bruno Nofri. Tokyo. 1959. – OTELLO, Verdi. M : Herbert Graf. Teatro Massimo, Palermo. 1962.

MORALIS, Yannis.
(Greece)
Born : Arta. 23 Apr. 1916.
Educated : School of Fine Arts, Athens, and École des Arts et Métiers, Paris. Pupil of Jean CEPHALLINOS and disciple of DERAIN.
Stage Designs : 16.
SIX POPULAR IMAGES, Manos Hadzidakis. M : Rallou Manou – Manos Hadzidakis. Cotopouli Rex Theatre, Athens. 1951. – PLUTUS, Aristophanes. Mu : Manos Hadzidakis. M : Karolos Koun. Art Theatre, Athens. 1957. – THE SHOEMAKER'S WIFE, Federico Garcia Lorca. M : Alexis Solomos. National Theatre, Athens. 1958.

MÖRK, Lennart.
(Sweden)
Born : Falköping. 1 Aug. 1932.
Educated : Konstfackskolan and Konsthögskolan, Stockholm. Disciple of Olle NYMAN.
Stage Designs : 6.
HAMLET, Shakespeare. M : Alf Sjöberg. Royal Dramatic Theatre, Stockholm. 1960. – THE LIFE AND DEATH OF KING JOHN, Shakespeare. M : Alf Sjöberg. Ch : Birgit Akesson. Royal Dramatic Theatre, Stockholm. 1961.

MÖRNER, Stellan.
(Sweden)
Born : Örebro. 3 Feb. 1896.
Educated : Kungl. Konstakademien, Stockholm.
Stage Designs : About 20.
TWELFTH NIGHT, Shakespeare. M : Alf Sjöberg. Royal Dramatic Theatre, Stockholm. 1946. – SALOME, Richard Strauss. M: Göran Gentele. Ch: Birgit Cullberg. Royal Opera, Stockholm. 1956. – THE CHERRY ORCHARD, Chekhov. M : Henning Jensen. Frederiksberg Theatre, Copenhagen. 1952. – THE CHERRY ORCHARD, Chekhov. M : Bengt Ekerot. City Theatre, Stockholm. 1961.

MOULAERT, René.
(Belgium)
Born : Brussels. 7 Nov. 1901.
Educated : Académie des Beaux-Arts, Brussels. Disciple of Jacques COPEAU.

Stage Designs : 1950 and 110 designs for films.
LUCIFER, Vondel. M : Johan de Meester. Het Vlaamsche Volkstoneel, Brussels and Flanders. 1925. – JUDITH, Jean Giraudoux. M : Louis Jouvet. Pigalle Theatre, Paris. 1931. – THE WINTER'S TALE, Shakespeare. M : Julien Bertheau. Comédie Française, Paris. 1950.

MUMCU, Hüseyin.
(Turkey)
Born : Bursa. 1926.
Educated : Academy of Fine Arts, Istanbul. Disciple of Bedri Rahmi EYÜBOGLU and Turgut ZAIM.
Stage Designs : Over 50.
TEAHOUSE OF THE AUGUST MOON, John Patrick. M : Mahir Canova. State Theatre, Ankara. 1954. – LOVE AND PEACE, Suat Taser. M : Suat Taser. State Theatre, Ankara. 1960. – THE CHERRY ORCHARD, Chekhov. M : Ziya Demirel. State Theatre, Ankara. 1962.

MUNIZ FREIRE, Napoleão.
(Brazil)
Born : Rio de Janeiro. 1929.
Educated : Escola Nacional de Engenharia, Rio de Janeiro.
Stage Designs : About 12.
PLUFT, Maria Clara Machado. M : Maria Clara Machado. Tablado, Rio de Janeiro. 1955. – OUR TOWN, Thornton Wilder. 1955. – O MAMBEMBE, Arthur de Azevedo. M : Gianni Ratto. Companhia dos Sete. Copacabana Theatre, Rio de Janeiro. 1959. – THE CONNECTION, Jack Gelber. Studio de Produção, Rio de Janeiro.

MUNOZ, Gori.
(Argentina)
Born : Valencia (Spain). 26 July 1906.
Educated : School of Fine Arts, Madrid and Valencia. Disciple of Salvator ALARMA.
Stage Designs : Over 125.
THE BEST ALCADE IS THE KING, Lope de Vega. M : Javier Farias. Casa de Castilla Theatre, Buenos Aires. 1957. – EL ANZUELO DE FENISA (Fenisa's Bait), Lope de Vega. M : Alejandro Casona. Liceo Theatre, Buenos Aires. 1958. – LOS INTERESES CREADOS (The Bonds of Interest), Jacinto Benavente. M : Lola Membrives. Comedy Theatre, Buenos Aires. 1959.

N

NAVICKS, Felikss.
(U.S.S.R.)
Born : Lithuania. 5 Nov. 1922.
Educated : Fine Arts Academy, Vilnius.
Stage Designs : About 20.
GENERALMEGINAJUMS (The Dress Rehearsal), Kazis Binkis. M : F. Vencevicius. Mu : V. Baumplas. Kaunas Dramatic Theatre. 1958.

NAVON, Arieh.
(Israel)
Born : Dunayevtsa (Russia). 22 May 1909. Educated : Israeli teachers and the Académie de la Grande Chaumière, Paris.
Stage Designs : Over 35.
HU HALAH BASADOT (He Walked in the Fields), Moshe Shamir. M : Joseph Millo. Cameri Theatre, Tel Aviv. 1956. – RASHOMON, Kanin. M : Joseph Millo. Haifa City Theatre. 1961. – PUNDAK HARUHOT (The Haunted Inn), Natan Alterman. M : Gershon Plotkin. Cameri Theatre, Tel Aviv. 1962.

NEGRI, Richard.
(Great Britain)
Born : London. 27 June 1927.
Educated : Old Vic Theatre School. Disciple of Michel SAINT-DENIS.
Stage Designs : About 60.
BRAND, Ibsen. M : Michael Elliot. Lyric, Hammersmith, London. 1959. – PLATONOV, Chekhov. M : George Devine - John Blatchley. Royal Court, London. 1960. – As YOU LIKE

IT, Shakespeare. M : Michael Elliott. Royal Shakespeare Theatre, Stratford-upon-Avon. 1961.

NESJAR, Carl.
(Norway)
Born : Larvik, 6 July 1920.
Educated : Pratt Institute, Brooklyn, and Fine Arts Academy, Oslo.
Disciple of R. ROSTRUP-BOEYESEN (Copenhagen) and MEYER-SHAPIRO (Columbia University, New York).
Stage Designs : 3.
THE DISCOVERY OF THE NEW WORLD, Morvan Lebesque, after Lope de Vega. M : Arne Thomas Olsen. People's Theatre, Oslo. 1956. – DON JUAN, Molière. M : Arne Thomas Olsen. National Theatre. Oslo. 1960.

NEUMANN-SPALLART, Gottfried.
(Austria)
Born : Vienna. 29 March 1915.
Educated : Technische Hochschule, Vienna.
Stage Designs : 105.
TORQUATO TASSO, Gœthe. M : Raoul Aslan. Burg Theatre, Vienna. 1955. – PARSIFAL, Richard Wagner. M : Josef Witt. San Carlo Theatre, Naples. 1955. – THE LIAR. Goldoni. M : Arno Assman. Josefstadt Theatre, Vienna. 1961.

NOBILI, Lila de.
(France)
Born : Cassarate (Italy). 3 Sep. 1916.
Educated : Fine Arts, Rome. Disciple of Christian BÉRARD and Marcel VERTÈS.
Stage Designs : About 30.
CYRANO DE BERGERAC, Edmond Rostand. M : Raymond Rouleau. Sarah Bernhardt Theatre, Paris. – LA TRAVIATA, Verdi. M : Luchino Visconti. Scala, Milan.

NOËL, Jacques.
(France)
Born : Ivry. 7 Nov. 1924.
Educated : École Boulle. Disciple of Christian BÉRARD.
Stage Designs : About 100.
THE PANTOMIMES OF THE MARCEL MARCEAU MIME COMPANY. M : Marcel Marceau. The principal plays of Eugène Ionesco in productions by Jacques Mauclair, Robert Postec, J.M. Serreau, Nicolas Bataille, Marcel Cuvelier, José Quaglio and Jean-Louis Barrault.

NORDEN, Hans van.
(Netherlands)
Born : Bussum. 3 Dec. 1915.
Educated : Rijksacademie van Beeldende Kunsten, Amerstam. Disciple of Heinrich CAMPENDONK.
Stage Designs : About 80.
JENUFA. Mu : Leos Janácek. M : Abraham van der Vies. City Theatre, Amsterdam. 1951. – THE FORCE OF DESTINY, Verdi. M : Wolf-Dieter Ludwig. Ch : Françoise Adret. City Theatre, Amsterdam. 1956. – THE SPANISH CITIZEN OF BRABANT, Bredero. M: Ton Lutz. Rotterdam City Theatre, Rotterdam. 1961.

NURMIMAA, Seppo.
(Finland)
Born : Helsinki. 19 April 1931.
Educated : Helsinki Institute of Arts and Crafts.
Stage Designs : 23.
CSARDAS PRINCESS. Mu : Kálmán. M : Sven - Aage Larssen. Finnish National Opera, Helsinki. 1959. – SHOWBOAT. Mu : Kern. M : Sven-Aage Larssen. Finnish National Opera, Helsinki. 1960.

NÝVLT, Vladimir.
(Czechoslovakia)
Born : Prague. 23 Mar. 1927.
Educated : Vysoká Skola Umelecko-Prumyslová. Disciple of Otto ROTTMAYER (architect).
Stage Designs : Over 100.
WHITE NIGHTS, Dostoievsky. M: Emil Frantisek Burian. D. 34 Theatre, Prague. 1956. – BEFORE SUNSET,

Gerhard Hauptmann. M : Václav Spidla. J.K. Tyl Theatre, Pilsen. 1959. – HAMLET, Shakespeare. M : Milos Horansky. City Theatre, Ostrava. 1960.

O

ÖBERG, Barbara W.
(Sweden)
Born : Berlin (Germany). 28 Oct. 1930.
Educated : Konstfackskolan and Kungl. Konstakademien, Stockholm. Disciple of Sven ERIXON and Olle NYMAN.
Stage Designs : About 25.
LYSISTRATA, Aristophanes. M : Olof Thunberg. City Theatre, Norrköping-Linköping. 1957. – THE HOSTAGE, Brendan Behan. M : Lars Barringer. City Theatre, Norrköping-Linköping. 1960. – QUEEN CHRISTINA, August Strindberg. M : John Zacharias. City Theatre, Norrköping-Linköping. 1961.

O'BRIEN, Timothy.
(Great Britain)
Born : Shillong (Assam-India). 8 March 1929.
Educated: Yale University. Disciple of Donald OENSLAGER.
Stage Designs : 10.
THE FLYING DUTCHMAN, Wagner. M : Dennis Arundell. Sadler's Wells Theatre, London. 1958. – DREAMING BANDSMEN, Jeremy Sandford. M : Ted Kotcheff. Belgrade Theatre, Coventry. 1960.

ODA, Otoya.
(Japan)
Born : Tokyo. 6 Apr. 1920.
Educated : Arts School, Tokyo. Disciple of Kisaku ITÔ.
Stage Designs : 100.
TATSUMI KÔDAN (At the South-East of Tokyo), Kyôka Izumi - Mantarô Kubota. M: Mantarô Kubota. Shimpa, Tokyo. 1952. – GOJU NO Tô (The Five-storied Pagoda), Rohan Kôda - Ton Satomi. M : Ton Satomi. Kabukiza, Tokyo. 1953. – SHUNDEINI (Priestess Shundei), Tôkô Kon - Matsutarô Kawaguchi. M : Takeo Hodoshima. Shimpa, Tokyo. 1958.

OECHSLIN, Ary.
(Switzerland)
Born : Berlin (Germany). 26 June 1914.
Educated : Reimann Kunstschule, Staatliche Hochschule für bildende Künste, and Meisterschule der Stadt Berlin, Berlin.
Stage Designs : Over 100.
OF MICE AND MEN, John Steinbeck. M : Adolf Spalinger. Atelier Theatre, Berne. 1954. – THE EGG, Félicien Marceau. M : Hermann Kutscher. Atelier Theatre, Berne. 1959. – HAMLET, Shakespeare. M: Harald Benesch. Komödie, Basle. 1961.

OENSLAGER, Donald.
(U.S.A.)
Born : Harrisburg. 7 Mar. 1902.
Educated : Philips Exeter Academy and Harvard University.
Stage Designs : About 200.
GIRL CRAZY, Guy Bolton - John MacGowan. Mu : George and Ira Gershwin. M : Alexander Leftwich. Ch : George Hale. Alvin Theatre, New York. 1930. – OF MICE AND MEN, John Steinbeck. M : George S. Kaufman. Music Box Theatre, New York. 1937. – THE BALLAD OF BABY DOE, John Latouche. Mu : Douglas Moore. M : Hanya Holm. Central City Opera, Denver. 1956.

OLIVA BALUJA, Raul.
(Cuba)
Born : Ciego de Avila. 25 May 1935.
Educated : University of Havana (architecture).
Stage Designs :
RONDAS INFANTILES (Children's Games). Ch : Ramiro Guerra. Teatro Experimental de Danza, Havana. 1956. – DEATH OF A SALESMAN, Arthur Miller. Teatro Estudio, Sala

Nico López, Havana. 1960. – DOÑA ROSITA, Federico Garcia Lorca. Teatro Estudio. Sala Nico López, Havana. 1961.

OLOFSSON, Pierre.   (Sweden)
Born : Paris (France). 4 Feb. 1921.
Educated : Konsthögskolan. Stockholm. Disciple of SKÖLD.
Stage Designs : 3.
NARREN (The Fool), Lars Forsell. M : Hans Dahlin. City Theatre, Uppsala. 1953. – KRÖNINGEN (The Coronation), Lars Forsell. Mu : G. Bucht. M : Bengt Ekerot. Ch : Birgit Cullberg. Royal Dramatic Theatre, Stockholm. 1956.

OTTO, Teo.   (Switzerland)
Born : Remscheid (Germany). 4 Nov. 1904.
Educated : Academy of Fine Arts, Kassel, and Bauhaus, Weimar.
Stage Designs : Over 500.
THE FLIES, Jean-Paul Sartre. M : Leonhard Steckel. Playhouse, Zurich. 1944. – DON JUAN OR THE LOVE OF GEOMETRY, Max Frisch. M : Oskar Wälterlin. Playhouse, Zurich. 1952. – THE VISIT OF THE OLD LADY, Friedrich Dürrenmatt. M : Oskar Wälterlin. Playhouse, Zurich. 1957.

P

PACE.   (France)
Born : Tunis. 22 July 1935.
Educated : École des Beaux-Arts, Paris.
Stage Designs : Over 20.
IN THE JUNGLE OF THE CITIES, Bertolt Brecht. M : Antoine Bourseiller. Champs-Élysées Theatre Studio, Paris. – RODOGUNE, Corneille. Sarah Bernhardt Theatre, Paris. – AS YOU DESIRE ME, Luigi Pirandello. Champs-Élysées Theatre Studio, Paris.

PAES LEME, Bellá.   (Brazil)
Born : Sao Paulo. 1933.
Pupil of Pedro CORREIA DE ARAUJO.
Stage Designs : About 20.

PÁN, József.   (Hungary)
Born : Budapest. 1900.
Educated : High School of Fine Arts, Berlin.
Stage Designs : 100 (plus 100 films).
UNCLE VANYA, Chekhov. M : Endre Gellért. Katona Jozsef Theatre, Budapest. 1952. – THE MAIDEN DISGUISED, Kovnyer. M : György Székely - Miklós Szinetár. City Operette Theatre, Budapest. 1954.

PAYOT, Tom   (Belgium)
Born : Antwerp. 2 Apr. 1921.
Educated : Antwerp Academy. Disciple of Carl DEROOVER.
Stage Designs : Over 70.
THE MARIAGE OF FIGARO, Mozart. M : Lode Verstraeten. Royal Flemish Opera, Antwerp. – THE ALCHEMIST, Ben Jonson. M : Cas Baes. Nederlands Kamertoneel, Antwerp. – A MOON FOR THE MISBEGOTTEN, Eugene O'Neill. M : Jo Dua. Koninklijke Vlaamse Schouwburg, Brussels.

PEDREIRA, Luis Diego.
          (Argentina)
Born : Buenos Aires. 30 Oct. 1921.
Educated : High School of Fine Arts, Buenos Aires. Disciple of Rodolfo FRANCO.
Stage Designs : 59.
THE WOMEN'S GOSSIP, Goldoni. M : Cecilio Madanes. Caminito Theatre, Buenos Aires. 1957. – NARCISA GARAY, MUJER PARA LLORAR (Narcisa Garay, a Woman for Crying), Juan Carlos Ghiano. M : Francisco Silva. Carpa - Belgrano Theatre, Buenos Aires. 1959. – THE ROBBERS, Schiller. M : Fernando Labat - Ernesto Bianco.

Teatro del Botánico, Buenos Aires. 1960.

PEETERMANS, Mimi.   (Belgium)
Born : Antwerp. 13 Apr. 1929.
Educated : Académie Royale des Beaux-Arts, Brussels and Studio of Flemish National Theatre. Disciple of Anto CARTE, Fred ENGELEN and Herman TEIRLINCK.
Stage Designs : Over 300.
A MIDSUMMER NIGHT'S DREAM, Shakespeare. M : Ben Rooyaards. Ch : J. Brabants. Koninklijke Nederlandse Schouwburg, Antwerp. 1954. – ELCKERLYC, adaptation : Herman Teirlinck. M : Fred Engelen. Koninklijke Nederlandse Schouwburg, Antwerp. 1958. – THE FAN, Goldoni. M : Jo Dua. Koninklijke Vlaamse Schouwburg, Brussels. 1959.

PELLETIER, Jacques.   (Canada)
Born : Montreal. 10 Jan. 1922.
Educated : École des Beaux-Arts, Montreal. Disciple of Jo MIELZINER, New York.
Stage Designs : Over 80.
TWELFTH NIGHT, Shakespeare. M : Jan Doat. Théâtre-Club, Montreal. 1955. – A SIMPLE SOLDIER, Marcel Dubé. M : Jean-Paul Fugère. Canadian Comedy Theatre, Montreal. 1958. – THE MAGIC FLUTE, Mozart. M : M. Cohen. Canadian Comedy Theatre, Montreal. 1960.

PERAHIM, Jules.   (Rumania)
Born : Bucharest. 24 May 1914.
Pupil of the painter Costin PETRESCU.
Stage Designs : Over 80.
THE ARISTOCRATS, Nicolai Pogodin. M : Horia Popescu. Railway Workers' Theatre, Bucharest. 1959. – THE BATH HOUSE, V. Maiakovski. M : Horia Popescu. Railway Workers' Theatre, Bucharest. 1960. – DE PRETORE VINCENZO, Eduardo de Filippo. M : Dinu Cernescu. Youth Theatre, Bucharest. 1961.

PETRITZKI, Anatoli.   (U.S.S.R.)
Born : Kiev. 12 Feb. 1895.
Educated : School of Fine Arts, Kiev and Art Studios (Vkhutemas), Moscow. Disciple of Alexander MURASHKO and Grigori DIADCHENKO.
Stage Designs : Over 100.
CHEREVICHKI, opera by Tchaikovsky. M : Ruben Simonov. Ch : Vasili Vainonen. Bolshoi Theatre, Moscow. 1941. – THE DECEMBRISTS, opera by Yuri Shaporin. M : Nicolai Okhlopkov. Ch : Leonid Lavrovski. Bolshoi Theatre, Moscow. 1953. – BOGDAN KHMELNITSKI, opera by Konstantin Dankievich. Libretto by Wanda Wassilewska-Alexander Korneichuk. M : Marian Krushelnitski. Ch : Serge Sergeyev. Shevchenko Opera and Ballet Theatre, Kiev. 1958.

PHOCAS, Antonis.   (Greece)
Born : Athens. 1903.
Stage Designs : Several thousand costumes (Especially for nearly every ancient tragedy and most of Shakespeare at the Greek National Theatre, since 1931).

PIGNON, Edouard.   (France)
Born : Bully-Marles les Mines. 12 Feb. 1905.
Stage Designs : 7 or 8.
MOTHER COURAGE AND HER CHILDREN, Bertolt Brecht. M : Jean Vilar. People's National Theatre, Paris. – PLATONOV, Chekhov. M : Jean Vilar. People's National Theatre, Paris. – NO TRIFLING WITH LOVE, Musset. M : René Clair. People's National Theatre, Paris.

PIMENOV, Yuri.   (U.S.S.R.)
Born : Moscow. 26 Nov. 1903.
Educated : Art Studios (Vkhutemas).

Disciple of Serge MALIUTIN, Mikhail SHEMIAKIN, Vladimir FAVORSKI.
Stage Designs : About 50.
THE SLUT, Labiche. M : Boris Aphonin. Central Soviet Army Theatre, Moscow. 1945. – STEP SHIROKAYA (The Vast Steppes), Nicolai Vinnikov. M : Alexei Popov. Central Soviet Army Theatre, Moscow. 1949. – I PAGLIACCI, Leoncavallo. M : Boris Pokrovski. Subsidiary of the Bolshoi Theatre, Moscow. 1957.

PIPER, John.   (Great Britain)
Born : Epsom. 1903.
Educated : Royal College of Art.
Stage Designs : 30.
DON GIOVANNI, Mozart. M : Carl Ebert. Glyndebourne Opera. 1951. – THE TURN OF THE SCREW, Benjamin Britten. M : Coleman. Fenice Theatre, Venice. 1954. – THE PRINCE OF THE PAGODAS, Benjamin Britten. M : Cranko. Royal Opera House, Covent Garden, London. 1957.

PIZZI, Pier Luigi.   (Italy)
Born : Milan. 15 June 1930.
Educated : Faculty of Architecture, University of Milan.
Stage Designs : 150.
LE MORBINOSE (The Good-Humoured Ladies), Goldoni. M : Giorgio De Lullo. Teatro La Fenice, Venice. 1959. – IL TROVATORE, Verdi. M : Giorgio De Lullo. Scala, Milan. 1962.

PONNELLE, Jean-Pierre.
          (West Germany)
Born : Paris. 19 Feb. 1932.
Educated : Sorbonne (History of Art and Philosophy) then with Fernand LÉGER and the Grande Chaumière.
Has worked as designer in most of the theatres in West Germany, Vienna, Rome, Paris, London, San Francisco. In recent years has concentrated on directing plays.

POPOV, Assen.   (Bulgaria)
Born : Pordim. 24 Jan. 1895.
Educated : Fine Arts Academy, Leningrad. Pupil of O.E. BRAZ. Disciple of GOLOVIN and the German theatre.
Stage Designs : Over 350.
AIDA, Verdi. M : Dragan Kardzhiev. Bulgarian National Opera, Sofia. 1949. – I QUATTRO RUSTEGHI, Wolf-Ferrari. M : Dragan Kardzhiev. Bulgarian National Opera, Sofia. 1952. – KAM PROPAST (To the Abyss), Ivan Vazov. M : Stephan Sarchedjiev. "Ivan Vazov" National Theatre, Sofia, 1959.

POPOV, Dmitri.   (U.S.S.R.)
Born : Tambov. 4 Aug. 1911.
Educated: Lunacharski Worker's University, Moscow and Fine Arts Academy, Leningrad. Disciple of Anna OSTROUMOVA - LEBEDEVA and Mikhail BOBYSHOV.
Stage Designs : Over 50.
THE SEAGULL, Chekhov. M : Leonid Vivien. Pushkin Academie Theatre, Leningrad. 1954. – LEVSHA (Left Handed), operetta by Anatoli Novikov after Nicolai Leskov. M : Andrei Tutyshkin. Musical Comedy Theatre, Leningrad. 1959.

POPOVA, Mariana.   (Bulgaria)
Born : Munich. 16 Dec. 1914.
Educated : Institute of Fine Arts, Sofia. Disciple of Ivan PENKOV.
Stage Designs : Over 120.
MARIA STUART, Schiller. M : Krastu Mirski. Youth Theatre, Sofia. 1958. – COSI FAN TUTTE, Mozart. M : Nicolai Nikolov. National Opera, Varna. 1959. – TURANDOT, Puccini. M : Emile Boshnakov. Bulgarian National Opera, Sofia. 1960.

PRÉVOST, Robert.   (Canada)
Born : Montreal. 21 Mar. 1927.
Disciple of Christian BÉRARD.
Stage Designs : Over 90.
VENICE PRESERVED, Morvan Lebesque-Thomas Otway. M : Jean Gascon. New World Theatre, Montreal. 1959. – OTHELLO, Shakespeare. M : Jean Gascon - Georges McCowan. Festival Theatre, Stratford, Ontario. 1959.

PRIDE, Malcolm.   (Great Britain)
Born : London. 5 July 1930.
Educated : Old Vic Theatre School, London. Disciple of Michel SAINT-DENIS.
Stage Designs : 35.
TWELFTH NIGHT, Shakespeare. M : John Gielgud. Royal Shakespeare Theatre, Stratford-upon-Avon. – ORPHEUS IN THE UNDERWORLD, Offenbach. M : Wendy Toye. Sadler's Wells Theatre, London. – THE MARRIAGE OF FIGARO, Mozart. M : Douglas Seale. Sadler's Wells Theatre, London.

R

RABINOVICH, Isaac.   (U.S.S.R.)
Born : Kiev. 27 Feb. 1894.
Educated : School of Fine Arts and Alexander Murashko Studio, Kiev. Disciple of Alexander MURASHKO and Alexandra EXTER.
Stage Designs : About 100.
LYSISTRATA, Aristophanes. M : Vladimir Nemirovich-Danchenko - Leonid Baratov. Mu : Reinhold Glière. Musical Studio of the Moscow Art Theatre. 1923. – THE STORM, Alexander Ostrovsky. M : Vladimir Nemirovich-Danchenko - Ilia Sudakov. Moscow Art Theatre. 1934. – HAMLET, Shakespeare. M : Boris Zakhava - Mikhail Astangov. Mu : Visarion Shebalin. Vakhtangov Theatre, Moscow. 1958.

RAFFAËLLI, Michel.   (France)
Born : Marseilles. 26 June 1929.
Stage Designs : About 30.
MOSES UND ARON, Schönberg. M : G.R. Sellner. Berlin Opera. 1960. – IMPROVISATIONS SUR MALLARMÉ. Mu : Pierre Boulez. Ch : Deryk Mendel. Deutsche Oper, Berlin. 1961. – THE TRIP TO THE COUNTRY, Carlo Goldoni. M : Jacques Rosner. City Theatre, Villeurbanne. 1963.

RAJKAI, György.   (Hungary)
Born : Budapest. 1914.
Educated : Munich Academy. Disciple of Kurt WELTE, Mátyás VARGA and Gusztáv OLAH.
Stage Designs : About 500.
LA BELLE HÉLÈNE, Jacques Offenbach. M : Miklós Szinetár. City Operette Theatre, Budapest. 1959. – THE THREEPENNY OPERA, Bertolt Brecht. M : Kurt Weill. M : Miklós Szinetár. Petöfi Theatre, Budapest. 1960. – CRIME AND PUNISHMENT, Dostoyevski. M : István Egri. Jókai Theatre. Budapest. 1962.

RAPP, Jacques.   (France)
Born : Strasbourg. 16 May 1930.
Educated: Arts Décoratifs, Strasbourg. Disciple of L. Ph. KAMM.
Stage Designs : Over 85.
LA NOCE FORAINE (The Wedding on the Road), J.M. Damase. M : Joseph Lazzini. Marseilles Opera. 1961. – THE SEVEN DEADLY SINS, Bertolt Brecht. Mu : Kurt Weill. M : Milko Sparembleck. Strasbourg Opera. 1962. – SIMONE BOCCANEGRA, Verdi. M : J.J. Brothier. Strasbourg Opera. 1963.

RATTO, Gianni.   (Italy)
Born : Milan. 27 Aug. 1916.
Educated : Faculty of Architecture, University of Milan, and Experimental Cinema Centre, Rome.

Stage Designs :
LA PARISIENNE, Henri Becque. M : Giorgio Strehler. Piccolo Teatro, Milan. 1950. – LULU, Carlo Bertolazzi. M : Giorgio Strehler. Piccolo Teatro, Milan. 1953. – Gianni RATTO has been working in Brazil since 1954.

REINKING, Wilhelm.
(West Germany)
Born : Aachen. 18 Oct. 1900.
Educated : Technische Hochschule, Karlsruhe, and University of Munich.
Stage Designs : About 400 (12 unrealised).
JULIUS CAESAR, Handel. M : Arthur Maria Rabenalt. Ch : Clare Eckstein. Hessisches Landestheater, Darmstadt. 1927. – THE MASKED BALL, Verdi. M : Oscar Fritz Schuh. State Opera, Vienna. 1942. – ALCMENE, after Kleist. Mu : Giselher Klebe. M : Gustav Rudolf Sellner. Deutsche Oper. West Berlin. 1961.

RENARD, Raymond. (Belgium)
Born : Auderghem. 6 Feb. 1929.
Educated : École Nationale Supérieure d'Architecture et des Arts Décoratifs, Brussels.
Stage Designs :
KISS ME KATE, Sam and Bella Spewack-Cole Porter. M : Ernst Pichler. Théâtre Royal de la Monnaie, Brussels. 1961. – BOULEVARD DURAND, Armand Salacrou. M : André Reybaz. Northern Dramatic Centre, Tourcoing. 1962. – IT'S RAINING IN MY HOUSE, Paul Willems. M : Pierre Laroche. Rideau de Bruxelles, Brussels. 1962.

RICE, Peter Anthony Morrish.
(Great Britain)
Born : Simla (India). 13 Sept. 1928.
Educated : Royal College of Art, London.
Stage Designs : 70.
TIME REMEMBERED, Jean Anouilh. M : William Chappell. Lyric Theatre, London. 1954. – ROMEO AND JULIET, Serge Prokofiev. Ch : Sir Fredrick Ashton. Royal Danish Ballet, Copenhagen. 1955. – CASTLE IN SWEDEN, Françoise Sagan. M : Peter Coe. Piccadilly Theatre, London. 1962.

RIECHETOFF, Nina. (France)
Born : Angiers. 18 Dec. 1929.
Educated : École des Métiers d'Art, Paris.
Stage Designs :
THE ALCHEMIST, Ben Jonson. M : André Steiger. Bourgogne Theatre. 1961. – FEAR AND MISERY IN THE THIRD REICH, Bertolt Brecht. M : André Steiger. Bourgogne Theatre. 1962. – THE STAR TURNS RED, Sean O'Casey. M : G. Garran. Récamier Theatre, Paris. 1962.

RINFRET, Jean-Claude. (Canada)
Born : Shawiningan. 3 Sep. 1929.
Educated : École des Beaux-Arts, Montreal. Worked at École des Arts Décoratifs, Paris. Disciple of LABISSE.
Stage Designs : Over 100.
CINNA, Corneille. M : Jean Valcourt. Théâtre-Club, Montreal. 1959. – COSI FAN TUTTE, Mozart. M : Florent Forget. Montreal Festival. Canadian Comedy Theatre, Montreal. 1962. – THE MERCHANT OF VENICE, Shakespeare. M : Jacques Létourneau. Théâtre-Club, Montreal. 1963.

RISTIĆ, Dušan. (Yugoslavia)
Born : Bucharest (Rumania). 22 Oct. 1913.
Educated : Fine Arts Academy, Belgrade. Disciple of Peter DOBROVIC.
Stage Designs : Over 100.
ORPHÉE. Mu : Igor Stravinsky. Ch : D. Parlic. Narodno Pozorište, Belgrade. 1952. – VARIATIONS ON A THEME BY FRANK BRIDGE. Mu : Benjamin Britten. Ch : D. Parlic. Vienna State Opera. 1959.

RODHE, Lennart. (Sweden)
Born : Stockholm. 15 Nov. 1916.
Educated : Kungl. Konstakademien, Stockholm. Disciple of P. Rostrup BOEYESEN (Copenhagen) and Sven ERIXON (Stockholm).
Stage Designs : 2.
RITER (Rites), Erik Lindegren. Mu : Ingvar Lidholm. Ch : Birgit Akesson. Royal Opera, Stockholm. 1960. – THE FLYING DUTCHMAN, Richard Wagner. M : Bengt Peterson. Royal Opera, Stockholm. 1960.

RODRIGUEZ, Aida. (Uruguay)
Born : 1924.
Education and Stage Designs, see TOSAR, Beatriz.

ROGNONI, Franco. (Italy)
Born : Milan. 20 Sept. 1913.
Stage Designs : 3.
MAVRA, Igor Stravinsky. M : Tatiana Pavlova. RAI - Italian TV, Milan. 1957. – THE TEMPEST, Shakespeare. M : Franco Enriquez. Ch : Luciana Novaro. Villa Giusti Gardens, Verona. 1957.

ROLF, Elli. (Austria)
Born : Vienna.
Educated : Akademie für Angewandte Kunst, Vienna. Disciple of Professor WIMMER-WISSGRILL.
Stage Designs : About 100 costume designs.
DER SCHWIERIGE (The Fastidious Man), Hugo von Hofmannsthal. M : Rudolf Steinböck. Josefstadt Theatre, Vienna. 1954. – MEASURE FOR MEASURE, Shakespeare. M: Leopold Lindtberg. Burg Theatre, Vienna. 1956. – LUMPACIVAGABUNDUS, Johann N. Nestroy. M : Leopold Lindtberg. Salzburg Festival. 1962.

RÖTHLISBERGER, Max.
(Switzerland)
Born : Berthoud (Burgdorf). 27 Nov. 1914.
Studied : Reinhardtseminar, Vienna.
Stage Designs : Over 300.
JUDITH, Arthur Honegger. M: Leopold Lindtberg. City Opera, Zurich. 1948. – THE TEMPEST, Frank Martin. M: Hans Zimmermann. City Opera, Zurich. 1959. – BLUEBEARD'S CASTLE, Bartok. M : Walter Oberer. City Theatre, Berne. 1961.

RYNDIN, Vadim. (U.S.S.R.)
Born : Moscow. 15 Jan. 1902.
Educated : Art Studios (Vkhutemas), Varonezh and Moscow. Disciple of Philippe MALIAVIN, Nicolai MAXIMOV and Serge ROMANOVICH.
Stage Designs : About 150.
THE OPTIMISTIC TRAGEDY, Vsevolod Vishnevski. M : Alexander Tairov. Mu : Lev Knipper. Kamerny Theatre, Moscow. 1938. – HAMLET, Shakespeare. M : Nicolai Okhlopkov. Mayakovski Theatre, Moscow. 1954. – THE MIRACULOUS MANDARIN, Bela Bartok. M : Leonid Lavrovski. Bolshoi Theatre, Moscow. 1961.

S

SAINTHILL, Loudon.
(Great Britain)
Born : Hobart (Australia). 9 Jan. 1919.
Stage Designs : 37.
THE TEMPEST, Shakespeare. M : Michael Benthall. Royal Shakespeare Theatre, Stratford-upon-Avon. 1951. – THE GOLDEN COCKEREL, Rimsky-Korsakov. M : Robert Helpmann. Royal Opera House, Covent Garden, London. 1953. – PERICLES, Shakespeare. M : Tony Richardson. Royal Shakespeare Theatre, Stratford-upon-Avon. 1959.

SALAS, José. (Venezuela)
Born : Juan Griego. 2 Jan. 1941.
Educated : School of Plastic Arts, Caracas. Disciple of Jacobo BORGES.
Stage Designs : 7.
LO QUE DEJO LA TEMPESTAD (In the Wake of the Storm), Cesar Rengifo. M : Humberto Orsini. La Comedia Theatre, Caracas. 1961. – THE RESPECTABLE PROSTITUTE, Jean-Paul Sartre. M : Rafaél Brieño. Central University, Caracas. 1961. – LOS INSURGENTES (The Rebels), José Ignacio Cabrujas. M : Carlos Denis. Juares Theatre, Barquisimeto. 1962.

SARYAN, Martiros. (U.S.S.R.)
Born : Nakhichevan (Armenia).28 Feb. 1880. Educated : School of Painting, Sculpture and Architecture. Disciple of Konstantin KOROVIN and Valentin SEROV.
Stage Designs : About 20.
THE GOLDEN COCKEREL, Rimsky-Korsakov. M: Konstantin Stanislavski - Vladimir Alexeyev. Stanislavski Opera Theatre, Moscow. 1932. – THE VALIANT NAZAR. Mu : Aro Stepanian. M : Arkadi Burdzhalian. Yerevan Opera and Ballet Theatre. 1936.

SCANDELLA, Mischa. (Italy)
Born : Venice. 5 Dec. 1921.
Educated : Venice.
Stage Designs : About 200.
L'AMANTE MILITARE (The Soldier in Love), Carlo Goldoni. M : Giorgio Strehler. Piccolo Teatro, Milan. 1951. – ANTONELLO CAPOBRIGANTE, Ghigo De Chiara. M : Gianfranco. De Bosio. Teatro Stabile, Turin. 1960. – JOAN OF ARC AT THE STAHE, Paul Claudel. Mu : Arthur Honegger. M : Vittorio Gassman. Teatro Massimo Bellini, Catania. 1960.

SCHADE, Gerhard. (East Germany)
Born : Frankfurt-on-the-Oder. 20 May 1922.
Educated : Hochschule für Angewandte Kunst, Berlin. Disciple of H. Kilger.
Stage Designs : About 80.
THE LOVE OF THREE ORANGES, Serguei Prokofiev. M : Hinko Leskovsek. Ch : Tom Schilling. State Opera, Dresden. 1958. – SAINT JOAN OF THE STOCKYARDS, Bertolt Brecht. M : Prof. Dr. Gaillard - Hannes Fischer. Staatstheater, Dresden. 1961. – TROILUS AND CRESSIDA, Shakespeare. M : Hannes Fischer. Staatstheater, Dresden. 1962.

SCMID, Georg. (Austria)
Born : Vienna. 18 Jan. 1928.
Educated : Akademie für Angewandte Kunst, Vienna.
Stage Designs : 7.
DIE CHINESISCHE MAUER (The Chinese Wall), Max Frisch. M : Gustav Manker. People's Theatre, Vienna. 1956. – THE DIE IS CAST, Jean-Paul Sartre. M : Gustav Manker. People's Theatre, Vienna. 1959. – DANTON'S DEATH, Georg Büchner. M : Gustav Manker. People's Theatre, Vienna. 1960.

SCHMIDT, Willi. (West Germany)
Born : Dresden. 19 Jan. 1910.
Educated : Berlin.
Disciple of Rochus GLIESE and Jürgen FEHLING.
Stage Designs : 143.
THE SATIN SLIPPER, Paul Claudel. M : Willi Schmidt. Schiller Theatre, West Berlin. 1952. – L'APOLLON DE BELLAC, Jean Giraudoux. M : Willi Schmidt. Schlosspark Theatre, West Berlin. 1958. – INTRIGUE AND LOVE, Schiller. M : Willi Schmidt. Institute for Advanced Studies in the Theater Arts, New York. 1960.

SCHULZ, Rudolf. (West Germany)
Born : Gnesen. 2 July 1909.
Educated : Berlin. Disciple of Ernst SCHÜTTE and Caspar NEHER.
Stage Designs : About 160.
THE TRIAL, Kafka-Gide. M : Kurt Ehrhardt. Landestheater, Hanover. 1951. – THE ORESTEIA, Aeschylus. M : Günther Fleckenstein. Landestheater, Hanover. 1960. – THE WOMAN FROM ANDROS, Yvonne Georgi. Mu : Henk Badings. Ch : Yvonne Georgi. Landestheater, Hanover. 1960.

SHWAB, Per. (Norway)
Born : Stockholm (Sweden). 8 Nov. 1911.
Educated : Kungliga Akademien, Stockholm. Disciple of Isaac GRÜNEWALD and Per LINDBERG.
Stage Designs : About 400.
THE DEFEAT, Nordahl Grieg. M : Hans Jacob Nilsen. National Theatre, Bergen. 1938. – A MIDSUMMER NIGHT'S DREAM, Shakespeare. M : Ivo Cramer. Ch : Ivo Cramer. National Theatre, Bergen. 1958.

SCHWENK, Eberhard.
(East Germany)
Born : Kiel. 28 April 1923.
Educated : Kunstgewerbeschule, Magdeburg. Disciple of Professors DEFFKE and LERETZ.
Stage Designs : About 150.
DON JUAN. Mu : Vaclav Kaslik. Ch : Veith Büchel. Städtische Bühnen, Magdeburg. 1957. – PEER GYNT. Mu : Werner Egk. M : Helmut von Senden. Ch : Veith Büchel. Städtische Bühnen, Magdeburg. 1959. – JULIUS CAESAR, Shakespeare. M : Herbert Körbs. Städtische Bühnen, Magdeburg. 1960.

SCILTIAN, Gregorio. (Italy)
Born : Rostov-on-Don (Russia). 20 Aug. 1904.
Educated : Vienna and Rome.
Stage Designs : 9.
WAR AND PEACE, Serguei Prokofiev. M : Tatiana Pavlova. Ch : Nives Poli. Teatro Comunale, Florence. 1953. – MAVRA, Igor Stravinsky. M-Ch : Tatiana Gsovski. Scala, Milan. 1955. – ABU HASSAN, Weber. M : Frank De Quell. Piccola Scala, Milan. 1958.

SCOTT, J. Hutchinson.
(Great Britain)
Born : Northumberland. 1 Aug. 1924.
Educated : University of Durham.
Stage Designs : 45.
THE ICEMAN COMETH, O'Neill. Arts Theatre, London. 1957. – THE ELDER STATESMAN, T.S. Eliot. Edingburgh Festival and Cambridge Theatre. London. 1957. – CAESAR AND CLEOPATRA, Bernard Shaw. Crest Theatre, Toronto. 1962.

SEBREGTS, Lode. (Belgium)
Born : Antwerp. 28 Nov. 1906.
Educated : Institut des Beaux-Arts, Antwerp, and Drama School of Koninklijke Nederlandse Schouwburg, Antwerp. Disciple of Baron OPSOMER, Albert SAVERYS, Joris DIELS and Lea DAAN.
Stage Designs : About 35.
ROMEO AND JULIET, Shakespeare. M : Charles Gilhijs. Koninklijke Nederlandse Schouwburg, Antwerp. 1951. – MOTHER COURAGE AND HER CHILDREN, Bertolt Brecht. M : Fred Engelen. Koninklijke Nederlandse Schouwburg, Antwerp. 1959. – DE SPIEGEL DER MINNEN (The Mirror of the Troubadours), Colijn van Rijssele. M : Fred Engelen. Koninklijke Nederlandse Schouwburg, Antwerp. 1960.

SERBAN, Milenko. (Yugoslavia)
Born : Cerovic. 4 Apr. 1907.
Educated : Académie André Lothe, Paris. Disciple of André LOTHE.
Stage Designs : Over 350.

PERA ŠEGEDINAČ (Pera Shegedinats), Laza Kostic. M : Josip Kulundžić. Serbian National Theatre, Novi Sad. 1939. – KING LEAR, Shakespeare. M : Mata Milošević. Yugoslav Drama Theatre, Belgrade. 1952. – DON CARLOS, Schiller. M: Tomislav Tanhofer. Yugoslav Drama Theatre, Belgrade. 1955.

SHAHN, Ben. (U.S.A.)
Born : Lithuania. 12 Sept. 1898.
Stage Designs :
JAZZ BALLET, Jerome Robbins. Mu : Robert Prince. Ch-M : Jerome Robbins. Festival of Two Worlds, Spoleto. 1958. – EVENTS, Jerome Robbins. Mu : Robert Prince. M-Ch : Jerome Robbins. Festival of Two Worlds, Spoleto. 1961.

SHIFRIN, Nisson. (U.S.S.R.)
Born : Kiev. 28 June 1892.
Disciple of Alexander MURASHKO and Alexandre EXTER.
Stage Designs : About 100.
FEAR, Alexander Afinogenov. M : Ilia Sudakov. Moscow Art Theatre. 1931. – THE TAMING OF THE SHREW, Shakespeare. M : Alexei Popov. Mu : Alexander Golubentsev. Central Soviet Army Theatre, Moscow. 1947. – VIRGIN SOIL UPTURNED, after the novel by Mikhail Sholokhov. M : Alexei Popov - Alexander Shatrin. Central Soviet Army Theatre, Moscow. 1957.

SIERCKE, Alfred. (West Germany)
Born : Hanover. 1 Feb. 1910.
Educated : Frankfurt-on-Main. Disciple of GOWA.
Stage Designs : About 400.
DER MOND (The Moon), Carl Orff. M : Rudolf Scheel - Günther Rennert. Hamburg State Opera, Hamburg. 1938. – PALLAS ATHENE WEEPS, Ernst Krenek. M : Günther Rennert. Hamburg State Opera, Hamburg. 1955. – BELSHAZZAR, Handel. M : Joachim Herz. Hamburg State Opera, Hamburg. 1959.

SIKI, Emil. (Hungary)
Born : Ivándárda. 1914.
Educated : High School of Decorative Arts, Budapest. Disciple of Vilmos ABA NOVÁK and Sandor BENKOVSZKI.
Stage Designs : About 500.
IL TROVATORE, Verdi. M : László Vámos. Csonokai Theatre, Debrecen. 1954. – BÁNK BÁN, József Katona. Mu: Ferenc Erkel. M : László Vámos. Csonokai Theatre, Debrecen. 1955. – THE DIARY OF ANNE FRANK, Goodrich - Hackett. M : Ottó Ádám. Mádách Theatre, Budapest. 1957.

ŠIMÁČEK, Oldřich.
(Czechoslovakia)
Born : Prague. 2 Sep. 1919.
Educated : Vysoká Skola Umelecko-Prumyslová, Prague. Disciple of J. BENDA and A. KRATOCHVÍL.
Stage Designs : Over 200.
DIE CHINESISCHE MAUER (The Chinese Wall), Max Frisch. M : Karel Novák. O. Stibor Theatre, Olomouc. 1957. – THE IMAGINARY INVALID, Molière. M: Jaromir Pleskot. National Theatre, Prague. 1960. – KAMENNYI TSVETOK (The Stone Flower). Mu : Serguei Prokofiev. Ch. Jiří Nemecek. National Theatre, Prague. 1961.

SIMONINI, Pierre. (France)
Born : Italy. 27 Jan. 1927.
Educated: Fine Arts Academy, Brera-Milan. Disciple of Professor REINA.
Stage Designs : 18.
THE TIDINGS BROUGHT TO MARY, Paul Claudel. M : Pierre Franck. Théâtre de l'Œuvre, Paris. 1961. – MON FAUST (My Faust), Paul Valéry. M : Pierre Franck. Théâtre de l'Œuvre, Paris. 1962. – VALENTINE'S MAUVE DRESS,

Françoise Sagan. M : Yves Robert. Ambassadeurs Theatre, Paris. 1963.

SITTER, Inger. (Norway)
Born : Trondheim. 18 Oct. 1929.
Educated : Fine Arts Academy, Oslo, Higher Institute of Fine Arts, Antwerp, and "Atelier 17", Paris. Disciple of André LHOTE and S.W. HAYTER. Wife of Carl NESJAR, (see NESJAR).

SKALICKI, Wolfram. (Austria)
Born : Vienna. 10 June 1925.
Educated : Akademie der Bildenden Künste and University of Vienna (Theaterwissenschaft). Disciple of Emil PIRCHAN and Josef GREGOR.
Stage Designs : 330.
ARMUT (Poverty), Anton Wildgans. M : Walter Davy. Akademie Theatre, Vienna. 1951. – THE MAGIC FLUTE, Mozart. M : André Diehl. Graz Opera. 1956. – THE RAKE'S PROGRESS, Igor Stravinsky. M : Paul Hager. San Francisco (U.S.A.). 1962.

SKULME, Otto. (U.S.S.R.)
Born : Latvia 7 Aug. 1889.
Educated : Stiglits School, St. Petersburg. Disciple of Yakov ROSENTHAL.
Stage Designs : About 100.
THE YEAR 1905. Andrei Upit. M : Eduard Smilgis. Riga Art Theatre. 1940. – THE VICTORY, Vilis Lacis. M : Eduard Smilgis. Riga Art Theatre. 1945. – FIRE AND NIGHT, Janis Rainis. M : Eduard Smilgis. Mu : Marters Zarins. Riga Art Theatre. 1947.

SMITH, Gary. (U.S.A.)
Born : New York. 1 July 1935.
Educated : Carnegie Institute of Technology.
Stage Designs : 200 (principally for Television).
PERRY COMO SHOW. N.B.C. T.V. Producer : Nick Vanoff. M : Dwight Hemion. Ch : Peter Gennaro. New York. From 1960 to 1963. – JUDY GARLAND SHOW. C.B.S. T.V. M : Norman Jewison. Los Angeles. 1962.

SMITH, Oliver. (U.S.A.)
Stage Designs :
MY FAIR LADY, Allan J. Lerner - Frederick Lowe. M : Moss Hart. Ch : Hanya Holm. Marc Hellinger Theatre, New York. 1955. – WEST SIDE STORY, Arthur Laurents. Mu : Leonard Bernstein. M-Ch : Jerome Robbins. Winter Garden Theatre, New York. 1957. – CAMELOT, Allan J. Lerner. Mu : Frederick Lowe. M : Moss Hart. Ch : Hanya Holm. Majestic Theatre, New York. 1960.

SOKOLIČ, Dorian. (Yugoslavia)
Born : Zemun. 24 Nov. 1928.
Educated : Academy of Applied Arts, Belgrade. Disciple of Milenko ŠERBAN.
Stage Designs : Over 60.
MACBETH, Shakespeare. M : Andjelko Stimac. "Ivan Zajc" National Theatre, Rijeka. 1958. – PROMETHEUS, Marijan Matković. M : Leo Tomašić. "Ivan Zajc" National Theatre, Rijeka. 1959.

STEGARS, Rolf. (Finland)
Born : Helsinki. 4 Oct. 1914.
Educated : Finnish National Theatre (disciple of Matti WARÉN aad Karl FAGER) and School of Design (disciple of Uuno ALANKO).
Stage Designs : 150 (+ 100 in collaboration).
THE CRUCIBLE, Arthur Miller. M : Edvin Laine. Finnish National Theatre, Helsinki. 1956. – THE DREAM PLAY, August Strindberg. Mu : Heikki Aaltoila. M : Arvi Kivimaa. Ch : Elsa Sara. Finnish National Theatre, Helsinki. 1959. – SCHOOL FOR SCANDAL, Sheridan. M : Denis Arundell. Finnish National Theatre, Helsinki. 1960.

STENERSEN, Christian. (Norway)
Born : Moss. 27 Nov. 1899.
Educated : Statens Handverk-og Kunstindustriskole, Oslo.
Stage Designs : Over 200.
MARIANA PINEDA, Federico Garcia Lorca. M : Knut Hergel. National Theatre, Oslo. 1956. – THE SPANISH TRIANGLE, Kurt Becsi. M : Arne Thomas Olsen. National Theatre, Oslo. 1961.

STEPHANELLIS, John. (Greece)
Born : Lesbos. 28 Aug. 1915.
Educated : Athens Art Theatre Drama School. Disciple of Karolos KOUN.
Stage Designs : 140.
THE THREE SISTERS, Chekhov. M : Karolos Koun. National Theatre, Athens. 1951. – SUMMER AND SMOKE, Tennessee Williams. M : Karolos Koun. Art Theatre, Athens. 1957. – SAMSON AND DELILAH, Saint Saëns. M : R. Moresco. Ch : Tatiana Varouti. National Opera (Theatre of Herodus Atticus), Athens. 1960.

STONE, Alix. (Great Britain)
Born : Isle of Wight. 18 Nov. 1918.
Educated : Central School of Arts and Crafts, London. Disciple of Jeanetta COCHRANE.
Stage Designs : 9.
SWEENEY TODD, Malcolm Arnold. M : John Cranko. Royal Opera House, Covent Garden, London. 1959. – TWELFTH NIGHT, Shakespeare. M : Colin Graham. Old Vic Theatre, London, 1961.

STRENGER, Friedhelm.
(West Germany)
Born : Berlin. 30 Jan. 1912.
Educated : Dessau. Disciple of KLEE, FEININGER, HILBERSHEIMER and SCHMIDT.
Stage Designs : About 250.
VASCO, Schéhadé. M : Hans Bauer. Landestheater, Hannover. 1958. – CAMINO REAL, Tennessee Williams. M: Günther Fleckenstein. Landestheater, Hannover. 1959.

SUOMINEN, Paul Rafael. (Finland)
Born : Helsinki. 7 Feb. 1930.
Educated : Swedish Theatre, Helsinki.
Stage Designs : 30.
THE MAGIC FLUTE, Mozart. M : Josef Witt. Finnish National Theatre, Helsinki. 1956. – TURANDOT, Puccini. M: Erich Bohrmann. Finnish National Opera, Helsinki. 1960.

SVOBODA, Josef.
(Czechoslovakia)
Born : Cáslav. 10 May. 1920.
Educated : Vysoká Skola Umelecko-Prumyslová, Prague, and Akademie Muzickych Umeni, Prague. Disciple of Jan SMETANA (architect) and Frantisek TRÖSTER.
Stage Designs : Over 200.
SPRONOVA NEDELE (An August Sunday), Frantisek Hrubín. M : Otomar Krejca. National Theatre, Prague. 1958. – JEJICH DEN (Their Day), Josef Topol. M : Otomar Krejca. J.K. Tyl Theatre, Prague. 1959. – DRAHOMIRA A JEJI SYNOVE (Drahomira and her Sons), Josef Kajetán Tyl. M : Otomar Krejca. National Theatre, Prague. 1960.

SYNEK, Vladimir. (Czechoslovakia)
Born : Pilsen. 24 Sep. 1922.
Educated: Akademie Muzickyck Umeni, Prague. Disciple of Professor TRÖSTER.
Stage Designs : Over 200.
UKRADENA PRAHA (The Stolen City), Egon Erwin Kisch. M : Jirina Martínková. S.K. Neumann Theatre, Prague. 1958. – A VIEW FROM THE BRIDGE, Arthur Miller. M : Jaroslav Dudek. S.K. Neumann Theatre, Prague. 1959. – THE ARISTOCRATS, Nikolai Pogodin.

M : Jaroslav Dudek. S.K. Neumann Theatre, Prague. 1960.

T

TAGG, Alan. (Great Britain)
Born : Sutton-in-Ashfield. 13 April 1928.
Educated : Old Vic Theatre School, London. Disciple of Michel SAINT-DENIS.
Stage Designs : About 50.
LOOK BACK IN ANGER, John Osborne. M : Tony Richardson. Royal Court, London. 1956. – BIEDERMANN AND THE FIRE RAISERS, Max Frisch. M : Lindsay Anderson. Royal Court, London. 1961.

TAIVASSALO, Reino. (Finland)
Born : Pyhäjärvi. 1 June 1920.
Educated : City Theatre, Viipuri (disciple of Viljo TERÄS and Toivo DROCKILA) and Turku School of Design.
Stage Designs : About 150.
THE CIRCLE OF CHALK, Klabund. M : Helmi Lehosti. Kemi City Theatre. 1953. – UNCLE VANYA, Chekhov. M : Urho Lauri. Kemi City Theatre. 1955. – DEATH OF A SALESMAN, Arthur Miller. M: Matti Tapio. Oulu Theatre. 1959.

TAKATA, Ichirô. (Japan)
Born : Tokyo. 1 July 1929.
Educated : Arts School, Tokyo.
Stage Designs : 10.
MARIA NO KUBI (Saint Mary's Head), Chikao Tanaka. M : Chikao Tanaka - Yasuyuki Shimada. Shinjinkai, Tokyo. 1959. – TWELFTH NIGHT, Shakespeare. M : Eitarô Ozawa. Haiyûza, Tokyo. 1959. – ALTONA, Jean-Paul Sartre. M : Toshirô Hayano. Haiyû Shogekijô, Tokyo. 1961.

TANAKA, Beatrice. (Brazil)
Born : Cernauti (Rumania). 1932.
Educated : Belo Horizonte and Paris. Disciple of GUIGNARD and Paul COLIN.
Stage Designs : About 10.
THE DOCTOR IN LOVE, Molière. Théâtre de l'Humour, Paris. 1955. – The THREEPENNY OPERA, Bertolt Brecht. Theatre School of the University of Bahia. 1959.

TER-ARUTUNIAN, Rouben.
(U.S.A.)
Born : Tiflis (Russia), 24 July 1920.
Educated : Reimann Schule, Berlin and École des Beaux-Arts, Paris.
Stage Designs :
FESTIVAL STAGE, for the American Shakespeare Festival Theatre, Stratford, Connecticut. 1956-1960. NEW FESTIVAL STAGE. 1960-1961. – THE SEVEN DEADLY SINS, Bertolt Brecht. Mu : Kurt Weill. M-Ch : George Balanchine. New York City Ballet, New York. 1958. – BLOOD MOON, Norman Dello Joio. M : Dino Yannopoulos. San Francisco Opera. 1961.

TERRY, Alberto. (Peru)
Born : Lima. 12 March 1927.
Educated : Escuela Nacional de Arte Escenio. Disciple of Santiago ONTAÑON.
Stage Designs : About 150.
ANTIGONE, Jean Anouilh. M : Mario Rivera. Segura Theatre, Lima. 1955. – COLLACOCHA, Enrique Solari Swayne. M : Luis Alvarez. Asociacion de Artistas Aficionados, Lima. 1956. – TWELFTH NIGHT, Shakespeare. M : Pedro Orthous. City Theatre, Lima. 1957.

TIMIN, Alexander. (U.S.S.R.)
Born : Kamin (Altai). 1910.
Educated : Repin School, Omsk. Disciple of Vikenti TROFIMOV.
Stage Designs : About 50.
NA BAIKALE (On Lake Baikal). Mu : Lev Knipper. M : Gombo Tsydyn-

THIS Designer's Who's Who does not claim to list *all* the leading designers of the 30 odd countries included. The National Centres of the I.T.I. were merely asked to send us short biographies of the artists responsible for at least one of the designs chosen for reproduction : some omissions are therefore inevitable. At all events, we are sure that the reader will find here the names of leading designers that are not to be found in any other work.

As we had requested, each of the biographies contains the titles of three or four works that have constituted landmarks in the designer's career. The manner in which these titles are presented calls for a few words of explanation. When the work is well known in English, we have given the title in English, as in the case of *The Servant of Two Masters*. When the work is little known in English, or not at all, we have, as a rule, given the original title followed by a translation of our own in brackets, for instance : *Donde la Muerte clava sus Banderas* (Where Death fastens his Flags). M : denotes the director, Mu : the composer and Ch : the choreographer.

Over a thousand works are listed. To some extent, they reveal the characteristics of the repertory performed throughout the world during the past ten years.

A

ACQUART, André. (France)
Born : Vincennes. 22 Nov. 1922.
Educated : École Nationale des Beaux-Arts, Algiers.
Stage Designs : 55.
THE BLACKS, Jean Genet. M : Roger Blin. Lutèce Theatre, Paris. 1959. – BIEDERMANN AND THE FIRE RAISERS, Max Frisch. M : Jean-Marie Serreau. Lutèce Theatre, Paris. 1960. – THE RESISTIBLE RISE OF ARTURO UI, Bertolt Brecht. M : Jean Vilar – Georges Wilson. People's National Theatre, Paris. 1960.

ADAR, Arnon. (Israel)
Born : Dresden (Germany). 1 Apr. 1923.
Educated : Yale University Drama School (U.S.A.).
Stage Designs : Over 30.
MILHEMET BNEY OR (The War of the Sons of Light). Moshe Shamir. M : Gershon Plotkin. Cameri Theatre, Tel Aviv. 1956. – LOOK HOMEWARD ANGEL, Thomas Wolfe - Ketti Frings. M : Peter Frye. Cameri Theatre, Tel Aviv. 1958. – THE TWELVE ANGRY MEN, R. Rose. M : Avraham Ninio. Habima Theatre, Tel Aviv. 1959.

AEBERLI, Hans. (West Germany)
Born : Aachen. 5 Apr. 1916.
Educated : Düsseldorf. Disciple of Carl Wilhelm VOGEL.
Stage Designs : About 130.
DANTON'S DEATH, Georg Büchner. M : Dr. E. Schumacher. Vereinigte Städt. Bühnen Krefeld - M. Gladbach. Krefeld. 1954. – ALTONA, Jean-Paul Sartre. M : Erwin Piscator. Bühnen der Stadt Essen. 1959. – BECKET OR THE HONOUR OF GOD, Jean Anouilh. M : Erwin Piscator. Bühnen der Stadt Essen. 1960.

AHLBOM, Martin. (Sweden)
Born: Helsinki (Finland). 28 Feb. 1895.
Educated : Academy of Fine Arts, Abo (Finland). Disciple of Victor WESTERHOLM.
Stage Designs : Over 400.
YERMA, Federico Garcia Lorca. M : Bengt Ekerot. City Theatre, Malmö. 1949. – VÄRMLÄNNINGARNA (The People of Värmland), Fredrik August Dahlgren. Mu : Gert Ove Andersson. M : Ingmar Bergman. Ch. : Ingrid Tönshager. City Theatre, Malmö. 1959. – ANDROMAQUE, Jean Racine. M : Yngve Nordwall. City Theatre, Malmö. 1960.

AKIMOV, Nicolai. (U.S.S.R.)
Born : Kharkov. 16 Apr. 1901.
Educated : Private Studio of the painter SEIDENBERG and Fine Arts Academy, Petrograd. Disciple of Vasili SHUKHAEV, Alexander YAKOVLEV and Mstislav DOBOUJINSKI.
Stage Designs : About 200.
RAZLOM (The Breach), Boris Lavrenev. M : Alexei Popov. Vakhtangov Theatre, Moscow. 1927. – TEN (The Shadow), Evgeni Shvarts. M : Nicolai Akimov. Comedy Theatre, Leningrad. 1953. – THE TREES DIE STANDING, Alejandro Casona. M : Nicolai Akimov. Comedy Theatre, Leningrad. 1957.

ALKAZI, Ebrahim. (India)
Born : Poona. 18 Oct. 1925.
Educated : Royal Academy of Dramatic Art, London.
Stage Designs : About 50.
THE FATHER, August Strindberg. M : Ebrahim Alkazi. Theatre Unit, Jai Hind College Theatre, Bombay. 1955. – TARTUFFE, Molière. M : Ebrahim Alkazi. Theatre Unit, Jai Hind College Theatre, Bombay. 1959. – MEDEA, Euripides. M : Ebrahim Alkazi. Meghdoot Terrace Theatre, Bombay. 1960.

ALLIO, René. (France)
Born : Marseilles. 8 Mar. 1924.
Stage Designs : About 50.
HENRY IV, Shakespeare. M : Roger Planchon. Villeurbanne. 1958. – THE GOOD SOLDIER SCHWEIK, Bertolt Brecht. M : Roger Planchon. Villeurbanne. 1961. – CRIME AND PUNISHMENT, Dostoievsky - Arout. M : Michel Vitold. Comédie Française, Paris. 1963.

ALME, Gunnar. (Norway)
Born : Bergen. 18 Dec. 1924.
Educated : University of Valparaiso, Chile, and the Central School of Arts and Crafts, London.
Stage Designs : About 50.
THE WITCH, Hans Wiers-Jenssen. M : Agnes Mowinckel. National Theatre, Bergen. 1955 – MURDER IN THE CATHEDRAL, T.S. Eliot. Mu : Pauline Hall. M : Alfred Solaas. Nye Theatre, Oslo. 1958.

ALTINDAĞ, Seza. (Turkey)
Born : Istanbul. 1921.
Educated : Professor Helmut JÜRGENS's Fine Arts School, Munich. Disciple of Karl BLOCHERER and Kurt HALLEGGER.
Stage Designs : Over 50.
UN CASO CLINICO (A Clinical Case),
Dino Buzzati. M : Ziya Demirel. State Theatre, Ankara. 1960. – THE EARS OF KING MIDAS, Güngör Dilmen. M : Sahap Akalin. State Theatre, Ankara. 1961. – THE FLYING DUTCHMAN, Wagner. M : Feridun Altuna. State Theatre, Ankara. 1961.

ALTMANN, Nathan. (U.S.S.R.)
Born : Vinnitsa. 22 Dec. 1889.
Educated : Art School, Odessa. Disciple of Kiriak KOSTANDI and Efim LADYZHENSKI.
Stage Designs : About 50.
MYSTERY-BOUFFE, Vladimir Mayakovski. M : Alexander Granovski. State Circus, Moscow. 1921. – KING LEAR, Shakespeare. M : Grigori Kozintsev. Mu : Dmitri Shostakovich. Gorki Grand Dramatic Theatre, Leningrad. 1940. – HAMLET, Shakespeare. M : Grigori Kozintsev. Mu : Dmitri Shostakovich. Pushkin Academic Theatre, Leningrad. 1954.

ANEMOYANNIS, Georges. (Greece)
Born : Candia (Crete). 15 Dec. 1917.
Educated : Reinhardt Seminar, Vienna and Wienerspezialschule für Bühnenbild.
Stage Designs : 210.
ANNE OF THE THOUSAND DAYS, Maxwell Anderson. Mu : Manolis Skouloudis. M : Demètre Murat. Cotopouli - Rex Theatre, Athens. 1950. – THE SERVANT OF TWO MASTERS, Goldoni. M : Takis Muzenidis. Cotopouli - Rex Theatre, Athens. 1952. – PATOUCHAS (from the novel by Condylakis), A. Nikas. M : Manos Katrakis. Mu : Jean Macropoulos. Ch : N. Dimoglou. Greek People's Theatre - Pedion Areos, Athens. 1960.

APPEN, Karl von. (East Germany)
Born : Düsseldorf. 12 May 1900.
Educated : Kunstgewerbeschule, Frankfurt/Main. Disciple of F.K. DELAVILLA and Ludwig SIEVERT.
Stage Designs : About 500.
THE CAUCASIAN CHALK CIRCLE, Bertolt Brecht. M : Bertolt Brecht. Berliner Ensemble, East Berlin. 1955. – THE RESISTIBLE RISE OF ARTURO UI, Bertolt Brecht. M : Manfred Weckwerth. Berliner Ensemble, East Berlin. 1958. – THE DAYS OF THE COMMUNE, Bertolt Brecht. M : Manfred Weckwerth - Joachim Tenschert. Berliner Ensemble, East Berlin. 1962.

ARLE, Asmund Johannes. (Sweden)
Born : Klagstorp. 29 May 1918.
Educated : Kungl. Konsthögskolan,
Stockholm. Disciple of Eric GRATE.
Stage Design :
MODELL BEATRICE (Beatrice Model), Tore Zetterholm. M : Alf Sjöberg. Royal Dramatic Theatre, Stockholm. 1954.

ARMISTEAD, Horace. (U.S.A.)
Born : England. 1898.
Educated : London Polytechnic.
Stage Designs : About 50.
THE RAKE'S PROGRESS, Igor Stravinsky. M : Balanchine. Metropolitan Opera, New York. 1953. – FIDELIO, Beethoven. Metropolitan Opera, New York. 1957. – LE MISANTHROPE, Molière. M : George Hamlin. Loeb Drama Centre, Harvard University. Cambridge, Massachusetts. 1960.

ARMSTRONG, Will Steven. (U.S.A.)
Born : New Orleans. 26 Mar. 1930.
Educated: Bachelor of Arts, Louisiana State University and Master of Arts, Yale University.
Stage Designs : About 12.
CALIGULA, Albert Camus. M : Sidney Lumet. 54th Street Theatre, New York. 1959. – CARNIVAL, Michael Stewart - Helen Deutsch. Mu : Bob Merrill. M : Gower Champion. Imperial Theatre, New York. 1961. – CHIN-CHIN, François Billetdoux. M : Peter Glenville. Plymouth Theatre, New York. 1962.

ARONSON, Boris. (U.S.A.)
Born : Kiev (Russia). 15 Oct. 1900.
Educated : Institute of Fine Arts, Kiev, then Moscow.
Disciple of Alexandra Exter.
Stage Designs : About 90.
A VIEW FROM THE BRIDGE, Arthur Miller. M : Martin Ritt. Martin Beck Theatre, New York. 1955. – THE FIRSTBORN, Christopher Fry. M : Anthony Quayle. Coronet Theatre, New York. 1958. – J.B., Archibald MacLeish. M : Elia Kazan. ANTA Theatre, New York. 1959.

ARROCHA FERNANDEZ, Eduardo. (Cuba)
Born : Guanabacoa. 17 May 1934.
Educated : Escuela Nacional de Bellas Artes " San Alejandro " and Uffizi Gallery, Florence.
Stage Designs :
THE ITALIAN STRAW HAT, Labiche. Compañia Andrés Castro. 1961. – CANTO CAMPESINO (Peasant Song). Mu : A. Roldán. Ch : Lorna Burdsall. Conjunto Nacional de Danza Moderna, Cuba. 1962.

zhapov. Opera and Ballet Theatre, Ulan-Ude. 1948. – V BURYU (The Storm). Mu : Tikhon Khrennikov. Libretto : Alexei Faiko - Nicolai Virta. M : Gombo Tsydynzhapov. Opera and Ballet Theatre, Ulan-Ude. 1957.

TOFAN, Mihai. (Rumania)
Born : Tigheci (U.S.S.R.). 8 Nov. 1926.
Educated : Institute of Plastic Arts, Bucharest. Disciple of Professor I. COVALENCU.
Stage Designs :
OAMENI ARE TAC (The Silent Ones), Alexander Voitin. M : Mihai Berechet. National Theatre, Bucharest. 1960. – ORPHEUS DESCENDING, Tennessee Williams. M : Moni Ghelerter. National Theatre, Bucharest. 1962.

TOMS, Carl. (Great Britain)
Born : Kirkby-in-Ashfield. 29 May 1927.
Educated : Royal College of Art, London, and Old Vic Theatre School, London.
Stage Designs : 16.
LA REJA. Mu : Scarlatti. Ch : John Cranko. Ballet Rambert. Sadler's Wells Theatre, London. 1959. – LA CENERENTOLA, Rossini. M : Douglas Craig. Sadler's Wells Theatre, London. 1959. – NEW CRANKS, John Cranko. M : John Cranko. Lyric Theatre, Hammersmith, London. 1960.

TOSAR, Beatriz. (Uruguay)
Born : Montevideo. 24 Oct. 1924.
Educated : Faculty of Architecture, University of Urugay. Disciple of Rubén DUFAU.
Stage Designs : More than 6.
LAS DE BARRANCO, Gregorio de Laferrere. M : Concepcion Zorrilla. Comedia Nacional. Teatro Solis, Montevideo. – TIME REMEMBERED, Jean Anouilh. M : Emilio Acevedo Solano. Compañia Eva di Carlo. Teatro Artigas, Montevideo. 1954. – EL SUEÑO ANCLADO (The Anchored Dream), Elzear De Camilli. M : Emilio Acevedo Solano. Compañia de Actores Profesionales Uruguayos (Capu). Sala Verdi, Montevideo. 1954.

TOSI, Piero. (Italy)
Born : Florence. 10 Apr. 1927.
Educated : Fine Arts Academy, Florence. Disciple of Ottone ROSAI.
Stage Designs : 9.
MIRANDOLINA (Mine Hostess), Carlo Goldoni. M : Luchino Visconti. Teatro La Fenice, Venice. 1954. – CAT ON A HOT TIN ROOF, Tennessee Williams. M : Raymond Rouleau. Teatro Manzoni, Milan. 1956. – MACBETH, Verdi. M : Luchino Visconti. Teatro Nuovo, Spoleto. 1958.

TRAUTVETTER, Paul. (U.S.A.)
Born : Patterson. 1921.
Educated : Carnegie Institute of Technology.
Stage Designs : 55.
RUINS AND VISIONS. Mu : Benjamin Britten. Ch : Doris Humphrey. Connecticut College Theatre, New London. 1953. – THE SOLDIER'S TALE. Mu : Igor Stravinsky. M : William Steinberg - Henry Boettcher. Carnegie Institute of Technology, Pittsburgh. 1955. – ROMEO AND JULIET, Shakespeare. M : Mary Morris. Carnegie Institute of Technology, Pittsburgh. 1960.

TRÖSTER, František.
(Czechoslovakia)
Born : Vrbicany. 20 Dec. 1904.
Educated : Vysoké Uceni Technické, Prague. (Specialising in architecture). Disciple of Pavel JANÁK.
Stage Designs : Over 350.
CHUDAK (The Eccentric), Nazim Hikmet. M : Otomar Krejca. J.K. Tyl

Theatre, Prague. 1957. – SMIR TANTALUV (Tantalus Reconciled), Jaroslav Vrchlicky. Mu : Zdenek Fibisch. M : Ladislav Boháč. Smetana Theatre, Prague. 1958. – WOZZECK, Büchner. Mu : Alban Berg. M : Ferdinand Pujman. National Theatre, Prague. 1959.

TSAROUCHIS, Yannis. (Greece)
Born : Piraeus. 1910.
Educated : School of Fine Arts, Athens and in Paris (painting).
Stage Designs : Over 50.
UNCLE VANYA, Chekhov. M : Karolos Koun. Greek National Theatre, Athens. 1953. – THE MEDIUM, Gian-Carlo Menotti. National Opera, Athens. 1958. – MEDEA, Cherubini. M : Alexis Minotis. Dallas, Texas. 1958. Royal Opera House, Covent Garden, London. 1959. Scala, Milan. 1959. Epidaurus Festival. 1961.

TYSHLER, Alexander. (U.S.S.R.)
Born : Kiev. 26 July 1898.
Educated : School of Fine Arts, Kiev. Disciple of painters DIADCHENKO, SELEZNIOV and STRUNNIKOV.
Stage Designs : About 100.
RICHARD III, Shakespeare. M : Konstantin Tverskoi. Mu : Valeri Zhelobinski. Gorki Grand Dramatic Theatre, Leningrad. 1935. – MYSTERY BOUFFE, Vladimir Mayakovski. M : Valentin Pluchek. Mu : Rodion Chedrin. Theatre of Satire, Moscow. 1957. – NE TOLKO LYUBOV (Not Love Alone). Mu : Rodion Chedrin. Libretto : Vasili Katanian. M : Georgi Ansimov. Bolshoi Theatre, Moscow. 1961.

U

UPOR, Tibor. (Hungary)
Born : Budapest. 1904.
Educated : Faculties of Architecture, Milan, Rome and Braunschweig. Disciple of Sándor HEVESI.
Stage Designs : About 800.
SUCH A LOVE, Pavel Kohout. M : István Kazán. Gaiety Theatre, Budapest. 1958. – PESTI EMBEREK (People of Budapest), Lajas Mesterházi. M : Károly Kazimir. Gaiety Theatre, Budapest. 1958. – THE VISIT OF THE OLD LADY, Friedrich Dürrenmatt. M : István Kazán. Gaiety Theatre, Budapest. 1959.

V

VAKALO, Georges. (Greece)
Born : Constantinople (Turkey). 26 Oct. 1902.
Educated : Grande Chaumière, École du Louvre and École de l'Atelier, Paris (teacher, Charles DULLIN).
Stage Designs : About 200.
THE PEACE, Aristophanes. Mu : Darius Milhaud. M : Charles Dullin. Atelier Theatre, Paris. 1935. – THE WOULD-BE GENTLEMAN, Molière. Mu : J.B. Lulli. M : Socrate Carantinos. National Theatre, Athens. 1952. – THE CAUCASIAN CHALK CIRCLE, Bertolt Brecht. M : Karolos Koun. Art Theatre, Athens. 1957.

VANARELLI, Mario. (Argentina)
Born : Buenos Aires. 20 Oct. 1917.
Educated : High School of Fine Arts, Buenos Aires. Disciple of Rodolfo FRANCO.
Stage Designs : 150.
EL ULTIMO PERRO (The Last Dog), Carlos Gorostiza. M : Armando Discepolo. Cervantes National Theatre, Buenos Aires. 1954. – PROSERPINA Y EL EXTRANJERO (Proserpine and the Stranger), Omar del Carlo. M : Boya Diaz Ulloque. Verano Theatre, Buenos Aires. 1957. – THE HOUSE OF BERNARDA ALBA, Federico Garcia

Lorca. M : Margarita Xirgu. Cervantes National Theatre, Buenos Aires. 1958.

VAN NEROM, Jacques. (Belgium)
Born : Uccle. 13 Oct. 1903.
Self-taught.
Stage Designs : Over 300.
SAINT JOAN, Bernard Shaw. M : Marcelle Dambremont. Théâtre Royal des Galeries, Brussels. 1957. – ORFEO, Monteverdi. M : Jean-Marc Landier. Ch : Milko Sparemblek. Théâtre Royal de la Monnaie, Brussels. 1960. – CALIGULA, Albert Camus. M : Jean-Pierre Jorris. Théâtre Royal des Galeries, Brussels. 1962.

VARDAUNIS, Edgar. (U.S.S.R.)
Born : Cesis (Latvia).
Educated : Fine Arts Academy, Riga. Disciple of Wilhelm PURVIT.
Stage Designs : Over 20.
ROMEO AND JULIET, ballet by Serguei Prokofiev. Ch : Yevgeni Changa. Academic Opera and Ballet Theatre of the Republic of Latvia, Riga. 1953. – SPARTACUS, ballet by Aram Khachaturian. M : Yevgeni Changa. 1960.

VARGA, Mátyás. (Hungary)
Born : Budapest. 1910.
Educated : High School of Decorative Arts, Budapest. Disciple of Nándor Lajos VARGA.
Stage Designs : About 700.
AZ EMBER TRAGEDIÁJA (The Tragedy) of Man), Imre Madách. Mu : Gyula Dávid. M : Tamas Major. Ch : Imre Eck. National Theatre, Budapest. 1960. – THE CRUCIBLE, Arthur Miller. M : Andre Marton. National Theatre, Budapest. 1961. – AIDA, Verdi. M : András Mikó. Szeged Festival. 1962.

VASILESCU, Valer. (Rumania)
Born : Cluj. 22 Oct. 1924.
Educated : " Ion Andreescu " Institute of Plastic Arts, Cluj.
Stage Designs : Over 15.
THE PEOPLE OF SOIMARESTI (The Saga of Soimaresti), Mihail Sadoveanu - Tudor Jarda. M : Ilie Balea. Ch : Taub Gabriela. State Opera, Cluj. 1959. – ROMEO AND JULIET, Ballet by Lavrovski. Mu : Serguei Prokofiev. M-Ch : Taub Gabriela. State Opera, Cluj. 1961.

VASILIEV, Alexander. (U.S.S.R.)
Born : Kuibyshev. 11 Jan. 1911.
Educated : " 1905 " School of Fine Arts, Moscow. Disciple of Serge NICOLAYEV.
Stage Designs : About 140.
THE FRUITS OF ENLIGHTENMENT, Leo Tolstoi. M : Mikhail Kedrov. Moscow Art Theatre. 1951. – DALI NEOGLYADNYE (Far, Far Away), Nicolai Virta. M: Yuri Zavadski. Mossoviet Theatre, Moscow. 1957. – BUNT ZHENSHCHIN (The Revolt of the Women), Nazim Hikmet - Victor Komissarzhevski, after Knud Sonderby. M : Yuri Zavadski. Mu: Kara Karayev. Mossoviet Theatre, Moscow. 1961.

VERTÈS, Marcel. (France)
Born : Ujpest (Hungary). 10 Aug 1895.
Stage Designs : 15.
THE DISPUTE, Marivaux. Comédie Française, Paris. 1930. – LA BELLE HISTOIRE (The Lovely Tale), G.H. Clouzot. Madeleine Theatre, Paris. 1935. – LA BELLE HÉLÈNE, Jacques Offenbach. Paris Opera. 1960.

VESSEUR, Wim. (Netherlands)
Born : Utrecht. 5 Apr. 1919.
Disciple of Edward Gordon CRAIG.
Stage Designs : 150 to 175.
COLOMBE, Jean Anouilh. M : Cees Laseur. Theatre Royal, The Hague. 1951. – ORPHEUS, Gluck. M : Hans Hartleb. City Theatre, Amsterdam.

1959. – THE PERSIANS, Aeschylus. M : Erik Vos. Carré Theatre, Amsterdam. 1963.

VIDROVITCH, Nina. (France)
Born : Barcelonnette. 16 Nov. 1930.
Disciple of Paul COLIN and Yves-BONNAT.
Stage Designs : 10.
THE TWO OGRES. M : Jacques Fornier. Théâtre de Bourgogne, Beaune and Arras Festival. 1959. – IBERIA. Mu : Claude Debussy. Ch: Salvador Vargas. Opera-Comique, Paris. 1961.

VIGON, Ruben. (Cuba)
Born : Cienfuegos. Las Villas. 10 Aug. 1917.
Stage Designs :
OUR TOWN, Thornton Wilder. Escuela Municipal de La Habana. Teatro E. Normal. 1947. – BLOOD WEDDING, Federico Garcia Lorca. M : T. Stockdale. New Haven. Conn. (Yale). 1948. – PROMETHEUS BOUND, Aeschylus. M : Baralt. University Theatre, Plaza Cademas. 1956. – DON JUAN, Guilherme Figueiredo. M : Pedro Alvarez. Sala Arlequin. Havana. 1960.

VILIAMS, Piotr. (U.S.S.R.)
Born : Moscow. 30 Apr. 1902.
Educated : Vasili MESHKOV Studio and Art Studios (Vkhutemas), Moscow.
Stage Designs : Over 50.
THE PICKWICK CLUB, after Charles Dickens. M : Victor Stanitsin. Moscow Art Theatre. 1934. – ROMEO AND JULIET, ballet by Serguei Prokofiev. Ch: Leonid Lavrovski. Kirov Opera and Ballet Theatre, Leningrad. 1940. Bolshoi Theatre, Moscow. 1946. – TRUDNIYE GODY (The Difficult Years), Alexei Tolstoi. M : Alexei Popov. Moscow Art Theatre. 1946.

VILKS, Girts. (U.S.S.R.)
Born : Durba (Latvia). 1 Jan. 1909.
Educated : Faculty of Architecture, University of Latvia and Art Studio, University of Riga. Disciple of Wilhelm PURVIT.
Stage Designs : About 100.
PUT, VEZHINI (Blow, Breeze), Janis Rainis. M : Eduard Smilgis. Mu : Indulis Kalnins. Riga Art Theatre. 1947. – LYUBOV YAROVAYA, Konstantin Trenev. M : Eduard Smilgis. Mu : Marters Zarins. Riga Art Theatre. 1952. – SPELEZHU, DANCOZHU (I played, I danced), Janis Rainis. M : Eduard Smilgis. Mu : Indulis Kalnins. Ch : Erika Ferda. Riga Art Theatre. 1957.

VINOGRADOV, Mily. (U.S.S.R.)
Born : Varnitsi. 27 Apr. 1910.
Educated : " 1905 " School of Fine Arts, Moscow. Disciple of Serge NICOLAYEV.
Stage Designs : Over 50.
OTHELLO, Shakespeare. M : Yuri Zavadski. Mu : Yuri Biriukov. Mossoviet Theatre, Moscow. 1944. – RUSKI LES (The Russian Forest), after the novel by Leonid Leonov. Stage adaptation by Leonid Leonov and Fedor Bondarenko. Mu: Tchaikovsky. Vakhtangov Theatre, Moscow. 1961. – STRIAPUKHA (The Canteen Woman), Anatoli Sofronov. M: Ruben Simonov. Mu : Boris Mokrusov. Vakhtangov Theatre, Moscow. 1959.

VIRSALADZE, Simon. (U.S.S.R.)
Born : Tbilisi. 24 Jan. 1909.
Educated : Fine Arts Academy, Tbilisi, Art Institute (Vkhutein) and Fine Arts Academy, Leningrad. Disciple of Joseph CHARLEMAGNE, Isaac RABINOVICH, Nisson SHIFRIN and Mikhail BORYSHOV.
Stage Designs : About 100.

SEMYA TARASA (The Taras Family), opera by Dmitri Kabalevski. M : Ilia Shlepianov. Kirov Opera and Ballet Theatre, Leningrad. 1950. – OTHELLO, ballet by Alexei Machavariani. Ch : Vakhtang Chabukiani. Paliashvili Opera and Ballet Theatre, Tbilisi. 1957. – THE STONE FLOWER, ballet by Serguei Prokofiev. Libretto : Mirra Mendelson - Prokofieva and Leonid Lavrovski. Ch : Yuri Grigorovich. Kirov Opera and Ballet Theatre, Leningrad. 1961.

VIUDES, Vicente. (Spain)
Born : Murcia. 29 Nov. 1916.
Educated : School of Fine Arts, Madrid.
Stage Designs : 60.
THE PEASANT IN HIS ACRES, Lope de Vega. M : Cayetano Luca De Tena. Teatro Español, Madrid. 1950. – CELESTINA, Fernando de Rojas. M : Luis Escobar. Teatro Eslava, Madrid. 1957. – THE STAR OF SEVILLE, Lope de Vega. M : José Tamayo. Teatro Español, Madrid. 1959.

VOLKOV, Boris. (U.S.S.R.)
Born : Moscow. 26 Mar. 1900.
Educated : Stroganov School and Art Studios (Vkhutemas), Moscow. Disciple of Vasili POLENOV, pupil of Georgi YAKULOV, Aristarkh LENTULOV and Vladimir TATLIN.
Stage Designs : About 200.
THE STORM, opera by Tikhon Khrennikov. Libretto : Alexei Faiko - Nicolai Virta. M : Vladimir Nemirovich-Danchenko - Pavel Zlatogorov - Pavel Markov. Stanislavski and Nemirovich-Danchenko Musical Theatre, Moscow. 1939 (Revival in 1952). – MOZART AND SALIERI, Rimsky-Korsakov. M : Pavel Markov. Stanislavski and Nemirovich-Danchenko Musical Theatre, Moscow. 1944. – WAR AND PEACE, Serguei Prokofiev. M : Leonid Baratov - Pavel Zlatogorov. Stanislavski and Nemirovich-Danchenko Musical Theatre, Moscow. 1957.

VOS, Marik. (Sweden)
Born : Leningrad (U.S.S.R.). 3 June 1923.
Educated : Otte Skölds Malarskola. Teknikaskolan and the Studio of the Royal Dramatic Theatre, Stockholm. Disciple of Sven-Erik SKAWONIUS.
Stage Designs : About 40.
THE DREAM PLAY, August Strindberg. M : Olof Molander. Royal Dramatic Theatre, Stockholm. 1955. – THE SEAGULL. Chekhov. M : Ingmar Bergman. Royal Dramatic Theatre, Stockholm. 1961.

VYCHODIL, Ladislav.
(Czechoslovakia)
Born : Hácky u Litovle. 28 Feb. 1920.
Educated : Vysoké Uceni Technické, Prague (architecture), and Akademie Muzickych Umeni, Prague. Disciple of Frantisek TRÖSTER.
Stage Designs : About 200.
THE OPTIMISTIC TRAGEDY, Vsevolod Vishnevski. M : Josef Budsky. Slovakian National Theatre, Bratislava. 1957. – THE WHITE PLAGUE, Karel Capek. M : Josef Budsky. Slovakian National Theatre, Bratislava. 1958. – GALILEO GALILEI, Bertolt Brecht. M : Tibor Rakovsky. Slovakian National Theatre, Bratislava. 1958.

W

WAKHÉVITCH, Georges. (France)
Born : Odessa (Russia). 18 Aug. 1907.
Educated : École Supérieure des Arts Décoratifs, Paris. Disciple of Edwin SCOTT, Lazare MEERSON and Jean PERRIR.
Stage Designs: About 80 (50 in France, 30 abroad).
BORIS GODUNOV, Mussorgsky. M : Peter Brook. Covent Garden, London. 1948. – FAUST, Charles Gounod. M : Max De Rieux. Paris Opera. 1955. – DON CARLOS, Verdi. M : Margherita Wallmann. Scala, Milan. 1960.

WALENTIN, Arne. (Norway)
Born : Oslo. 26 Oct. 1915.
Educated : Fine Arts Academy, Oslo. Disciple of Per KROHG.
Stage Designs : 200.
BRAND, Henrik Ibsen. M : Hans Jacob Nilsen. People's Theatre, Oslo. 1953. – THE TEMPEST, Shakespeare. M : Ivo Cramer. Norwegian Theatre, Oslo. 1960.

WENIG, Adolf. (Czechoslovakia)
Born : Prague. 28 Apr. 1912.
Educated : Akademie Vytvarnych Umeni, Prague.
Disciple of Jakub OBROVSKY and T.F. SIMON.
Stage Designs : Over 300.
GENEVA, Bernard Shaw. M : Bohus Stejskal. Chamber Theatre, Prague. 1947. – THE RAINMAKER, Richard Nash. M: Rudolf Hrusinsky. Chamber Theatre, Prague. 1957. – THE GLASS MENAGERIE, Tennessee Williams. M : Ota Ornest. Chamber Theatre, Prague. 1960.

WEYL, Roman. (East Germany)
Born : Mainz. 21 July 1921.
Educated : Staatl. Kunsthochschule.

Dresden. Pupil of Professor MANKE.
Stage Designs : About 100.
WILLIAM TELL, Schiller. M : Fritz Wisten. Volksbühne, East Berlin. 1954. – FIESKO. Schiller, M : Fritz Wisten. Volksbühne, East Berlin. 1955. – NEKRASSOV, Jean-Paul Sartre. M : Fritz Wisten. Volksbühne, East Berlin. 1956.

WICH, Harry. (Netherlands)
Born : Eindhoven. 13 Feb. 1927.
Educated : Slade School of Fine Arts, London, and Württemberg State Theatres, Stuttgart. Disciple of Robert MEDLEY (London) and Gerd RICHTER (Stuttgart).
Stage Designs : 25.
PERESPHONE. Mu : Antonio Vivaldi. Ch : Robert Joffrey. Sadler's Wells Theatre, London. 1955. – A VIEW FROM THE BRIDGE, Arthur Miller. M : Henk Rigters. City Theatre, Amsterdam. 1956. – MUCH ADO ABOUT NOTHING, Shakespeare. M : Cees Laseur. Theatre Royal, The Hague. 1958.

WIJNBERG, Nicolaas. (Netherla ds)
Born : Amsterdam. 22 Nov. 1918.
Educated : Rijksacademie van Beeldende Kunsten, Amsterdam. Pupil of Frits LENSVELT, disciple of Christian BÉRARD.
Stage Designs : About 100.
MOORTJE, Bredero. M : Ton Lutz. Theatre Royal, The Hague. 1957. – HET LIED VAN DE MOORDENAAR (The Murderer's Song), Hugo Claus. M : Ton Lutz. Rotterdam City Theatre, Rotterdam. 1957. – COMEDY OF ERRORS, Shakespeare. M : Ton Lutz. Rotterdam City Theatre, Rotterdam. 1960.

WILCOX, Richard Kent. (U.S.A.)
Born : San Luis Obispo. 20 Feb. 1933.
Educated : Universities of California and Yale.
Stage Designs : 20.
ON BORROWED TIME, Paul Osborn. M : Ralph Freud. University of California Theatre, Los Angeles. 1957. – THE FLOWERING PEACH, Clifford Odets. M : Nikos Psacharopoulos. Yale University Theatre. New Haven. 1960.

WOTRUBA, Fritz. (Austria)
Born : Vienna. 23 Apr. 1907.
Educated : Kunstgewerbeschule and Akademie der Bildenden Künste, Vienna. Disciple of A. HANAK.
Stage Designs : 3.
ŒDIPUS REX, Sophocles. M : Gustav Rudolf Sellner. Burg Theatre, Vienna.

1960. – ANTIGONE, Sophocles. M : Gustav Rudolf Sellner. Burg Theatre, Vienna. 1961. – ELECTRA, Sophocles. M : Gustav Rudolf Sellner. Burg Theatre, Vienna. 1962.

Y

YUNOVICH, Sophia. (U.S.S.R.)
Born : Vitebsk. 28 Sep. 1910.
Educated : Repin Institute (Fine Arts Academy), Leningrad. Disciple of Mikhail BOBYSHOV.
Stage Designs : About 40.
INVASION, Leonid Leonov. M : Leonid Vivien. Leningrad Pushkin Academic Theatre, Novosibirsk. 1943. – SADKO, Rimsky-Korsakov. M : Yevgeni Sokovnin. Ch : Yuri Grigorovich. Kirov Opera and Ballet Theatre, Leningrad. 1953. – THE LEGEND OF THE INVISIBLE CITY OF KITEZH AND OF THE VIRGIN, FEVRONIA. Rimsky - Korsakov. M : Yevgeni Sokovnin. Kirov Opera and Ballet Theatre, Leningrad. 1958.

Z

ZEFFIRELLI, Franco. (Italy)
Born : Florence. 12 Feb. 1923.
Educated : Faculty of Architecture, University of Florence.
Stage Designs : 15.
TROILUS AND CRESSIDA, Shakespeare. M : Luchino Visconti. Boboli, Florence. 1949. – THE THREE SISTERS, Chekhov. M : Luchino Visconti. Teatro Eliseo, Rome. 1952.

ZOLOTARIEV, Nicolaï. (U.S.S.R.)
Born : Orel. 1 June 1915.
Educated : Repin Institute (Fine Arts Academy), Leningrad. Disciple of Mikhail BOBYSHOV.
Stage Designs : About 25.
VELIKI GOSUDAR (The Great Sovereign), Vladimir Soloviev. M : Vasili Poznanski. Dramatic Theatre, Noginsk. 1946. – POVEST O NASTOYASHCHEM CHELOVEKE (The Story of a True Man), Opera by Serguei Prokofiev. M : Georgi Ansimov. Bolshoi Theatre, Moscow. 1960. – A VIEW FROM THE BRIDGE, Arthur Miller. M : Andrei Goncharov. Dramatic Theatre, Moscow. 1959.

ZUFFI, Piero. (Italy)
Born : Imola (Bologna). 28 Apr. 1919.
Educated : Fine Arts Academy, Florence.
Stage Designs : 83.
JULIUS CAESAR, Shakespeare. M : Giorgio Strehler. Piccolo Teatro, Milan. 1954. – ŒDIPUS REX, Sophocles. M : Vittorio Gassman. Italian Popular Theatre, Rome. 1955.

INDEX TO ILLUSTRATIONS
LISTED UNDER DESIGNERS

The name in the third column represents the author in the case of a play (I), the composer in the case of an opera or a musical comedy (II), the choreographer in the case af a ballet (III).

Designer	Original title and translation in English	Author, choreographer or composer	Page
CAGLI, Corrado	II. Macbeth	Bloch, Ernest	122
CAMURATI, Jacques	I. Prométhée enchaîné *Prometheus Bound*	Beer, Jean de	78
CARBONI, Erberto	II. Agnese di Hohenstaufen *Agnes of Hohenstaufen*	Spontini, Gaspare	122
CARL, Joseph	I. King Lear	Shakespeare	118
CARLSTEDT, Birger	I. L'Œuf *The Egg*	Marceau, Félicien	203
CASSON, Hugh	II. The World of Paul Slickey	Whelan, Christopher	215
CASTILLO, Carlos Aïtor	I. Les Bonnes *The Maids*	Genet, Jean	163
CASTILLO, Carlos Aïtor	I. La Endemoniada *The She-devil*	Schoenherr, Carl	163
CHIARI, Mario	I. Enrico IV *Henry IV*	Pirandello, Luigi	123
CHIFRINE, Nisson	I. Jenitba *The Wedding*	Gogol, Nicolaï	179
CHIFRINE, Nisson	I. The Merry Wives of Windsor	Shakespeare	180
CHIFRINE, Nisson	I. Podniataïa Tsélina *Virgin Soil Upturned*	Sholokhov, Mikhaïl	180
CHIFRINE, Nisson	I. Stalingradzi *The People of Stalingrad*	Tchépourine, Youri	180
CHRISTIANSEN, Rolf	II. Angigone	Honegger, Arthur	58
CIULEI, Liviu	I. Anii Negri *The Dark Years*	Baranga, Aurel - Moraru, Nicolae	173
CIULEI, Liviu	I. Na Dnye *The Lower Depths*	Gorki, Maxim	173
COCTEAU, Jean	II. Pelléas et Mélisande	Debussy, Claude	85
COLASANTI, Veniero - MOORE, John	II. La Traviata *The Lost One*	Verdi, Giuseppe	123
COLONNELLO, Attilio	I. The Taming of the Shrew	Shakespeare	124
COLTELLACCI, Giulio	II. Amahl and the Night Visitors	Menotti, Gian-Carlo	124
CORTEZO, Victor Maria	I. Fuente Ovejuna *The Sheep-Well*	Vega, Lope de	77
COSTA, Valeria	I. Venezia Salvata *Venice Preserved*	Bontempelli, Massimo	124
COUTAUD, Lucien	I. Protée *Proteus*	Claudel, Paul	87
CREUZ, Serge	I. Arlecchino, Servitore di due Padroni *The Servant of Two Masters*	Goldoni, Carlo	28
CRUDDAS, Audrey	I. Macbeth	Shakespeare	215
CSELENYI, József	I. Biedermann und die Brand-stifter *Biedermann and the Firebugs*	Frisch, Max	139
CSELENYI, József	I. A Midsummer Night's Dream	Shakespeare	139
CURREL, Nicolas	I. Twelfth Night	Shakespeare	243

D

Designer	Original title and translation in English	Author, choreographer or composer	Page
DALI, Salvador	I. Don Juan Tenorio	Zorrilla, José	78
DALI, Salvador	I. Don Juan Tenorio	Zorrilla, José	79
DAMIANI, Luciano	I. El Nost Milan *Our Milan*	Bertolazzi, Carlo	251
DAMONTE, Marcelo	I. An Inspector Calls	Priestley, J.B.	163
DAMONTE, Marcelo	I. Volpone	Jonson, Ben	164
DASZEWSKI, Wladyslaw	I. Parady *Parade*	Potocki, Jan	166
DAYDÉ, Bernard	II. Orphée aux Enfers *Orpheus in the Underworld*	Offenbach, Jacques	88
DECAMP, Olivier	I. Prometheus desmotes *Prometheus Bound*	Aischylos	88
DECKWITZ, Franz	II. Pluk een een Ster *Pluck a Star*	Kous, Walter	137
DELFT, Hep van	I. Die Herberge *The Inn*	Hochwälder, Fritz	143
DEL NERI, Cino	I. O Pagador de Promessas *Payer of Promises*	Gomes, Dias	35
DE PAZ Y MATEO, Alberto	I. La Casa de Bernarda Alba *The House of Bernarda Alba*	Lorca, Federico Garcia	244
DMITRIEV, Vladimir	I. Bespridannitza *The Poor Bride*	Ostrovski, Alexandre	182
DMITRIEV, Vladimir	I. Diadia Vania *Uncle Vanya*	Chekhov, Anton	182
DMITRIEV, Vladimir	I. Ounijennié i Oskorblionnié *The Humble and the Offended*	Dostoïevsky Féodor - Olchvanger, Ilia	182
DMITRIEV, Vladimir	II. Pikovaïa Dama *The Queen of Spades*	Tchaikovsky, Piotr	181
DMITRIEV, Vladimir	I. Tri Sestri *The Three Sisters*	Chekhov, Anton	181
DORRER, Valeri	III. Tropoïou Groma *The Path of Thunder*	Sergheev, Konstantin	183

Designer	Original title and translation in English	Author, choreographer or composer	Page
DOUKING, Georges	II. Vol de Nuit *Night Flight*	Dallapiccola, Luigi	89
DUPONT, Jacques	I. Château en Suède *Castle in Sweden*	Sagan, Françoise	89

E

Designer	Original title and translation in English	Author, choreographer or composer	Page
ECHAVE, José	I. La Cuisine des Anges *My Four Angels*	Husson, Albert	241
ECHAVE, José	III. La Danse de Mort *The Dance of Death*	Veltcheck, Vaslav	241
ECKART, William-Jean	II. Damn Yankees	Adler, Richard - Ross, Jerry	233
ECKART, William-Jean	I. Mister Johnson	Cary, Joyce - Rosten, Norman	233
EGG, Lois	I. Parisian Comedy	Saroyan, William	155
EGG, Lois	I. Torquato Tasso	Gœthe, Johann Wolfgang	155
ELDER, Eldon	I. Henry V	Shakespeare	234
ELSON, Charles	II. Don Giovanni *Don Juan*	Mozart, Wolfgang Amadeus	234
EREN, Refik	I. Hörrem Sultan *Sultana Hürrem*	Asena, Orhan	213
EREN, Refik	I. Oidipous Tyrannos *Oedipus Rex*	Sophocles	214
ERIXON, Sven II.	II. Aniara	Blomdahl, Karl-Birger	208

F

Designer	Original title and translation in English	Author, choreographer or composer	Page
FARRAH, Abd'El Kader	I. Mille Francs de Récompense *1000 Francs Reward*	Hugo, Victor	89
FARRAH, Abd'El Kader	II. Oedipus Rex	Stravinsky, Igor	90
FAUCHEUR, Yves	I. La Famille Arlequin *Harlequin's Family*	Santelli, Claude	90
FAUCHEUR, Yves	I. The Merry Wives of Windsor	Shakespeare	90
FAVORSKI, Vladimir	I. Twelfth Night	Shakespeare	183
FEDOROVSKI, Fedor	II. Kniaz Igor *Prince Igor*	Borodine, Alexandre	184
FERNANDEZ, Salvador - OLIVA, Raúl	I. Santa Juana de América *Saint Joan of America*	Lizárraga, Andrés	48
FINI, Léonor	I. Le Garçon d'Honneur *The Man of Honour*	Wilde - Blondin - Guimard	91
FISHER, Randi - MORK, Lennart	I. Drottningens Juvelsmycke *The Jewels of the Queen*	Almqvist, C.J.L.	210
FIUME, Salvatore	II. Nabucco	Verdi, Giuseppe	126
FJELL, Kai	I. Fruen fra Havet *The Lady from the Sea*	Ibsen, Henrik	151
FRANCINI, Mauro	I. La Regina e gli Insorti *The Queen and the Rebels*	Betti, Ugo	35
FRANCINI, Mauro	I. Volpone	Jonson, Ben	35
FRANÇOIS, André	III. Pas de Dieux	Kelly, Gene	91
FRIGERIO, Ezio	I. Andromaque	Racine, Jean	126
FRIGERIO, Ezio	I. Arlecchino, Servitore di due Padroni *The Servant of Two Masters*	Goldoni, Carlo	125
FRISCH, Max	I. Biedermann und die Brand-stifter *Biedermann and the Firebugs*	Frisch, Max	110
FRITZSCHE, Max	I. Die Dreigroschenoper *The Threepenny Opera*	Brecht, Bertolt	58
FÜLÖP, Zoltán	III. Furfangos Diakok *The Witty Students*	Harangózó, Gyula	140
FÜLÖP, Zoltán	II. Salome	Strauss, Richard	140

G

Designer	Original title and translation in English	Author, choreographer or composer	Page
GALUP, Mario	I. Na Dnye *The Lower Depths*	Gorki, Maxim	241
GALUP, Mario	I. Moon on a Rainbow Shawl	John, Erroll	242
GAMLIN, Yngve	I. Vävaren i Bagdad *The Weaver of Baghdad*	Bergman, Hjalmar	209
GAMREKELI, Irakli	I. Die Räuber *The Robbers*	Schiller, Friedrich	184
GANEAU, François	I. La Zapatera Prodigiosa *The Shoemaker's Wife*	Lorca, Federico Garcia	92
GARBUGLIA, Mario	I. A View from the Bridge	Miller, Arthur	126
GAUGUIN, Paul René	I. Clochemerle	Aymé, Marcel	152
GEENENS, Robert	I. Sire Halewijn	Closson, Herman	29
GISCHIA, Léon	I. Le Triomphe de l'Amour *Love's Triumph*	Marivaux	92
GONDOLF, Walter	II. Bluthochzeit *Blood Wedding*	Fortner, Wolfgang	59

262

263

264

265

266

INDEX OF ILLUSTRATIONS LISTED UNDER PLAYWRIGHTS, COMPOSERS AND CHOREOGRAPHERS

This index is in three parts.

The first part contains spoken plays (those preceded in the captions by a Roman I) listed under authors. The second contains operas or musical comedies (those preceded in the captions by a Roman II) listed under composers. The third contains ballets (those preceded in the captions by a Roman III) listed under choreographers.

I

PLAYWRIGHTS

II

COMPOSERS

CONTENTS

ILLUSTRATIONS

Printed in Belgium